Property Finance Negligence:

Claims Against Solicitors and Valuers

To Caroline, Sarah, Miranda

Property Finance Negligence:

Claims Against Solicitors and Valuers

Hugh Tomlinson *Barrister*
New Court Chambers Gray's Inn
Jonathan Seitler *Barrister*
Wilberforce Chambers Lincoln's Inn
Thomas Grant *Barrister*
New Court Chamber, Gray's Inn

LAW & TAX

© Pearson Professional Limited 1996

Hugh Tomlinson, Jonathan Seitler and Thomas Grant have asserted their right under the Copyright, Designs and Patents Act 1988 to be identified as the authors of this work

ISBN 075200 2163

Published by
FT Law & Tax
21–27 Lamb's Conduit Street
London WC1N 3NJ

A Division of Pearson Professional Limited

Associated offices
Australia, Belgium, Canada, Hong Kong, India, Japan, Luxembourg, Singapore, Spain, USA

First edition 1996

A CIP catalogue record for this book is available from the British Library.

Printed in Great Britain by Biddles

Contents

Foreword

The law of negligence has been in torment for some years. Decisions of high authority have brought about great changes. There is, however, never any final and conclusive view on the law. Inevitably, one is witnessing a developing and dynamic evolution of principles. But the fact that no perfect system is attainable is no excuse for lawyers not to strive to improve the qualify of our law of negligence, which is the most important branch of the law of tort.

The most acute problems arise in the content of the provision of professional services. To a large extent this is caused by a major structural defect in English contract law: the discredited privity of contract rule. The inconvenience and injustice of this rule compels courts to invest remedies in negligence where contractual remedies would be more appropriate. After the Law Commission's careful and closely reasoned report of July 1996 recommending the abolition of the rule by statute one can but hope that legislation will follow swiftly. But even such law reform will not eliminate many of the problems of negligence in the field of professional services. Those problems have been highlighted by the burgeoning case law resulting from the lending boom and property collapse of the late 1980s and early 1990.

This book is a valuable contribution to understanding the law of negligence as it applies to claims against solicitors and valuers. The authors have throughout adopted a contextual approach: they have set the particular problems and possible solutions in this field against the background of a coherent study of the law of obligations. I unreservedly commend this book to readers.

Lord Steyn
House of Lords
November 1996

Preface

In the early 1990s the trickle of cases against professionals arising out of property lending turned into a flood. We were among the many practitioners swept along by the rapidly advancing waters. As waves of new cases appeared, it was difficult to pause long enough to chart their course. The general textbooks dealing with the law of professional negligence are of high quality but were not able to provide extended treatments of the special difficulties which arise in lender cases. We became acutely aware of the absence of a book dealing specifically with the problems which arise in cases brought by lenders against professionals who have advised in relation to property lending.

The idea that we might write such a book began to crystallise in early 1994 when the transcript of *BBL v Eagle Star* first began to circulate. Before the case had been reported, it became the subject of considerable discussion among practitioners and in the courts. It seemed to us that the case raised several important issues which would be at the centre of a book on what we had begun to call 'property finance negligence'. This term is a convenient shorthand for those cases in which lenders who have made loans secured on real property bring claims against the professionals who advised them in relation to the transaction.

When we first discussed the proposal with Daniel Perkins at FT Law & Tax it was decided that the book should be written to a tight time table and completed when the decision of the Court of Appeal in *BBL v Eagle Star* was available. Fortunately for the hard pressed authors, when judgment was given in February 1995, the Court of Appeal gave leave to appeal to the House of Lords. When the decision of the House of Lords came in June 1996 we were bereft of further excuses. The time had come for us to try and produce our own chart of this area of the law of professional negligence.

In the period of two years between conception and execution a large number of new issues had been raised and decided in the courts. Many of the dog-eared 'samizdat' transcripts which passed from hand to hand had been reported. A number of the issues which initially caused difficulty to practitioners have now been resolved. We have tried to explain, in each instance, the form that the resolution has taken and the gaps which remain. We are, however, confident that the rhizomatic growth of the common law will continue to outflank our best attempts at orderly exposition.

We have been greatly assisted in writing this book by the input of a number of friends and colleagues. The Appendix on Methods of Valuation was written in conjunction with Peter Tobin FRICS FCI Arb of Messrs Strettons, for whose assistance we are very grateful. David Heffron (of Booth & Co) was an invaluable source of new cases and points. Many people read and commented on all or part of the type-script. We would mention, in particular, Gilead Cooper, John Hawkins (of Sparling Benham and Brough), Alex Pelling and John Wardell. A large number of other friends and colleagues have assisted us in many ways. We would mention, in particular, John McDonnell QC, David Hughes and Amanda Ryding (of Dibb Lupton Alsop), Frederic Reynold QC, Terry Bergin, Andrew Davies and Joel Donovan. We would also like to thank our publisher at FT Law & Tax, Joanna Hicks, without whose tenacity and persistence the book would never have been completed and our editor, Donna Murphy. Finally, we are extremely grateful to Lord Steyn for writing the Foreword at a time when his diary was already full.

The law is stated as at 1 October 1996.

Hugh Tomlinson
Jonathan Seitler
Thomas Grant
21 October 1996

Table of Cases

Table of Statutes

Statutory Instruments

Introduction

The purpose of the book

This book sets out to provide an up-to-date exposition of the legal principles applicable in cases brought by lenders against their professional advisers arising out of property loans which went wrong. The volume of litigation in this area has increased dramatically in recent years as a result of the combination of the lending boom and property collapse of the late 1980s and early 1990s.

The creativity of lawyers acting for both sides has led to a large number of decided cases. Two examples illustrate the rapid developments which have taken place. First in 1991, lenders successfully argued that a solicitor was liable for a breach of trust on paying away the advance for a different transaction.[1] In 1993, the Court of Appeal was persuaded to award damages for breach of trust without proof of causation.[2] This decision was overturned by the House of Lords in July 1995.[3] A few weeks later, it was held that a lender had a claim for breach of fiduciary duty against a negligent solicitor.[4] This decision was overturned by the Court of Appeal in July 1996.[5] Second in 1993 valuers successfully persuaded a judge to reduce an award of damages so as to exclude the fall in the property market.[6] This decision was reversed by the Court of Appeal in 1995[7] but in June 1996 the House of Lords allowed the appeal, imposing a different type of 'damages reduction'.[8] As Staughton LJ said in a recent case:

> Such has been the volume of litigation on the topic of loss to lenders following negligent professional advice and the collapse of the property market that judges risk being overtaken by new authority.[9]

---

[1] See *Alliance & Leicester Building Society and others v Edgestop and others; sub nom Alliance & Leicester Building Society v Hamptons* [1993] 1 WLR 1462.

[2] *Target Holdings v Redferns* [1994] 1 WLR 1089.

[3] [1996] 1 AC 421.

[4] *Bristol & West Building Society v Mothew* (1995) unreported, 27 July, Chadwick J.

[5] (1996) unreported, 24 July.

[6] *BBL v Eagle Star* [1995] 2 All ER 769.

[7] [1995] QB 375.

[8] [1996] 3 WLR 87.

[9] *Bristol & West Building Society v Mothew* (1996) unreported, 24 July, judgment, p 42.

This book aims to provide a reliable guide to the law relating to property finance claims.

The property collapse

The lending boom and the property collapse affected, at different times, both the commercial and the residential sectors. In relation to the former, the rising prices of the late 1980s produced an increased demand by borrowers for financing and an increased willingness by lenders to engage in property lending. Between 1985 and 1991 the total debt owed by the property sector had increased from £7 billion to £40 billion. The market pressures on lenders to increase the volume of business, the entry of new lenders into the market and the lack of experienced staff meant that poor credit risk decisions became more common as traditional conservative lending criteria were relaxed. In order to finance this debt, borrowers needed either to find tenants for the property or, more usually, to sell it. The collapse of the commercial property market which, in London, began early in 1990 drove many property companies into insolvency. The combined effect of all these factors was to produce very high rates of borrower default in the early 1990s. In addition, the prevalent but misplaced optimism made valuers and lenders increasingly vulnerable to borrower fraud. Many such frauds were exposed in the early 1990s, producing large losses for commercial lenders.

The pattern in the residential sector was similar. From the mid-1980s residential property prices began to show rapid increases. The residential market peaked in July 1988 after a rush to purchase properties was precipitated by the advance notification in March 1988 that double MIRAS relief would be abolished from 1 August 1988. From August 1988 to about January 1989 prices stabilised and then, through 1989, 1990 and 1991, they fell steadily, in London at first and then throughout the country. Despite a deceleration in the rate of fall following the general election in April 1992, prices continued to drop after 'Black Wednesday' in September 1992 until the middle of 1993. They then began to stabilise and have now started to rise again at a modest pace. As in the commercial sector, commercial pressures had led lenders to relax previously conservative lending criteria. There were high levels of domestic mortgage fraud. The exposure of such frauds, allied to the borrower default caused by the recession, produced unprecedented levels of mortgage repossessions in the early 1990s. Most of these resulted in substantial shortfalls for the lenders.

The seeds of the current litigation explosion were therefore sown in the late 1980s. Property prices were rising and new lenders entered the market. In the case of residential property, the new entrants were UK banks—who had not previously been involved in domestic mortgages—and centralised lenders who could provide competitive interest rates because they had low overheads. In the case of commercial property, foreign banks and even some building societies who had no previous experience of the commercial market began to lend. Lenders fought among themselves to make loans (a prospective lender would often dispense with the requirement of a previous lender's references for fear that the previous lender might underbid the prospective lender) with offers of 'low start' and 100 per cent mortgages and mortgage certificates which gave borrowers an assurance of funds even before they had identified a property on which to secure them. This enthusiasm to lend created a culture where valuers and solicitors were put under pressure to carry out their duties quickly and cheaply.

In itself this would have created the conditions for mistakes to be made. But in addition, the competition to make loans forced lenders to advance monies on ever smaller loan-to-value ratios and with ever fewer checks on the credit-worthiness of the borrower. They took comfort in mortgage indemnity guarantee policies as a replacement for any real knowledge of the borrower's ability to make payments. This culminated in the phenomenon of the 'self-certifying' domestic loan: effectively an open acceptance by a lender that its security was the property and not the borrower's covenant. This was a cheap and simple procedure to operate and loans were often underwritten by junior staff with little experience or training. Self-certification was, as is now apparent, an invitation to borrower fraud.

The illusion of an ever-rising property market led valuers into a variety of traps. Valuers with no experience of the property collapse of the early 1970s had difficulty in conceiving of anything other than a rising market. In domestic cases, valuers were often very heavily reliant on the agreed purchase price as an indicator of value. Certain areas became 'fashionable' and valuers assumed that the properties in those areas would continue to show substantial rises in value. This phenomenon was particularly costly in relation to properties in London's Docklands. When the 'slowdown' came, many valuers over-optimistically assumed that it was simply a 'pause' and were slow to recognise the fact that prices were falling. Overvaluations of 100 per cent or more were common in both domestic and commercial cases.

Solicitors were under similar pressures and made a variety of errors. The property boom coincided with market pressure on conveyancing costs. Mistakes in reporting on the title to the security or on planning permission or on other matters to do with the property had always been made but the large volume of work and the necessity for swift completion of standardised documentation made them more common. Many of the problems in domestic cases arose from the much-criticised practice whereby a solicitor would act for both the borrower and the lender. In most domestic cases the solicitor acting in relation to the taking of security would have been chosen by the borrower. There would often be no previous connection with the lender and little contact during the transaction: it was easy for the solicitor to forget that he was acting for the lender at all. With increasing borrower fraud it became ever more important for solicitors to inform lenders of matters relating to the valuation or the borrower which might have led the lenders to investigate matters further. In many cases, the solicitors provided no information to lenders, consciously or unconsciously preferring the interest of what might be a long-standing borrower client.

When substantial borrower default occurred in the early 1990s, lenders were slow to pursue their remedies. Many lenders had administrative difficulties in coping with the large numbers of defaults and there were often substantial delays before possession proceedings were taken or pursued. Political pressure to reduce the volume of mortgage possessions led to a reluctance to obtain possession in cases where borrowers made some attempt to clear their arrears. When the lenders finally took possession of properties they obtained valuations which were often very substantially less than the sums outstanding. When retrospective valuations were commissioned, the lenders discovered many overvaluations. Further investigations revealed that many solicitors had not passed on information relevant to the lending decision to the lenders.

In a large percentage of domestic cases, the 'top slice' of the loan was covered by Mortgage Indemnity Guarantee policies (MIG policies). The insurance market had contributed to the process of expansion of domestic lending by relaxing the criteria which the lenders needed to satisfy in order to qualify for residential MIG policies. In most cases in which a MIG policy was in place, the insurance companies paid out the lenders and then brought claims against solicitors and valuers under subrogated rights.

The result of all this was that, from the early 1990s onwards, large numbers of claims began to be brought by lenders against solicitors and valuers. These professionals were usually insured and were, therefore, the best targets for litigation. There have been remarkably few cases against the other professionals involved in property finance cases: finance brokers and accountants. Most of the brokers were themselves victims of the property collapse. Numbers of them were involved in mortgage fraud. Few were insured or solvent. Many of the accountants who produced 'accounts' or 'certificates' for borrowers turned out to be unqualified. Most have proved difficult to trace and, if found, are often uninsured and insolvent.

The structure of typical transactions

It is not, of course, possible to give a comprehensive description of a typical property finance transaction. Commercial and domestic cases are, typically, structured in very different ways. Even within each lending sector, the mode of operation varies from lender to lender. There are substantial variations in the type and contents of the standard documentation. Nevertheless, it is useful to provide a basic outline of each type of transaction in order to show how the professionals are involved in a typical case.

In a domestic case, in the late 1980s and early 1990s, the transaction typically had the following stages:[10]

(1) *The application form*: This is a standard form supplied by the lender and completed by the borrower (often with the assistance of a 'broker'). It typically seeks details of the property (including its purchase price) and of the borrower's finances (including a limited amount of information about other commitments). In addition, the borrower nominates the solicitor who is acting for him and who will be acting for the lender. This form is not usually shown to either the solicitor or the valuer.
(2) *The valuation*: On the basis of the information about the property in the application form, the lender commissions a valuation. In the case of building societies, this is a standard form 'Report and Mortgage Valuation' (as required by s 13 of the Building Societies Act 1986). The typical valuation is two or three pages long, containing little information save for a short description of the property, references to substantial defects and a statement of what is usually expressed as the 'open market value for mortgage purposes' of the property. Such short form valuations occasionally draw attention to matters such as rights of way or planning permission which need to be specifically confirmed by the solicitor.
(3) *The offer of advance*: This sets out the sum which the lender is prepared to advance along with general conditions which had been completed and any special conditions arising from, for example, matters specifically raised in the valuation.
(4) *The instruction of the solicitors*: The solicitor is sent a letter of instruction and the offer of advance. This is usually accompanied by 'standard form instructions' to solicitors. In the majority of cases a copy of the valuation is not provided to the solicitor.
(5) *The report on title*: The solicitor completes the report on title. This is usually on a standard form and is often combined with the request for the advance cheque. The 'reporting' is usually confined to confirmation

---

[10] See the description by Chadwick J of some common features of building society procedure in *Bristol & West Building Society v May, May & Merrimans* [1996] 2 All ER 801, at 805g–809d.

that the title is 'good and marketable', that all the special conditions relating to the advance have been complied with and a confirmation to the effect that:

> ... the details of the transaction accord exactly with the particulars in the offer of advance and the requirements of the Solicitors' Instructions.[11]

The report on title form also often contains undertakings to complete the registration and to deliver the title deeds to the lender.

(6) *The release of the advance:* On receipt by the lender of the report on title the advance is paid over to the solicitor to be held by him pending completion of the advance.

(7) *Completion of the transaction*: The borrower executes the charge and the advance is released—either to the vendor's solicitor (in a purchase case) or to the previous mortgagee and borrower (in a remortgage case).

(8) *Registration of the charge*: The solicitor then completes the registration formalities by registering the charge at the Land Registry.

The transactions in commercial property lending cases were more varied than those in domestic cases. The following stages can be identified:

(1) *The offer letter:* It is rare to have a formal application form in a commercial case. Negotiations usually take place between the parties, sometimes through a broker. The borrower makes known his finance requirements and the security he is prepared to offer (often accompanied by a valuation prepared on his behalf). The lender considers the 'credit risk' and decides on the 'margin' he is prepared to offer. If the negotiations are successful they will result in an 'offer letter' from the lender to the borrower. This sets out the terms on which the lender is prepared to make the advance, setting out the conditions concerning valuation, other security and so on.

(2) *The instruction of the solicitors*: The solicitor is usually sent a letter of instruction, the offer letter and other relevant documents supplied by the borrower. It is rare for detailed letters of instruction to be sent to solicitors. In some cases, the solicitors are instructed at an earlier stage and consulted about the terms of the offer letter.

(3) *The valuation*: In a typical case, the lender would engage the valuer to report on title on the basis of limited written instructions. The valuer's report would normally be a substantial document containing description of the property and analysis. It is common for the lender to make further inquiries of the valuer to clarify points arising from the valuation report and to supply a copy to the solicitor for his comments.

---

[11]   The terms of the Bristol & West 'report on title' form; see *Bristol & West Building Society v May, May & Merrimans, ibid,* at 809a–b.

The valuation is sometimes provided to the lender at the negotiation stage and then a further copy is obtained, specifically addressed by the valuer to the lender.

(4) *The loan and security documentation*: In some commercial cases standard documentation is used. However, in most cases a loan agreement and security documentation is prepared by the lender's solicitors in consultation with the lender and with the borrower's solicitors. In addition to the legal charge over the property, the solicitor is involved in drafting other security documentation such as floating charges and guarantees.

(5) *The report on title*: The solicitor then completes a report on title. This is usually a relatively substantial document, describing the property and the title, reviewing leases, contracts, easements and so on, affecting the title. The lender relies on his solicitor to confirm that there is good and marketable title to the property and that his charge will rank ahead of any other claims on the property.

(6) *The release of the advance:* This is paid over to the solicitor to be held by him pending completion of the advance.

(7) *Completion of the transaction*: The borrower executes the loan agreement, the charge and the other security documentation. The advance is released when the conditions precedent in the loan agreement have been complied with.

(8) *Registration of the charge*: The solicitor then completes the registration formalities, at the Land Registry and usually the Companies Registry.

These outlines do not, of course, attempt to be comprehensive in any way. Their purpose is to provide initial orientation and guidance when the role of a professional at a particular stage of the transaction comes under scrutiny.

The contents of the book

The book sets out to analyse the law as it now stands in relation to property finance claims against solicitors and valuers. Chapter 1 deals with the duties owed by solicitors to lenders and the potential areas of claim. Chapter 2 analyses the position in relation to valuers. Chapter 3 covers the measure of damages available in claims in each case and Chapter 4 deals with interest claims. Chapter 5 discusses the law relating to limitation as applied in property finance cases. Chapter 6 deals with the apportioning of responsibility: between defendant and plaintiff when the defence of 'contributory negligence' is made out and between solicitor and valuer when both are liable for the same damage. Chapter 7 deals with the difficult questions of expert evidence in

property finance cases. Chapter 8 deals with the aspects of civil procedure which are of particular importance in such claims. The various
methods of valuation are considered in Appendix 1. Appendix 2 includes
relevant extracts from the RICS and ISVA guidelines to valuers acting
for mortgagees and the Law Society's 'Green Card' Guidance on mortgage fraud.

1 Solicitors' Duties

1.1 Introduction

A solicitor who acts for one or more of the parties to a loan transaction will owe a range of different duties to those involved.[1] Four sources of duty can be identified. The first will be the solicitor's contract of retainer. Under that contract he will owe express and implied obligations to his client. If the solicitor has been retained by more than one client involved in the same transaction then there will be more than one retainer. The express obligations owed to each client may differ. Secondly, a solicitor will owe tortious duties of care to both his client and some third parties who are foreseeably affected by his actions. Solicitors may owe duties of care in tort to non-client lenders who are members of syndicates. Duties may also be owed by solicitors who are acting for other parties to a transaction. Thirdly, a solicitor owes certain equitable obligations to his client. Some of these equitable duties arise out of the 'fiduciary' nature of the relationship between a solicitor and his client; others arise from the terms on which a solicitor holds client funds.

Finally, when a solicitor holds himself out as acting for a client, he represents that he has that client's authority to act. As a result, if it turns out that he does not have such authority, the solicitor is potentially liable for breach of warranty of authority.

In this chapter, we consider claims by lenders against solicitors under those four heads: claims for breach of contractual duties, claims in tort, claims for breach of fiduciary duty (including breach of trust) and claims for breach of warranty of authority.

1.2 Contractual duties

1.2.1 Introduction

The most important source of a solicitors' duties is the contract of

---

[1] See generally Jackson and Powell, *Professional Negligence* 3rd edn (1992), Chapter 4; *Cordery on Solicitors* (1995); Evans, *Lawyers' Liabilities* (1996).

retainer.[2] The terms of this contract regulate the solicitor's duties to the lender. In a property finance case the solicitor is usually retained by a lender to perform at least three basic tasks:

(a) to report on the title to the property being offered as security for the loan;

(b) to prepare and obtain the execution of the security documentation; and

(c) to take all necessary steps to register the security.

The solicitor is, of course, under an obligation to use reasonable skill and care in carrying out these and any other tasks which he is retained to carry out. But the exercise of reasonable skill and care is only one aspect of the solicitors' duty: analysis must begin with consideration of the retainer. As Oliver J put it:

> The extent of [the solicitor's] duties depends upon the terms and limits of that retainer and any duty of care to be implied must be related to what he is instructed to do ... The classical formulation of the claim in this sort of case [a solicitor's failure to register an option] as 'damages for negligence and breach of professional duty' tends to be a mesmeric phrase. It concentrates attention on the implied obligation to devote to the client's business that reasonable care and skill to be expected from a normally competent and careful practitioner as if that obligation were not only a compendious, but also exhaustive, definition of all the duties assumed under the contract created by the retainer and its acceptance. But of course it is not. A contract gives rise to a complex of rights and duties of which the duty to exercise reasonable care and skill is but one.[3]

When considering the contractual duties owed by a solicitor to a lender client it is first necessary to consider the express terms of the retainer and then to look at the terms which the law will imply into the contract of retainer.

1.2.2   Formation and express terms

It is rare for contracts of retainer to attempt to define solicitors' duties in comprehensive terms. In most cases, the retainer will not be contained in any formally agreed document but will be formed when the solicitor accepts the lender's instructions to act.

In domestic loan cases, the solicitor is commonly instructed by being sent a copy of the letter of instruction and the 'offer of advance' addressed to the borrower. This will usually be accompanied by 'standard form instructions' to solicitors. The formation of the contract of

---

2   See *Midland Bank Trust Co Ltd v Hett, Stubbs & Kemp* [1979] Ch 384, 402; *Groom v Crocker* [1939] 1 KB 194, 222.

3   *Midland Bank Trust Co Ltd v Hett, Stubbs & Kemp, ibid*, 434.

retainer in a typical domestic case has been described in the following way:

> The correct analysis, as it seems to me, is that the solicitor's letter contains an offer by the society to retain the solicitor as its solicitor for the purpose of the mortgage transaction described in the offer of advance ... [This offer] is one which, again prima facie, can be accepted by conduct. ... the offer is accepted, at the latest, when the solicitor returns the report on title and request for advance cheque.[4]

The contents of these 'standard form instructions' differ enormously from lender to lender. Many standard form instructions are printed on one or two pages and consist largely of formal requirements such as: that the solicitor lodge any application for registration within the priority period; that he ensure that full vacant possession of the property is available to the borrower on completion; that if the security is a leasehold property the lease contains appropriate covenants; that any necessary permissions and consents be obtained; and that documents be placed with the title deeds after completion.

In addition, the standard form instructions often contain general statements of the solicitor's duties, such as requirements that the solicitor ensure that the title is good and marketable[5] and that he advise the lender if any conditions of the offer of advance have not been complied with. Some lenders make specific provision for the reporting of matters such as second mortgages. For example, a condition to the effect that the solicitor should report:

> Any proposal that the applicant may create a second mortgage or enter into a promissory note or otherwise borrow in order to finance part of the purchase price.[6]

In some standard instructions drafted in recent years, lenders have expressly required solicitors to inform them of matters which have been the source of problems in the past. Examples include a provision that the solicitor advises the lender if he become aware of the existence of a sub-sale or if he considers that the borrower cannot comply with a condition of the loan, such as that the property be purchased as the principal residence of the borrower for his sole continuing occupation.

In other cases, the standard form conditions contain general 'sweeping up' clauses to the effect that the solicitor should report if there are any onerous or unusual covenants or if there are any matters of which the lenders should be aware which are likely to affect the value of the

---

4   *Bristol & West Building Society v May, May & Merrimans* [1996] 2 All ER 801, 809e–h.
5   The meaning of this term was recently considered in *Barclays Bank plc v Weeks Legg & Dean* [1996] EGCS 29.
6   Cheshunt Building Society Conditions, quoted in *Bristol & West Building Society v Mothew* (1996) unreported, 24 July, CA, judgment, p 3.

property or likely to impede the realisation of the security. For example, one building society gave solicitors instructions to report:

> Any matters which might prejudice the Society's security or which are at variance with the Offer of Advance should be notified to the Society in writing immediately they become known. Completion should not be arranged until the Society has indicated its willingness to proceed.[7]

The instructions which are given to the solicitor in domestic loan cases will generally be considered to be express terms of the contract of retainer.[8] However, even where there are fairly detailed solicitor's instructions, they will not generally be taken to be exhaustive of all that the lender expects the solicitor to do, or all that the law requires him to do, in the course of investigating title.[9]

In commercial property loan cases, it is unusual for a lender to have standard conditions for solicitors. Many commercial lenders have long-standing relationships with the solicitors which they use and neither party feels the need for detailed instructions. The instructions will often consist of a short letter accompanied by a copy of the proposed or actual offer letter. It is not uncommon for instructions in very substantial cases to be given and accepted orally.

In the absence of evidence of an express request for the solicitor to act for the lender the courts will infer such a request from the fact that legal services were provided[10] or from the request for a fee[11] even if the fee is to be paid not by the lender but by the borrower.[12]

1.2.3   Implied terms

In many cases presently proceeding through the courts no express instructions were given in relation to many relevant matters. In the absence of relevant express instructions lenders must rely upon 'implied terms'.

There is a considerable body of case law as to the terms to be implied into a contract of retainer.[13] The Law Society's *Guide to the Professional Conduct of Solicitors*[14] provides very useful guidance as to the ambit of solicitors' duties to their clients. However, it should be borne in mind

---

[7]   Bristol & West Building Society, quoted in *Bristol & West Building Society v May, May & Merrimans* [1996] 2 All ER 801, 808. See also *Bristol & West Building Society v Kramer* [1995] TLR 57.

[8]   *Bristol & West Building Society v Kramer, ibid.*

[9]   *Bristol & West Building Society v May, May & Merrimans* [1996] 2 All ER 801, 813.

[10]   *Bean v Wade* (1885) 2 TLR 157, CA.

[11]   *Gurd v A Cobden Soar & Son* (1951) 157 EG 415.

[12]   *Scholes v Brook* (1891) 63 LT 837.

[13]   See Jackson and Powell, *Professional Negligence* 3rd edn (1992), paras 4–38 *ff*.

[14]   7th edn (1996).

that this document provides guidance only: while it may assist the court in deciding what terms are to be implied into the retainer, a breach of its provisions 'cannot ipso facto and of necessity be negligence'.[15]

The fact that a solicitor is acting for both borrower and lender does not reduce his duties to the lender.[16] The duties which a solicitor owes to a lender are at least as extensive as those owed to a purchaser.

Three implied terms are of particular importance in property finance cases:

(a) the duty to use reasonable skill and care;
(b) the duty to keep the lender informed as to relevant matters; and
(c) the duty to inform the lender if a conflict of interest arises.

These are considered in the next three sections.

1.2.4   Duty to exercise reasonable skill and care

The contract of retainer contains an implied obligation by the solicitor to exercise reasonable skill and care in carrying out the terms of his retainer. The standard of reasonable skill and care is, in general, that of the 'reasonably competent practitioner'.[17] The classic formulation is that of McNair J in *Bolam v Friern Hospital Management Committee*[18] (often referred to as 'the Bolam test'):

> Where you get a situation which involves the use of some special skill or competence, the test as to whether there has been negligence ... is: the standard of the ordinary skilled man exercising and professing to have that special skill. A man need not possess the highest expert skill; it is well established that it is sufficient if he exercises the ordinary skill of an ordinary competent man exercising that particular art.

In other words, the court applies the ordinary standards of solicitors, not those of the particularly 'meticulous or conscientious' practitioner.[19] A solicitor is not expected to show perfect judgment and is not 'bound to know all the law'. However a solicitor must have sufficient knowledge of the fundamental issues and principles of law applicable to the particular work he has undertaken to enable him to perceive the need to ascertain the law on the relevant points.[20]

However, if the client retains a solicitor of high standing or experience—for example, a City solicitor specialising in complex property loans—he is entitled to expect something more than the 'reasonably

---

[15] See *Johnson v Bingley* (1995) *The Times*, 28 February, B Hytner QC.
[16] See *Mortgage Express Ltd v Bowerman Partners* [1996] 2 All ER 836, 841a–b.
[17] See *Midland Bank Co Ltd v Hett, Stubbs & Kemp*, [1979] Ch 384, 402–3.
[18] [1957] 1 WLR 582, at 586.
[19] Per Oliver J in *Midland Bank Trust Co Ltd v Hett, Stubbs & Kemp* [1979] Ch 384, 403.
[20] See *Central Trust Co v Rafuse* (1986) 31 DLR (4th) 481, 524.

competent'.[21] The fact that a solicitor holds himself out as an expert in a particular specialism entitles the client to expect, and obliges the solicitor to perform to, a higher standard than that of the reasonably prudent and competent solicitor.[22] The fact that a solicitor acts in accordance with the 'general practice' of solicitors in relation to a particular matter will not, of itself, provide him with a complete defence. Thus, in *Edward Wong Finance Co v Johnson Stokes & Master*,[23] the Privy Council held that a solicitor who had competently carried out a 'Hong Kong style' completion was negligent because of the inherent risks of the procedure. The general principle has been expressed as follows:

> The ultimate question, however, is not whether the defendant's conduct accords with the practice of his profession or some part of it, but whether it conforms to the standard of care demanded by the law. That is a question for the Court and the duty of deciding it cannot be delegated to any profession or group in the community.[24]

A solicitor's conduct must be judged by the standards of the time.[25] This is particularly important in mortgage fraud cases where the profession has become increasingly aware of problems over recent years. These issues of fraud were drawn to the attention of the profession by the issue of the Law Society's *Guidance on Mortgage Fraud*[26] in December 1990 and the *'Green Card' Warning on Property Fraud*[27] in March 1991. Any solicitor failing to take appropriate steps to deal with the 'warning signs' mentioned after March 1991 is likely to be held to be in breach of duty. However, despite the fact that these documents were the 'distillation or codification of existing good practice'[28] a solicitor who failed to detect signs of fraud in, say, 1988 or 1989 is unlikely to be subjected to the same standard of care.

The duty of care can be expressed as containing a number of general obligations.[29] Failures by solicitors to take appropriate steps in the performance of their duties are often simply expressed as a 'failure to take reasonable skill and care' rather than as breaches of more specific implied obligations.[30]

---

[21]   See *Duchess of Argyll v Beuselinck* [1972] 2 Lloyd's Rep 172, 183; whether these *dicta* were correct or not was left open by Simon Brown LJ in *Martin Boston & Co v Roberts* [1996] 1 PNLR 45. See generally, Jackson and Powell, *Professional Negligence* 3rd edn (1992), paras 4-52 *ff*.

[22]   *Benson v Thomas Eggar & Son* (1977) unreported, 2 December, Forbes J.

[23]   [1984] AC 1296.

[24]   *F v R* [1984] 33 SASR 189, 194.

[25]   See *Bell v Strathairn & Blair* (1954) 104 LJ 618.

[26]   *Guide to the Professional Conduct of Solicitors* 7th edn (1996), Annex 25F, p 426. At Appendix 2, below.

[27]   *Ibid*, Annex 25G, pp 427–8. At Appendix 2 below.

[28]   See *Mortgage Express Ltd v Bowerman & Partners* [1996] 2 All ER 836, 842c.

[29]   See, for example, *Tiffin Holdings v Millican* (1965) 49 DLR (2d) 216.

[30]   See Jackson and Powell, *Professional Negligence* 3rd edn (1992), para 4-05.

1.2.5 Duty to keep the lender informed

It is clear that when a solicitor is retained, he comes under a duty:

> ... to protect the client's interest and carry out his instructions in the matters to which the retainer relates, by all proper means. It is an incident of that duty that the solicitor shall consult with his client on all questions of doubt which do not fall within the express or implied discretion left to him, and to keep the client informed to such an extent as may be reasonably necessary according to the same criteria.[31]

In acting to protect a lender's interest in a property finance case, the solicitor must report on title and secure the execution and registration of the relevant charge documentation. The extent to which the solicitor's implied duties go beyond these 'core matters' has been a matter of controversy.

The case of *Mortgage Express Ltd v Bowerman & Partners*[32] dealt with the question of the solicitor's duty to report information which appeared to cast doubt on the valuation obtained by the lender. The borrower applied to the lender for a loan of £180,000. The defendants were solicitors who acted for both borrower and lender. On the basis of a valuation of £190,000 the lender made a mortgage offer of £180,150. The borrower's immediate vendor was simultaneously purchasing the property for £150,000. The defendants were aware of this price but did not give this information to the lender. The loan was completed and, some time later, the borrower defaulted. The central allegation of negligence against the defendants was that they failed to inform the lender of the two recent sales and the fact that the second was for a substantially lower amount than the valuation or the price paid by the borrower. The fact that the sub-vendor had bought at £150,000 cast serious doubt on the correctness of the valuation. Had the lender known these facts it would have sought another valuation, which, it was argued, would have revealed that the value of the property was considerably lower than the amount of the loan. This would have caused the lender to withdraw its offer of mortgage finance. The defendants argued that the £70,000 difference between the sale and sub-sale prices was not a matter giving rise to any cause for concern provided that the purchasing client understood and accepted the situation. There was no reason to suspect that the valuation was incorrect and the information had no effect on title, therefore there was no reason or obligation to report the price discrepancy to the plaintiff.

This argument was rejected by Arden J and the Court of Appeal. At

---

[31] Per Scott LJ in *Groom v Crocker*, [1939] 1 KB 194, 222; and see Principle 9.16 of the *Guide to the Professional Conduct of Solicitors* 7th edn (1996).

[32] [1996] 2 All ER 836.

first instance[33] Arden J held that:

(a) the solicitor's duties to a lender are not limited to advising on the purely technical aspects of the conveyance in hand. The scope of the solicitor's duties extends further than simply investigating and certifying title. It includes informing the lender of any matter which the reasonably competent solicitor ought to realise would or might affect the lender's decision and, if so, how much, to lend to the borrower. This includes matters which might have a bearing upon how a valuation of the security is viewed;

(b) the duty is equally onerous when the solicitor acts simultaneously for borrower and lender. In other words, the solicitor must act for each party with as much care and diligence as if he acted for one only; and

(c) in carrying out that duty the solicitor must consult with the lender on all questions of doubt which are outside his discretion to resolve unaided and keep the lender informed of relevant matters as far as may be reasonably necessary.

This decision was upheld on appeal. The Court of Appeal rejected the argument that, when acting for a lender, a solicitor's only duty is to report on title:

> A client cannot expect a solicitor to undertake work he has not asked him to do and will not wish to pay for such work. But if in the course of doing the work he is instructed to do he comes into possession of information which is not confidential and which is clearly of potential significance to the client, I think the client would reasonably expect the solicitor to pass it on and feel understandably aggrieved if he did not.[34]

As a result, the court accepted the lender's submission that:

> ... if in the course of investigating title a solicitor discovers facts which a reasonably competent solicitor would realise might have an effect on the valuation of the lender's security or some other ingredient of the lending decision then it is his duty to point this out.[35]

In short, although a solicitor does not, unless expressly instructed to do so, take on obligations to carry out detailed investigations on behalf of a lender client, he cannot 'shut his eyes' to the obvious: if relevant information comes to his attention he must pass it on to his lender client.

Whether or not a particular item of information is 'relevant to the lending decision' depends on a factual analysis of the circumstances of each case. However, it is clear that the duties imposed on solicitors have

---

[33]   [1994] 2 EGLR 156.
[34]   Per Sir Thomas Bingham MR, at 842.
[35]   At 842f–g. See also Chadwick J's formulation of the duty in *Bristol & West Building Society v May, May & Merrimans*, [1996] 2 All ER 801, 814.

become more onerous over the past ten years or so in the light of the increasing professional awareness of mortgage fraud, and the various danger signals which tend to indicate either a dubious valuation or a risk of borrower default.

It is submitted that information in the following areas is relevant and should be disclosed to a lender client:

(1) *Information casting doubt on the valuation*: It is clear that the following facts are relevant and should be reported by solicitors to lender clients:

- information affecting value which would be given to a purchaser client, concerning matters such as planning permission or building regulation;
- the fact that there has been a sub-sale to the borrower at a substantially increased price, or a chain of previous sales at substantially lower prices than the valuation or price being paid by the borrower;[36]
- the fact that the property has recently been sold for a significantly lower price than that stated in the valuation;[37] and
- in transactions after, say, 1990, the mere fact that there was a sub-sale.

In *Mortgage Express* the solicitor was sent the valuation document on which the lender was proposing to rely. He therefore knew precisely the discrepancy between the price of the sub-sale and what the lender thought the property was worth. However the fact that, as will often be the case, the solicitor is *not* sent the valuation (and so does not know the amount of the valuation upon which the lender is relying) will not mean that the solicitor comes under no obligation to disclose to the lender the fact of the sub-sale. The solicitor will generally know what the proposed advance sum is (because it will be stated in the offer of advance) and therefore can and will readily infer that the lender has been supplied with a valuation which values the property at a figure at least 10 per cent higher:

> In considering whether some fact which has come to his knowledge in the course of investigating title—for example, the price payable by the intermediate vendor who is selling on to the society's borrower by way of sub-sale—would or ought to have caused the solicitor to doubt the valuation (alternatively, would or ought to have caused him to realise that the lender might question the valuation) it cannot be without relevance that the solicitor does not know the valuation advice the Society has received in respect of the property. But the relevance, as it seems to me, is that in particular cases it may be more difficult to say that the solicitor ought to

---

[36] See *Mortgage Express* itself.
[37] See *BBL v Eagle Star* [1995] 2 All ER 769.

have realised that knowledge of the particular fact might have caused the lender to question the valuation.[38]

It remains unclear whether, in relation to pre-1991 transactions, the mere existence of a sub-sale should have been reported to a lender. This has been treated as a difficult point in a number of summary judgment applications. For example, in *Bristol & West Building Society v Heath & Co*[39] in relation to an argument that a sub-sale and direct deposit should have been notified to the lender, the judge said:

> ... the events occurred in 1989 before the first references in print to sub-sales and direct deposits being indicative of mortgage fraud. It is therefore arguable that at that time a reasonable solicitor would not have been aware that the sub-sale and deposit might prejudice the Society.

Although the issue does not appear to have been finally determined by any court, the consensus of opinion among conveyancers appears to be that, in the late 1980s, before 'mortgage fraud' became a matter of general concern, a reasonably competent solicitor would not, without more, have regarded a sub-sale as suspicious.

(2) *Information suggesting fraud by the borrower:* In *Mortgage Express,*[40] the court drew attention to the fact that, in December 1990, the Law Society had given guidance on mortgage fraud to solicitors in the following terms:

> Solicitors must not withhold information relevant to a transaction from any client and for a lender this includes not only straightforward price reductions but may also include other allowances (eg for repairs, payments of costs, the inclusion of chattels in the price and incentives of the kind offered by builders such as free holidays and part-subsidisation of mortgage payments) which amount to a price reduction and which would affect the lender's decision to make an advance.[41]

This guidance was said to represent 'the distillation or codification' of existing good practice.[42] In March 1991, the Law Society issued its *'Green Card' Warning on Mortgage Fraud*, drawing attention to 'signs to watch for'. A number of these are matters which, it is submitted, a solicitor should report to a lender if they are suspected to be present:

- the fact that unusual instructions have been given in relation to the payment of the purchase price—for example that it be remitted to the estate agent (*Green Card* (2));

---

[38] *Bristol & West Building Society v May, May &Merrimans* [1996] 2 All ER 801, 813.
[39] (1995) unreported, 26 July.
[40] At 842.
[41] *Guide to the Professional Conduct of Solicitors* 7th edn (1996), Annex 25F.
[42] *Mortgage Express*, at 842.

- the fact that the true cash price payable is different from the consideration stated in the contract or in the mortgage instructions (*Green Card* (3));
- the fact that the deposit is said to have been paid 'direct' by the borrower to the vendor (*Green Card* (4));
- the fact that the contract documentation is incomplete—because, for example, dates are missing (*Green Card* (5));
- the fact that adjustments have been made to the purchase price—particularly in high percentage mortgage cases (*Green Card* (6)); or
- the fact that the transaction does not follow its expected course according to the usual pattern of events (*Green Card* (7)).

Although there is no direct authority on the point, it is submitted the following matters are also relevant:

- the fact that there are or may be material inaccuracies in the information given to the lender by a domestic borrower is also relevant. These may, for example, concern income, existing financial commitments, the use of the property as a domestic residence or the fact that the borrower has other mortgages. While domestic lenders have not usually supplied a copy of the mortgage application form to the solicitor, this information may be known to the solicitor from other sources or be clear as a matter of inference; and
- the fact that the borrower's 'purchase' is not an arms length transaction (because, for example, he is the beneficial owner of the vendor company).

(3) *Information casting doubt on the borrower's ability to repay:* If the solicitor is aware of information which suggests that the borrower will not be able to repay the loan, he is under a duty to disclose this to his lender client. Thus the fact that, in a domestic purchase case of a modest property, the fact that the borrower is known to own other properties which are also mortgaged, will clearly be relevant to the decision whether or not to make a loan. However, the limits of the solicitor's duty under this head remain controversial. In *Birmingham Midshires v Parry*[43] Sir John Vinelott said:

> … a solicitor is not required to investigate the borrower's financial position and is entitled to assume that the mortgagee has himself made such inquiries as he thinks necessary.[44]

In *Halifax Mortgage Services Ltd v Howes Percival*[44a] the judge went

---

[43] (1995) unreported, 23 February, ChD.
[44] Transcript, p 21.
[44a] (1996) unreported, 4 March, Official Referee's Business, Mr Recorder Seymour QC.

further and appeared to suggest that the duty to disclose relevant matters was limited to matters relevant to the value of the property. The plaintiff in that case had sought summary judgment against the solicitor who had acted on a remortgage case but had failed to inform the lender that the borrower had fallen into arrears on the loan with their existing lender who had taken possession proceedings. The judge held that there was no duty to disclose this information and dismissed the action. In analysing the duty of solicitors he said:

> A prudent lender ... investigates, to the extent necessary to satisfy himself as to the borrower's ability to perform his obligations, the intending borrowers income and commitments. Unless specifically informed that such investigation has not been made, in my judgment a solicitor acting for a lending institution is entitled to assume that the lending institution has undertaken all of the investigations which it considers necessary to justify its lending decision.[44b]

It is submitted that the approach suggested by these cases is not correct. Although it is clear that, in the absence of specific instructions, a solicitor is not under a duty to make investigations into the borrower's finances, he is not entitled to 'shut his eyes' to relevant matters. The solicitor may be aware of information which would not be discovered by a lender's ordinary inquiries or which may have been concealed. Whatever assumptions the solicitor makes as to what investigations have been carried out, he is under a duty to report relevant information on the mortgagor's financial position to his lender client.

1.2.6   Duty to draw a lender's attention to a conflict of interest

A solicitor can, with the informed consent of the clients, act for both borrower and lender.[45] This is, of course, common practice in domestic property lending. However, the fact that a solicitor acts for more than one client does not cut down the duties of both confidentiality and disclosure owed to each:

> A solicitor who acts for more than one party to a transaction owes a duty of confidentiality to each client, but the existence of this duty does not affect the duty to act in the best interests of the other client. All information supplied by a client to his solicitor is confidential and may be disclosed only with the consent, express or implied, of his client.[46]

Where a solicitor acting for lender and borrower receives information confidential to the borrower and which is relevant to the lending

[44b] Judgment pp 12–13.
[45] See section 1.5.2 below.
[46] *Mortgage Express Ltd v Bowerman & Partners* [1996] 2 All ER 836, 844j , per Millett LJ.

decision, he must seek the borrower's consent to disclose it to the lender. In the absence of such consent:

> ... their duty to communicate the information to [the lender] was super-seded by a duty to tell [the lender] that they could no longer act for it because a conflict of interests had arisen.[47]

A solicitor who then continues to act after becoming aware that information confidential to the borrower is relevant to the lending decision will be in breach of this duty.

1.2.7   Claims for breach of contractual duty

The claims brought by lenders in property finance cases cover a wide range of areas. The most common include:

(a)   'Report on title errors', for example failure to discover title defects; failure to ensure that terms of a lease which is to stand as security are satisfactory for a lender's purposes; or failure to report difficulties with rights of way;

(b)   other conveyancing errors, for example failure to ensure that the necessary planning permissions are in place; failure to carry out local searches; failure to take proper steps to ensure that NHBC certificates or building regulation approvals have been obtained in relation to a new building;

(c)   failure to provide information relevant to valuation, for example information concerning previous sales at a lower price;[48]

(d)   failure to provide information relevant to borrower fraud, for example non-confidential information concerning direct deposits or sub-sales;

(e)   failure to withdraw when a conflict of interest arises, for example when the borrower refuses consent to the provision of confidential information concerning other mortgages into which he has entered; and

(f)   failure to register the lender's interest within the priority period or submit transfers for stamping outside the statutory period.

1.3   Duties in tort

1.3.1   General principles

It is now clear that a solicitor is under concurrent liability in both contract

---

[47]   *Halifax Mortgages Services Ltd v Stepsky* [1995] 3 WLR 701, 716E; see also *Mortgage Express Ltd v Bowerman & Partners*, [1996] 2 All ER 836, 841d.

[48]   For example, *Mortgage Express Ltd v Bowerman & Partners* [1994] 2 EGLR 156; [1996] 2 All ER 836.

and tort to his client. This was settled by the decision of the House of Lords in *Henderson v Merrett Syndicates Ltd*[49] in which Lord Goff said that:

> ... an assumption of responsibility coupled with the concomitant reliance may give rise to a tortious duty of care irrespective of whether there is a contractual relationship between the parties, and in consequence, unless his contract precludes him from doing so, the plaintiff, who has available to him concurrent remedies in contract and tort, may choose that remedy which appears to him to be the most advantageous.

In most cases a breach of express or implied terms of the retainer will also give rise to a liability in tort. This liability is of relevance when limitation issues arise.[50]

The House of Lords approved the decision to this effect by Oliver J in *Midland Bank Trust Co v Hett, Stubbs & Kemp*[51] in which he had declined to follow previous authority to the contrary.[52] As in a claim for breach of the contract of retainer, the standard to be applied is that of the 'ordinarily competent practitioner'. However, when a solicitor holds himself out as having a particular specialism (for example in acting for lenders on particular types of property finance transactions) then the standard of care is different:

> ... a [professional] who professes to exercise a special skill must exercise the ordinary skill of his speciality.[53]

1.3.2   Duties to opposing parties

In the leading case of *Gran Gelato v Richcliff (Group) Ltd*[54] it was held that, in a normal conveyancing transaction, a solicitor acting as agent of one party did not owe a duty of care to other parties. The basis of this finding was that, in general, where a principal owes a duty of care to a third party, the existence of a further duty of care owed by the agent to the third party is not necessary for the fair protection of the third party.[55] The *Gran Gelato* case is often thought to be an example of a special rule

---

[49] [1995] 2 AC 145. The issue of concurrent liability is also considered in *Caparo Industries plc v Dickman* [1990] 2 AC 605; *Smith v Eric S Bush* [1990] 1 AC 831; *Murphy v Brentwood District Council* [1991] 1 AC 398; and *Tai Hing Cotton Mill Ltd v Liu Chong Hing Bank Ltd* [1986] AC 80. See also *Lee v Thompson* [1989] 2 EGLR 151.

[50] See Chapter 5 and *Nitrigin Eireann Teoranta v Inco Alloys Ltd* [1992] 1 All ER 854.

[51] [1979] Ch 384.

[52] See *Groom v Crocker* [1939] 1 KB 194; generally, Jackson and Powell, *Professional Negligence* 3rd edn (1992), paras 4-08 *ff*.

[53] See *Maynard v West Midlands Regional Health Authority* [1985] 1 All ER 635, HL—a medical negligence case.

[54] [1992] Ch 560. See also *CEMP Properties (UK) Ltd v Denstply Research & Development Corp* [1989] 2 EGLR 205.

[55] *Ibid*, per Sir Donald Nicholls, at 571.

to the effect that 'a solicitor acting on behalf of a client, owes a duty of care only to his client'.[56]

There has, however, been a slow 'retreat' from *Gran Gelato* over the past four years.[57] In *White v Jones*[58] the House of Lords held that a solicitor was liable to an intended beneficiary under a will in circumstances where his negligence might result in the loss of an intended legacy. It was held that the assumption of responsibility of a solicitor towards his client extended to the intended beneficiary.

In *Penn v Bristol & West Building Society*,[59] a husband and wife were joint owners of a property. Unknown to his wife, the husband entered into an arrangement to sell the property, forging her signature on the documents. It was held that the solicitor, Mr Brill, who had been instructed by the husband, owed the wife a duty of care:

> ... although Mrs Penn was never a client of Brill she was reasonably within his contemplation when he received the title deeds (indeed, she was *necessarily* within his contemplation) and her interest as co-owner was sufficiently proximate to the transaction in which he was engaged (concerning as it did her jointly owned home) for Brill to owe her a duty of care according to the principles enunciated by the House of Lords in *White v Jones*.[60]

The duty owed by solicitors to third parties was analysed, *obiter*, by Hobhouse LJ in *McCullagh v Lane Fox & Partners*.[61] He pointed out that, when a solicitor was providing information to another party in answer to an inquiry:

> ... the duty in tort arises from the act of the solicitor in choosing to answer the inquiry. There is only one duty: it is the duty of the solicitor to take reasonable care in answering. The duty in tort is both created and broken by the solicitor. The *tortious* liability of the principal is, in this context, not for what he has done himself but is a vicarious liability for the tort of the solicitor.[62]

Hobhouse LJ drew attention to the fact that the 'governing principle' was still that of *Hedley Byrne & Co v Heller & Partners*[63] and that, in general, an agent was responsible for careless misrepresentation as much as his principal. He suggested that the 'special rule relating to solicitors' concerned only the exercise of *professional* duties:

[56] Per Lord Goff, *White v Jones* [1995] 2 AC 207, 256.
[57] See generally, Dirik Jackson, 'Liability on Sale and Purchase of Property', paper delivered to the PNBA, 20 January 1996.
[58] *Ibid*.
[59] [1995] 2 FLR 938.
[60] At 949E–F.
[61] [1996] 18 EG 104, 114–115; see also Evans, *Lawyers' Liabilities* (1996), Chapter 3.
[62] At 111, col 2.
[63] [1964] AC 465.

It is in the activities covered by the *rules and standards* of his profession and his *duties to the court as one of its officers* that the restriction applies. Within that framework and when exercising the *standard of skill and care appropriate to his status as a solicitor* his duty is confined to that to his client. In any other situation, or when it is a *reliance* (i.e. *Hedley Byrne*) case, the special rule does not apply.[64]

It is submitted that this approach is correct and that, as a result, a solicitor acting on a property finance transaction may be liable to a party who is not his client either in circumstances where there is a 'direct proximity' (as in *Penn*) or where the solicitor makes a representation to the other party which is relied on.

1.4   Claims in syndicated loan cases

1.4.1   Introduction

In a syndicated loan case, it is unusual for each member of the syndicate personally to instruct the solicitor to act. In the case of large commercial loans, where the syndicate may have dozens of members, this would be extremely expensive and unwieldy. In practice, the solicitor is instructed by the 'arranger' or 'lead lender'. In those circumstances, are the other members of the syndicate, who are not in direct contractual relationship with the solicitor and whose identity may not be known to him, owed duties in contract or tort by the solicitor?

Two types of syndication can be distinguished:

(a)   where the lead lender who retains the solicitors is acting as the agent for a syndicate whose membership and the extent of their 'participation' in the loan has been fixed by the date on which the advance is made; and

(b)   where the loan agreement provides for the 'sale down' of part of the loan to other lenders after the advance has been made. These banks then become parties to the loan transactions by assignment or novation, so that they acquire direct rights against the borrower.

Both types of syndication have been considered in the cases.

1.4.2   Original syndicate members

The first type of transaction was considered in *N M Rothschild & Sons v Berensons*.[65] In that case, the plaintiffs were a syndicate of lenders providing finance to a company which was the client of the defendant

---

[64]   *Ibid*, 113, col 1.
[65]   (1995) unreported, 22 June, ChD.

solicitors. The lead lender was the only party who had a contract with the solicitors. The defendants failed to report that lending criteria had not been adhered to and, in particular, that a proper security was not obtained. Knox J rejected the solicitors' argument that they did not owe duties to unknown members of the syndicate. He said:

> I see no reason for the duty not to extend to parties concurrently involved with [the lead lender] in advancing the relevant funds. The ambit of the duty is sufficiently defined by the amount advanced in the particular transaction. Fellow lenders are within a clearly identifiable class of persons engaged in the particular transaction … A duty of care to a lender as principal can properly extend to a duty of care to the same lender as agent for an undisclosed principal.[66]

Knox J emphasised the fact that the potential liability of the defendant was fixed by reference to the original transaction. A duty of care can be clearly identified which is based not on a knowledge of the identity of the persons who are going to rely upon or be affected by the defendant's statement, but rather upon the clear understanding by the defendant that a certain sum of money is being lent in reliance upon the defendant's advice.

1.4.3 Claims for loss suffered by sub-participants

There are two potential routes by which a claim could be made against the solicitor who advised the agent bank for losses suffered by sub-participants. First, it is possible that the agent bank might make a claim on behalf of the sub-participant under 'transferred loss' principles. Secondly, the sub-participant could make a direct claim in tort. We will consider these possibilities in turn.

The first possibility—claims by the agent—was considered in *BBL v Eagle Star*.[67] BBL were the agent bank in respect of a loan which was subsequently 'sold down' to a number of sub-participants. BBL claimed damages from the valuers of the properties which formed the security for syndicated loans. This claim reflected not simply BBL's eventual exposure, but the entirety of the loss sustained by the syndicate. This claim was based on two arguments.

First, it was contended that the principle of *res inter alios acta* applied so that the fact that BBL had received an indemnity from a third party in relation to a proportion of the loan amount could not be brought into account when assessing its damages. This argument was rejected by Phillips J who held that the principle did not apply:

---

[66] Transcript, pp 71–2.
[67] [1995] 2 All ER 769.

The principle of *res inter alios acta* requires the court to disregard an indemnity received by the plaintiff from a third party in respect of the loss caused by the defendant. It does not require or permit the court to assess damages on the basis of a fiction; to treat losses sustained by a third party as if they have been sustained by the plaintiff. The intervention of the syndicate banks did not indemnify BBL in respect of the consequences of entering into the loan transactions. It resulted in the syndicate banks suffering those consequences in place of BBL. The loss claimed by BBL is not suffered by BBL prior to syndication, but loss suffered by all the syndicate banks after syndication. The principle of *res inter alios acta* does not permit BBL to recover damages in respect of losses sustained by the syndicate banks.[68]

Secondly, it was argued that BBL were entitled to recover for the loss suffered by the syndicate members on the basis of the 'transferred loss' principles outlined in the case of *Linden Gardens Trust Ltd v Lenesta Sludge Disposals Ltd*.[69] In that case, the plaintiff had entered into a building contract and then later sold the building to a third party before the defendant's breaches of contract had been discovered. It appeared that the party with the cause of action (the plaintiff) had suffered no loss, and the party with the loss (the new owner of the building) had no cause of action, with the result that the loss had disappeared into a 'black hole' between the two. The House of Lords solved this conundrum by holding that an intention could be imputed to the parties that the plaintiff had entered into the original building contract 'on the footing that' it could recover for losses for the benefit of purchasers.

This argument was also rejected by Phillips J. He said that *Linden Gardens* was a case of breach of a contractual duty to supply work and materials whereas *BBL v Eagle Star* involved inducing a plaintiff to act to its detriment by negligent advice. He also held that in so far as 'substitute banks' had been induced by the valuation to join the syndicate they were likely to have independent causes of action against the valuers of their own. These points of distinction are unconvincing and it is submitted that, in an appropriate case, an agent bank could bring a *Linden Gardens* claim against a solicitor.

The second possible route for claims by sub-participants involves the making of direct claims in tort. The starting point for such claims is the fact that it is likely that the solicitor will have drafted the syndicated loan agreement, and will, therefore, be aware that it was intended that the loan would be 'sold down' to sub-participants. In these circumstances, if the sub-participant can show that it relied on advice given by the solicitor, then ordinary *Caparo v Dickman*[70] principles apply.

---

[68]   At 802h–j.
[69]   [1994] 1 AC 85.
[70]   [1990] 2 AC 605.

Even in the absence of proof of reliance, there is a strong argument that the solicitor would owe sub-participants a duty of care in any event. Thus, in *Punjab National Bank v De Boinville*[71] the Court of Appeal held that a professional owed a duty of care to someone who was known, at the time of the transaction, to be a prospective assignee of the benefit of the transaction. It is also clear that, at least in the case of an insurance syndicate, this duty may extend to future members of the syndicate, unidentified and unidentifiable at the time of the relevant transaction, who can be foreseen to be likely to suffer damage as a result of the negligent performance of the professional's duties in relation to the transaction.[72] It is submitted that analogous argument can be applied to the position of sub-participant lenders and that, as a result, they will be entitled to bring direct claims in tort against the solicitors who advised at the inception of the syndicated loan.

This argument receives further support from the House of Lords' decision in *White v Jones*.[73] Lord Nolan put the general principle as follows:

> A professional man or an artisan who undertakes to exercise his skill in a manner which, to his knowledge, may cause loss to others if carelessly performed, may thereby implicitly assume a legal responsibility toward them.[74]

Any solicitor acting for a lead bank in relation to a syndicated loan facility will obviously know that participants may join the syndicate at some later date. Secondly, he will obviously know that if such participants do join, they will reduce the participation of the lead bank. The result of this will be that the quantum of any potential damages claim by the lead bank will be reduced. If, therefore, no duty is owed to the sub-participants, the liability of the solicitor will be arbitrarily reduced to the extent that others participate, and the loss of the other participants will fall into the 'black hole' of irrecoverability. This is contrary to the policy considerations which found favour with the majority in *White v Jones*.

1.5 Fiduciary duties

1.5.1 Fiduciary relationships

There are particular categories of relationship in respect of which the

---

[71] [1992] 1 WLR 1138.
[72] See Potter J in *Aitken v Stewart Wrightson Members Agency* [1995] 1 WLR 1281, at 1307–13.
[73] [1995] 2 AC 207.
[74] At 294.

law will impose fiduciary duties. These include the relationship of trustee and beneficiary, director and company, agent and principal and, relevantly for present purposes, solicitor and client. There is no doubt that a solicitor stands in a fiduciary relationship to his client.[75]

No comprehensive definition of fiduciary duty is possible. It has been said recently that:

> A fiduciary is someone who has undertaken to act for or on behalf of another in a particular matter in circumstances which give rise to a relationship of trust and confidence. The distinguishing obligation of a fiduciary is the obligation to loyalty. The principal is entitled to the single-minded loyalty of his fiduciary.[76]

The obligation of a fiduciary has a number of aspects including the following:[77]

(a) a duty to act in good faith;

(b) a duty not to place himself in a position where his duty and interest may conflict;[78] and

(c) a duty not to act for his own benefit or for the benefit of a third party without the informed consent of his principal.

Where a fiduciary deals with his principal, who thereafter seeks to set aside the transaction or to claim damages, the fiduciary must prove that the transaction was fair and that he made full disclosure of material facts.[79]

When there is a contractual relationship between the parties, this regulates the basic rights and liabilities between them and will determine the nature and extent of the fiduciary duties owed. Indeed the contract may modify what are normally considered to be fiduciary duties.[80] Not all duties owed by a fiduciary are fiduciary duties.[81] In particular, as the Court of Appeal made clear in the leading case of *Bristol & West Building Society v Mothew*,[82] although a fiduciary owes his principal a duty of care, this is not a fiduciary duty:[83]

---

[75]   See *Nocton v Lord Ashburton* [1914] AC 932, 952.
[76]   *Bristol & West Building Society v Mothew* (1996) unreported, 24 July, CA, judgment, p 24.
[77]   *Ibid*, p 24 and see generally, Finn, *Fiduciary Obligations* (1977).
[78]   See section 1.5.2 below.
[79]   See *Demerara Bauxite v Hubbard* [1923] AC 673; and generally, Finn, *ibid*, pp 428–39.
[80]   See *Hospital Products v United States Surgical Corporation* (1984) 156 CLR 41, 97; approved *Kelly v Cooper* [1993] AC 205, 215, PC. See also *Henderson v Merrett Syndicates Ltd* [1995] 2 AC 145, 205–6, per Lord Browne-Wilkinson; *Clark Boyce v Mouat* [1994] 1 AC 428, 437, PC.
[81]   See *Girardet v Crease* (1987) 11 BCLR 361; and *LAC Minerals Ltd v International Corona Resources* (1989) 61 DLR (4th) 14, 28.
[82]   (1996) unreported, 24 July.
[83]   Judgment, pp 21–3, per Millett LJ; indorsing the comments of Ipp J in *Permanent Building Society v Wheeler* (1994) 14 ACSR 109, 157–8 and see *Henderson v Merrett Syndicates Ltd* [1995] 2 AC 145, 205–6, per Lord Browne-Wilkinson.

Breach of fiduciary obligation ... connotes disloyalty or infidelity. Mere incompetence is not enough. A servant who loyally does his incompetent best is not unfaithful and is not guilty of a breach of fiduciary duty.[84]

The result of this is that there is no advantage to a plaintiff in framing a claim against a solicitor for incompetence as a breach of an equitable obligation:

Although the remedy which equity makes available for breach of the equitable duty of skill and care is equitable compensation rather than damages, this is merely the product of history and in this context ... is a distinction without a difference. Equitable compensation for breach of the duty of skill and care resembles common law damages in that it is awarded by way of compensation to the plaintiff for his loss. There is no reason in principle why the common law rules of causation, remoteness of damage and measure of damages should not be applied by analogy in such case. It should not be confused with equitable compensation for breach of fiduciary duty ...[85]

As a result, a claim against a solicitor which amounts to an allegation of negligence cannot properly be framed as a breach of fiduciary duty. After *Mothew* it would appear that claims for breach of fiduciary duty will be limited to a case in which there is a breach of one of the specific fiduciary duties mentioned above. In particular, claims in property finance cases will commonly arise where the solicitor is placed in a position of conflict of interest.

1.5.2   Conflict of interest

In general, a fiduciary must avoid conflicting engagements because they may lead to his being unable adequately to discharge one engagement without conflicting with his obligation under another.[86] However, it is clear that:

There is no general rule of law that a solicitor cannot act for both parties to a transaction where their interest may conflict. Rather it is the position that he may act provided that he has obtained the informed consent of both to his acting. Informed consent means consent given in the knowledge that there is a conflict between the parties and that as a result the solicitor may be disabled from disclosing to each party the full knowledge which he possesses as to the transaction or may be disabled from giving advice to one party which conflicts with the interest of the other. If both parties are content to proceed upon this basis the solicitor may properly act.[87]

---

[84]   *Bristol & West Building Society v Mothew* (1996) unreported, 24 July, CA, judgment, p 25.

[85]   *Ibid*, judgment, p 23. See further Chapter 3, at section 3.8.

[86]   See, for example, *Commonwealth Bank of Australia v Smith* (1991) 102 ALR 453, 477.

[87]   See *Clark Boyce v Mouat* [1994] 1 AC 428, 435F–H.

On many occasions the courts have warned about the 'perils which a solicitor acting for more than one party can encounter'.[88] It is possible that when a solicitor acts for two parties, he may find his duties to his clients in such conflict that he will inevitably incur liability to one of them.[89] A solicitor who realises that a proposed transaction is potentially disadvantageous to one of his clients is obliged to give strong advice as to conflict to the potentially disadvantaged client. A failure to do so will render the solicitor liable for breach of duty.[90]

Nevertheless, in the context of domestic property finance transactions it is common for one solicitor to act for both borrower and lender. For the most part the interests of the lender and the borrower will coincide. Both are concerned to ensure that the purchaser obtains good and marketable title to the property.

The fact that a fiduciary has the informed consent of two parties with potentially conflicting interests does not relieve him of his fiduciary obligations. In *Bristol & West Building Society v Mothew*[91] Millett LJ identified a number of principles applying to a fiduciary who has potentially conflicting engagements:

(a) 'the duty of good faith'—the fiduciary must act in good faith in the interests of each and must not act with the intention of furthering the interests of one principal to the prejudice of those of the other;

(b) 'the no inhibition principle'—the fiduciary must not be inhibited by the existence of the other employment from serving the interests of his principal as faithfully and effectively as if he were the only employer; and

(c) 'the actual conflict rule'—the fiduciary must take care not to find himself in a position where there is an actual conflict of duty so that he cannot fulfil his obligations to one principal without failing in his obligations.

The effect of *Mothew* is that in order for conduct to be in breach of fiduciary duty it need not be dishonest but it must be intentional: negligent breach of these duties will not place the solicitor in breach of his fiduciary duty, though it will put him in breach of his ordinary duty of care. The fact that the solicitor has the means to know that a particular statement he has made is false, or that a particular step would put him in breach of his fiduciary duty, does not allow the court to conclude, without more, that he therefore 'knew' that he was making a misrepresentation or acting in breach of fiduciary duty. [92]

---

[88]   Per May J, *Mahoney v Purnell* [1996] 3 All ER 61; see also *O'Reilly v Law Society of NSW* (1988) 24 NSWLR 204.

[89]   See *Moody v Cox* [1917] 2 Ch 71, 91; and *Goody v Baring* [1956] 1 WLR 448.

[90]   See *Mahoney v Purnell* [1996] 3 All ER 61, 94e.

[91]   (1996) unreported, 24 July, CA.

[92]   *Ibid*, 19–20.

In *Mortgage Express Ltd v Bowerman & Partners* at first instance[93] the question of the nature of the solicitors' duties when acting for both borrower and lender in a mortgage transaction was confronted directly. The court identified two different sets of circumstances in each of which different principles relating to the disclosure of information by a solicitor to his client would apply.

The first is where a solicitor acting for lender and borrower receives information not confidential to either one or the other. In such a situation the question whether the solicitor is under a duty to disclose this information depends on the nature of that information and in particular whether it is in the interest of the party who might be told it, to learn of it. If it is relevant to that party, the information should be disclosed to him.

The second is where a solicitor acting for lender and borrower receives information confidential to one of them. In that event it would be necessary for the solicitor to obtain the consent of the client whose information it is, to disclose it to the other, and if consent is refused the solicitor may be obliged to cease to act for the other party or both parties.

The practical workings of such a rule can be seen in *Halifax Mortgages Services Ltd v Stepsky*.[94] A husband and wife remortgaged their property. The husband stated in the loan application form that the purpose of the remortgage was 'to buy family shares in business', whereas in fact, as the solicitors appointed by the borrowers—and later instructed by the lender—knew, the purpose of the loan was to discharge the husband's business debts. In the lender's proceedings for possession the wife claimed that the lender was fixed with constructive notice that the loan was not for the joint benefit of both husband and wife because of the solicitors' knowledge. This argument was rejected on the basis that although the solicitors, as the lender's agents, were under a *prima facie* duty to reveal to the lender the true purpose of the loan, that duty was in conflict with the duty of confidentiality to the borrowers. Because the solicitors were not free to pass the information to the lender a knowledge of the true purpose of the loan could not be imputed to the lender.

Finally, it should not be forgotten that even if a solicitor does allow a conflict of interest between two clients to arise and even if there is a failure to deal with such conflict on the basis of the principles outlined above, substantial equitable compensation will not be awarded unless it can be shown that a loss was suffered. Thus in *Elland Developments Ltd v Smith*[95] the defendant solicitors acted for both purchaser and

---

[93] [1994] 2 EGLR 156.
[94] [1995] 3 WLR 701.
[95] [1995] EGCS 141.

vendor in the sale of land. The purchaser sued the solicitors for failing to advise it concerning potential title problems relating to the land which made it subsequently difficult to sell. Rattee J dismissed the claim, holding *inter alia* that although the solicitors could be criticised for acting for both purchaser and vendor, they were not in breach of duty to the plaintiff. Although the solicitors had put themselves in a position of conflict of interest, as this was not of itself causative of loss, it did not of itself saddle the solicitors with any liability.

1.6   Solicitors as trustees

1.6.1   Trusts of advance monies

When the lender pays an advance to a solicitor pending its payment out to the borrower, the solicitor does not claim any beneficial interest in the money but holds on bare trust for the lender with the lender's authority to apply it to the completion of the transaction.[96]

The solicitor will be liable to a claim for breach of trust if the advance monies are paid away otherwise than 'in completion of the transaction': in other words, provided that the money is paid to the borrower or his nominee after the execution of the security documents, the solicitor will not commit a breach of trust.

However, where a solicitor pays the advance to the borrower before the charge is executed, he will have no answer to a claim for breach of trust. A claim of this type was made by the lender in the case of *Target Holdings v Redferns*.[97] The defendant solicitors were retained by lenders in a mortgage transaction in which the lenders lent £1.525 million to a company, P Ltd, secured on property valued, allegedly negligently, at £2 million. The solicitors were also retained by P Ltd. Another company, C Ltd, had initially bought the property for £775,000 and sold it on to K Ltd for £1.25 million which had in turn sold the property to P Ltd for £2 million. All three companies were owned by the same two people. Prior to completion the lenders paid the loan amount to the solicitors. The solicitors informed the lenders that the purchase of the property and the charge had been completed, when in fact these transactions had not yet taken place. Before completion actually took place the solicitors paid over the sums to P Ltd and K Ltd. Some days later the various transfers and the charge were completed. P Ltd defaulted on its loan obligations and the lenders repossessed the property and sold it for £5 million. It was conceded by the solicitors that they were guilty of breach of trust. The Court of Appeal held that, as a result, they

---

[96]   See *Target Holdings v Redferns* [1994] 2 All ER 337; [1996] 1 AC 421; and *Bristol & West Building Society v Mothew* (1996) unreported, 24 July, CA, judgment, p 32.

[97]   [1994] 2 All ER 337 CA; [1996] 1 AC 421, HL.

were liable to replace all the monies paid away. Their decision was over-turned by the House of Lords on the ground that the quantum of com-pensation for breach of trust was to be assessed at the date of judgment as the figure necessary to put the lenders in the position in which they would have been had there been no breach of trust. However, Lord Browne-Wilkinson made it clear that:

> … the circumstances under which the solicitor can part with money from the client account are regulated by the instructions given by the client: they are not part of the trust on which the property is held. I do not intend to cast any doubt on the fact that moneys held by solicitors on client account are trust moneys.[98]

A solicitor's authority to apply the advance to the completion of the transaction is not 'automatically vitiated'[99] by the fact that the money was paid over to the solicitor as the result of a misrepresentation (for example as to title). Therefore a payment away 'to complete the trans-action' by the solicitor after the advance monies have been received by reason of a misrepresentation or non-representation will not be a breach of trust. This is because a misrepresentation makes the transaction void-able, not void: if a solicitor makes misrepresentations in the report on title, this gives the lender the right to rescind the transaction. However:

> The right to rescind for misrepresentation is an equity. Until it is exercised the beneficial interest in any property transferred in reliance on the repre-sentation remains vested in the transferee.[100]

Although a lender could stipulate that the solicitor's authority to complete the transaction was 'conditional on having complied with his instructions':

> … it would … require very clear wording to produce so inconvenient and impractical a result. No solicitor could safely accept such instructions, for he could never be certain that he was entitled to complete.[101]

The recipient of trust money cannot be personally liable for payment away of the monies if, at the date of such payment, he is ignorant of the existence of the trust.[102]

1.6.2   Constructive trusts

In *Bristol & West Building Society v Mothew*[103] Chadwick J held that, when

---

[98]   At 436C.
[99]   See the reasoning of Chadwick J in *Bristol & West Building Society v May, May & Merrimans* [1996] 2 All ER 801, at 816–8.
[100] See *Bristol & West Building Society v Mothew* (1996) unreported, 24 July, CA, judg-ment, p 33.
[101] *Bristol & West Building Society v Mothew*, *ibid*, judgment, p 35.
[102] See *Westdeutsche Landesbanke v Islington Borough Council* [1996] 2 WLR 802.
[103] (1995) unreported, 27 July, ChD.

a solicitor submitted a misleading report on title to a lender, he held the advance which was paid over as a result of the report on constructive trust for the lender with an immediate obligation to repay. Chadwick J returned to the point in *Bristol & West Building Society v May, May & Merrimans*[104] where he gave detailed reasons. His analysis was based on the solicitor's obligations as fiduciary. He accepted that the Court of Equity would only intervene where the solicitor's obligations as fiduciary. He accepted that the Court of Equity would only intervene where the solicitor was guilty of 'unconscionable conduct' but held that this requirement was made out:

> ... where a solicitor who is acting for both borrower and lender misrepresents to the lender some fact which he knows, or must be taken to know, will or may affect the lender's decision to proceed with the loan. In those circumstances the solicitor is abusing his fiduciary relationship with one client, the lender, to obtain an advantage for his other client, the borrower.[105]

As a result:

> ... equity will give a remedy in respect of any loss which the [lender] may suffer as a result of its payment in reliance upon that request. That will be a remedy based upon breach of fiduciary duty and may, where necessary, take the form of the imposition of a constructive trust.[106]

When the solicitor paid the advance to the borrower he was acting in breach of this constructive trust.

In relation to causation, Chadwick J distinguished *Target Holdings* and applied the principle set out by the Privy Council in *Brickenden v London Loan & Savings*[107] to the effect that:

> ... where a fiduciary has failed to disclose material facts, he cannot be heard to say, in answer to a claim for equitable compensation, that disclosure would not have altered the decision to proceed with the transaction.[108]

As a result, when the plaintiff had advanced money based on a misleading report on title, it was unnecessary to try the question as to whether the plaintiff would have made the advance if it had been told the true facts.

This analysis was rejected by the Court of Appeal in *Bristol & West Building Society v Mothew*[108a] who held that:

(a) a failure to exercise reasonable care did not constitute a breach of fiduciary duty;

(b) an unconscious omission did not constitute a breach of a fiduciary duty.

---

[104] [1996] 2 All ER 801.
[105] At 817j–818a.
[106] At 818d–e.
[107] [1934] 3 DLR 465.
[108] 826h.
[108a] (1996) unreported, 24 July.

As a result, no constructive trust arose on the facts of that case. It was not, however, disputed that:

> ... a party who pays money to his solicitor in reliance on a representation *known* by the solicitor to be false has a remedy in breach of fiduciary duty.

In such a case the solicitor would clearly be 'abusing his fiduciary relationship' with his lender client. It appears, therefore, that the court could impose a 'remedial' constructive trust could arise in these circumstances.

Because no trust arose in *Mothew* case, the Court of Appeal did not consider Chadwick J's analysis of the *Brickenden* principle on causation. This principle has been applied in a number of recent Commonwealth cases but was *obiter* and appears to be inconsistent with a well established line of authority.[108b] The *Brickenden* case was referred to in the printed cases in *Target Holdings*[108c] but was not cited. It is submitted that any principle established by the case is inconsistent with the approach of the House of Lords in *Target Holdings*. As a result, if a solicitor is guilty of a breach of a construcitve trust, the lender will still have to establish that the breach of trust caused damage in accordance with ordinary 'common law' principles.

1.7   Solicitor's warranty of authority

When a solicitor represents that he is acting for a client and a third party relies on this representation to his detriment, the solicitor warrants the authority which he claims in representing his client.[109] This is an example of the general principle that:

> ... where a person by asserting that he has the authority of the principal induced another person to enter into any transaction which he would not have entered into but for that assertion and the assertion turns out to be untrue, to the injury of the person to whom it is made, it must be taken that the person making it undertook that it was proved, and he is liable personally for the damage that has occurred.[110]

Because it is based upon a warranty, the liability of a person who professes to act as agent arises whether or not he has been negligent in representing himself to have authority.[111] Furthermore:

> ... it is not necessary that the representation of authority should be made

---

108b See generally, J D Heydon, 110 LQR 328.
108c [1996] 1 AC 421.
109 *Yonge v Toynbee* [1909] 1 KB 215.
110 Per Lord Esher, *Firbanks' Executors v Humphries* (1886) 18 QBD 54.
111 See *Colleen v Wright* (1857) 8 E & B 647, 657.

expressly; merely purporting to act as agent will normally constitute a representation.[112]

The application of these principles to property finance negligence cases is illustrated by the case of *Penn v Bristol & West Building Society*.[113] In that case, the property was jointly owned by a husband and wife. The husband instructed solicitors to act on the 'sale' of the property to an accomplice. He forged the wife's signature on a purported contract of sale and the building society advanced the purchase price to the accomplice. The judge held that:

(a) the solicitors had made a continuing representation by conduct that they were authorised by the wife to act on the sale of the property; and

(b) the lender was induced by this representation to make an advance to the husband's accomplice.

As a result, the lender succeeded in its claim for damages for breach of warranty of authority against the solicitors.

---

[112] *Penn v Bristol & West Building Society* [1995] 2 FLR 938, 953B–C.
[113] *Ibid.*

2 Valuers' Duties

2.1 Introduction

A valuer who provides a report which is used by a lender can be potentially liable for breach of duties in both contract and tort.[1] The cause of action on which the duty is based may have a significant impact on the availability of 'limitation' defences.[2]

Recent decisions have clarified the relationship between these two types of duty. The debate which existed concerning whether a party in contractual relationship with another owed a concurrent duty in tort was resolved by the decision of the House of Lords in *Henderson v Merrett Syndicates Ltd*[3] where Lord Goff confirmed that a plaintiff could legitimately plead his case in both contract and tort.[4]

In practice, therefore, causes of action in tort and contract will generally be pleaded in the alternative and no practical distinction made between the two. As Sir Thomas Bingham MR said in the Court of Appeal in *BBL v Eagle Star*:[5]

> In the absence of special conditions, and whether the duty is contractual or tortious, [the valuer's] duty to [the lender] is the same: to take reasonable care to give a reliable and informed opinion on the open market value of the land in question at the date of valuation.

Furthermore, the High Court of Australia has suggested that in cases involving allegations against professionals of failures to discharge their duties, in deciding the question of liability, the court will look at the ordinary law of negligence, rather than attempt to imply into the particular contract terms not expressly set out.[6]

In professional negligence cases, any duty of care owed in tort will generally be co-extensive with the contractual duty. However parties to a contract may expressly narrow, modify or even exclude altogether

---

[1]   See generally Jackson and Powell, *Professional Negligence* 3rd edn (1992), Chapter 3; Murdoch & Murrells, *Law of Surveys and Valuations* 1st edn (1995); Joyce and Norris, *Valuers' Liability* 2nd edn (1994) (Aust).

[2]   See Chapter 5, below.

[3]   [1995] 2 AC 145; see also *Brickhill v Cooke* [1984] 3 NSWLR 396.

[4]   At 194; see 1.2.1, above.

[5]   [1995] 2 QB 375, at 403–4.

[6]   *Hawkins v Clayton Utz* (1988) 164 CLR 539, 574, per Deane J.

the duty which would otherwise arise in tort.[7] On the other hand the courts have recognised that the factual circumstances of a relationship between two parties may mean that, even though those parties have entered into a contract with each other at some stage during the course of the relationship, that contract (and any terms which can be implied into it) may not be finally determinative of the ambit or extent of the duty of care owed in tort. If, using the terminology of Lord Goff, there is an 'assumption of responsibility' by one person (A) to another person (B), and concomitant reliance by B (which founds the duty of care in tort), and that assumption of responsibility is referable to a wider set of factual circumstances than those which give rise to a concurrent contract between A and B, then there is no reason why the duty of care cannot impose wider obligations upon A than those arising under the contract:

> The difference in scope between the two will reflect the more limited factual basis which gave rise to the contract and the absence of any term in that contract which precludes or restricts the wider duty of care in tort.[8]

Of course, given the defined role of the valuer in most secured lending situations, the duty of care owed by the valuer to the lender, where there is a contract, will generally arise out of the same factual circumstances as those giving rise to the contract, and so the duties will be not only concurrent but also co-extensive.

It is nevertheless still important to be able to identify the relevant cause or causes of action, and to analyse what duties are owed in either tort and/or contract. In a property finance negligence case, this task will vary according to the facts of the particular lending transaction.

2.2   Contractual duties

The receipt and acceptance by a valuer of instructions for reward, whether the instructions are contained in a document or are given orally, will create a contract between client and valuer. Misunderstanding by the valuer as to the precise terms of the instructions, or failure on the client's part to properly instruct the valuer, can often lead to litigation, quite apart from failures to carry out instructions themselves.[9] If there has been a misunderstanding then it is likely that the valuer will be held responsible for failing to clarify with his client the precise basis and ambit of the valuation and the assumptions which have been

---

[7]   See *Henderson* per Lord Browne-Wilkinson, at 206G; and per Lord Goff at 194D.

[8]   Per Hirst LJ in *Holt v Payne Skillington* (1995) unreported, 12 December.

[9]   See, for example, *Predeth v Castle Phillips Finance Co Ltd* [1986] 2 EGLR 144; *South Australia Asset Management Corp v York Montague Ltd* [1995] 2 EGLR 219; and *Beaumont v Humberts* [1990] 2 EGLR 231.

made.[10] As a result, *Practice Statement* (henceforth 'PS') 2.1 of the *RICS Appraisal and Valuation Manual* (1996) (as amended) states that:

> To achieve client satisfaction and minimize the scope for misunderstand-ing and subsequent dispute, it is essential that whenever possible the valuer seeks to establish and understand at the outset the client's needs and requirements. (In some cases the use of standard Conditions of Engage-ment and a written agreement that they are to apply between the Client and the Valuer on a continuing basis will facilitate this) ... The valuer must seek to establish the purpose of the valuation or appraisal from the Client and/or his professional advisors, so that the Valuer can check that an appropriate basis of valuation is being specified ... Since disputes may arise many years after a valuation or appraisal has been provided, it is important to ensure that the agreement between the parties is contained in, or evidenced by, comprehensive documents.[11]

To this end, the RICS and the British Bankers' Association have drafted model conditions of engagement.[12]

If litigation is contemplated, analysis of the precise terms and ambit of the instructions will be vital, for it is these instructions, whether they were originally delivered orally or in a document, which will define the express duties which were undertaken by the valuer.

Where the client (in the sense of the person who retains and instructs the valuer) is the lender, and the consideration for the valuation is paid by the lender, no further difficulties arise: the lender can frame his cause of action in contract. The relevant contractual obligation which the valuer is alleged to have breached will generally be the same as the duty of care owed in negligence. Section 13 of the Supply of Goods and Services Act 1982 imports an implied term into any contract of valua-tion that the valuer will exercise reasonable care and skill in carrying out his instructions.

However, lenders in commercial loan transactions often do not them-selves commission or pay for the valuation upon which they rely in the making of the loan. The borrower pays for the valuation, whether at the request of the lender or even before making an application to the lender. In such cases it may be possible, on consideration of all the cir-cumstances, to spell out a contract between valuer and lender. It is note-worthy that, although the case was pleaded in both tort and contract, the judge in *B M Samuels Finance Group plc v Countrywide Surveyors Ltd*[13]

---

[10] See *Re Solomon* [1912] 1 Ch 261.
[11] Examples of actions generated by failures of valuers to clarify instructions in writing include *Shankie-Williams v Heavey Williams* [1986] 2 EGLR 139; and *Mirage Entertain-ment Corp Ltd v Arthur Young* (1992) 6 NZCLC 96–577.
[12] Set out at 'Valuation Guidance Note' (henceforth 'VGN') 12 (Annex) of the *Manual of Valuation Guidance Notes* and at 'PS 8' of the *Appraisal and Valuation Manual* (1996),which is extracted in Appendix 2 below.
[13] (1994) unreported, 15 June, HHJ Loyd QC.

considered the question whether there was indeed a contract between lender and valuer to be merely of 'academic importance', given the fact that, in the circumstances of the case, the valuer clearly owed the lender a duty of care.

2.3   Claims in tort

2.3.1   Introduction

It is common for there to be no contract between lender and valuer. Sometimes, for example, the borrower will obtain a valuation relating to the property he wishes to utilise as security and then produce that valuation to prospective lenders. The valuation, although initially directed to the borrower, may be redirected to the prospective lender at the instructions of the borrower, who remains liable at all times for the valuer's fees.[14] The potential pitfalls of this practice were revealed in *BBL v Eagle Star*[15] where the borrowers obtained a number of 'armchair' valuations from different valuers and then instructed the valuer who provided the highest of these to undertake a full valuation, which was then shown to the lender.

In such a case the plaintiff's claim can lie only in negligent misstatement.[16] The valuer will be liable in negligence to a lender only if:

(a)   a duty of care is owed by the valuer to the lender in relation to the preparation of the valuation report;

(b)   the valuer breaches that duty of care when he compiles the report; and

(c)   the lender is induced to advance money to the borrower in reliance upon the valuation report.

The first condition can give rise to legal difficulty and is considered in the next two sections. The second and third conditions are matters of expert and factual evidence and are considered below.[17]

2.3.2   Duty of care

The decision of the House of Lords in *Hedley Byrne & Co v Heller & Partners Ltd*[18] established that a person might owe a duty of care in relation to a negligent statement relied upon by a person who as a result suffered economic loss. The court emphasised the need to establish a

---

[14]   See, for example, *Private Bank & Trust v S (UK) Ltd* [1993] 1 EGLR 144.
[15]   [1995] 2 All ER 769.
[16]   The attempt in *BBL* to establish a contractual relationship between lender and valuer failed.
[17]   See 2.3.4 and 2.4 below.
[18]   [1964] AC 465.

'special relationship' between plaintiff and defendant, defined as an 'assumption of responsibility' by the defendant[19] prior to the imposition of such a duty.

There has been much controversy concerning the necessary elements for establishing the existence of a duty of care owed by one person to another person in negligent misstatement cases. The question was considered in *Caparo Industries plc v Dickman*[20] in which a three-stage test was proposed. Lord Bridge said[21] that:

> What emerges is that, in addition to the foreseeability of damage, necessary ingredients in any situation giving rise to a duty of care are that there should exist between the party owing the duty and the party to whom it is owed a relationship characterised by the law as one of 'proximity' or 'neighbourhood' and that the situation should be one in which the court considers it fair, just and reasonable that the law should impose a duty of a given scope on the one party for the benefit of the other party.

Lord Oliver analysed the relationship necessary to establish a duty of care between the maker of a statement or giver of advice and the recipient who acts in reliance upon it, and identified the following requirements:

(a) that the advice is required for a purpose, whether particularly specified or generally described, which is made known, either actually or inferentially, to the adviser at the time when the advice is given;

(b) that the adviser knows, either actually or inferentially, that his advice will be communicated to the advisee, either specifically or as a member of an ascertainable class, in order that it should be used by the advisee for that purpose;

(c) that it is known, either actually or inferentially, that the advice so communicated is likely to be acted upon by the advisee for that purpose without independent inquiry; and

(d) that it is so acted upon by the advisee, to his detriment.[22]

This approach is helpful in pragmatically applying the 'three-stage' test to the facts of any given case. It will be apparent that it reflects the law's recent concern not to impose too wide a potential liability upon professionals.[23]

The operation of these principles can be seen by comparing *Caparo* with *Smith v Bush*.[24] In *Caparo* the plaintiff owned shares in a public company and, having received the audited accounts produced by the

[19] Per Lord Devlin, at 528.
[20] [1990] 2 AC 605.
[21] At 617–618.
[22] *Ibid*, at 638.
[23] See also *James McNaughton Paper Group Ltd v Hicks Anderson & Co* [1991] 2 QB 113, 125 *ff*.
[24] [1990] 1 AC 831.

defendants, purchased more shares and eventually made a successful take-over bid for the company. The plaintiff alleged it had suffered loss by relying on the accounts, which overvalued the company, and purchasing the shares at an overvalue. The House of Lords held that the defendants did not owe the plaintiff a duty of care. The known purpose of the accounts was to enable shareholders to exercise the powers conferred on them by their ownership of the shares, not to enable them to speculate in the purchase of future shares. The fact that the 'purpose' of the accounts was not to assist investors in making further investment decisions was, for their Lordships, a crucial consideration for denying a duty situation.[25]

On the other hand, in *Smith v Bush* the fact that the purpose of the valuation was not to assist the purchaser in deciding whether to buy the particular property, or if so at what price (indeed there was a specific disclaimer to the effect that it should not be relied on for this purpose), did not deter the House of Lords from imposing a duty. The House found for the purchaser on the ground that the valuer would have known that in respect of a modest residential purchase the purchaser was unlikely, being in receipt of one valuation, to commission another for himself, and that therefore the valuer could be expected to have realised that his valuation, whatever caveats were imposed upon it, would be relied upon by the purchaser.

In property finance negligence cases there is usually little difficulty in establishing that where the borrower commissions a valuation which is clearly for mortgage purposes—so that the valuer knows, or can infer, that the valuation will be shown to a prospective lender—there is a duty owed by the valuer to the lender.[26] Often the valuation, although commissioned and paid for by the borrower, will be re-directed by the valuer himself to the lender, so that the valuer will know the precise identity of the lender who is intending to rely upon his valuation. In domestic purchaser cases, the position will generally be the direct opposite: the lender will commission the valuation which will then be shown to, and relied upon by, the purchaser.

In general, then, the absence of a direct contractual relationship between lender and valuer will not be determinative of (and may indeed be irrelevant to) the issue of whether a duty is owed, and, if so, whether a breach is actionable. The position was summarised in *Smith v Eric Bush*[27] in the following terms:

> A valuer who values property as security for a mortgage is liable either in contract or in tort to the mortgagee for failure on the part of the valuer to exercise reasonable skill and care in the valuation. The valuer is liable in

---

[25]   See, for example, per Lord Jauncey at 658.
[26]   See, for example, *Singer & Friedlander v Wood (John D) & Co* (1977) 243 EG 212.
[27]   [1990] 1 AC 831, per Lord Templeman, at 841.

contract if he receives instructions from and is paid by the mortgagee. The valuer is liable in tort if he receives instructions from and is paid by the mortgagor but knows that the valuation is for the purpose of a mortgage and will be relied on by the mortgagee.

2.3.3 Duties to lenders whose identities are unknown

The fact that the precise identity of the lender is not known to the valuer will generally be irrelevant to the existence of the duty of care. Thus, in *Assured Advances v Ashbee & Co*[28] the defendant valuer provided a valuation on the instructions of brokers who made it clear that the valuation was sought for lending purposes, but did not disclose to the defendants the name or type of lender who had commissioned it or the amount of the proposed loan. The valuation was passed to the plaintiff who made a loan in reliance upon it. The defendants argued that they owed no duty of care to the plaintiff, of whose identity they had not been aware when making the valuation. The judge held that the fact that the identity of the lender was unknown to the defendant valuers did not negative the existence of a duty of care as defined in *Caparo*, and that the reliance of the plaintiff lender fell within the contemplation of the valuers at the time of the valuation.

Counsel for the valuer in *Assured Advances* asked whether a valuer 'is to be held to owe a duty of care to anyone into whose hands that valuation might come?' While, in general terms, the answer to that question must be no, in that case the identity of the lender was 'easily ascertainable'. The judge held that it might have been a different matter 'if the valuation had then passed from hand to hand until a lender could be found', but held that, in the circumstances of the case:

> ... even in that event I tend to the view that, if the same brokers were involved, sufficient proximity would exist and ... the defendants would have owed a duty of care to the eventual lender.[29]

In the Australian case of *J B Plowman v K J McCarney & Associates Pty Ltd*[30] the court also considered the question of the circumstances when a duty of care will be owed to a lender whose identity is unknown to the valuer. In *Plowman* the valuation was made for a company, AHL, which lent in its own right and also acted as an intermediary between lenders and borrowers. The valuation came into the hands of a trustee who lent in reliance upon it. On the facts of the case, where it was not clear how the valuation had come into the hands of the lender (and indeed it appeared that the report may have been stolen from AHL) the

[28] 17 October 1994; [1994] EGCS 169, QBD.
[29] Transcript, p 3.
[30] (1990) unreported, 14 December, District Court of New South Wales.

claim failed: the judge rejected the plaintiff's argument that 'the relevant class of persons' to whom a duty was owed included 'all investors who lent money on the security of a mortgage over the property which had been valued'. He held that the relevant class was limited to AHL and any lender which might be induced by AHL to lend money in reliance on the valuation.[31]

A novel duty situation arose in *Scotlife Home Loans (No 2) Ltd v Gibson MacNeile*.[32] The valuer had provided a valuation, as requested, addressed to Scotlife Home Loans (No 1), although (No 2), which was a sister company, actually relied upon the valuation and made the loan. The mistake as to identity was the lender's. The argument that no duty of care was owed to (No 2) by the defendant was rejected: the defendant knew that the report would be relied upon, and had sufficient knowledge of the connection between the two companies to be under a duty of care to (No 2).

The analysis, however, will be more complex where the valuation is obtained by a lender who is the lead bank for a syndicate of other banks. In those circumstances, can the other participant banks, who are not in a direct contractual relationship with the valuer, and will probably not even be known to the valuer, maintain an action against the valuer in negligence?

In *BBL v Eagle Star*,[33] BBL were the agent bank in respect of a loan which was subsequently 'sold down' to a number of sub-participants. BBL claimed damages reflecting not simply their eventual reduced exposure, but the entirety of the loss sustained by the syndicate. This claim was rejected by Phillips J who suggested[34] that the syndicate banks probably had an independent cause of action in tort against the defendant valuer in so far as they could show that they were induced to join the syndicate by reliance upon the valuations provided by the valuer. The position is therefore that syndicate banks need to be joined as plaintiffs to any action against a negligent valuer.[35] Indeed, in *B M Samuels Finance Group plc v Countrywide Surveyors Ltd*[36] where the first plaintiff had syndicated the loan to 16 other lenders, all 16 lenders were joined as plaintiffs. It is submitted that if syndicate banks are able to show that they relied upon the valuation they will have a direct cause of action in tort against the valuer, whether their participation was con-temporaneous with, or subsequent to, the loan transaction.

---

31   This analysis accords with English law: see particularly *Smith v Eric Bush* [1990] 1 AC 831, per Lord Griffiths at 862 *ff*; and *Caparo v Dickman*, above.
32   [1995] EGCS 106.
33   [1995] 2 All ER 769.   34   At 801 *ff*.
35   For more detailed consideration of duties in syndicated lending see 1.4 above. Phillips J held that neither the *res inter alios acta* principle nor *Linden Gardens Trust Ltd v Lenesta Sludge Disposals Ltd* [1994] 1 AC 85 assisted the plaintiff.
36   (1994) unreported, 15 June, HHJ Loyd QC.

2.3.4 The need to establish reliance

'Reasonable reliance', as an objective principle, is a necessary precondition to the existence of a duty of care in negligent misstatement cases. However, even where the duty has been shown to have arisen (whether in tort or contract) and been breached, the plaintiff must prove, on the balance of probabilities, that it *in fact* relied upon the valuation in making the particular loan; ie that the breach caused the loss. The judge in *Nyckeln Finance Co Ltd v Edward Symmons*[37] stated the position in the following terms:

> In a claim for damages for breach of contract against a professional man it is necessary, if the plaintiff is to recover other than purely nominal damages, for the plaintiff to show that he would have acted differently if properly advised … in my judgment the same approach is to be adopted in tort, so that for the defendant who has allegedly given negligent advice to the plaintiff to be liable to the plaintiff, it is necessary for the plaintiff to prove not only that he has suffered damage, but also that he has done so as a result of relying upon the advice, in the sense that had he been properly advised he would have done something different.[38]

If the plaintiff is to show the necessary causal link between breach and loss, then it must establish that the valuation played a 'real and substantial part in inducing' him to make the loan. As was said in *JEB Fasteners Ltd v Marks Bloom & Co:*[39]

> As long as a misrepresentation plays a real and substantial part, though not necessarily a decisive part, in inducing a plaintiff to act, it is a cause of his loss and he relies upon it, no matter how strong or how many are the other matters which play their part in inducing him to act.[40]

The plaintiff therefore need not show that the valuation was the sole factor which caused it to enter into the loan transaction; indeed, that would generally be a hard task when other factors, such as the strength of the borrower's covenant and the existence of mortgage indemnity insurance or third party guarantees, will also influence the lending decision.[41]

The courts take a pragmatic view of issues of causation and reliance. So in an unreported appeal from Phillips' J's decision in *BBL v Eagle Star* it was held that the real test of whether negligence was the effective

---

[37] (1996) unreported, compare *Downs v Chappell* [1996] 3 All ER 344, 359; and see below at 3.2.4. In some limited circumstances reliance will not necessarily be an essential ingredient in a claim for negligent misstatement: see *Murphy v Brentwood District Council* [1991] 1 AC 398, 486.

[38] Transcript, pp 72–3.

[39] [1983] 1 All ER 583, 589, per Stephenson LJ.

[40] See also *Sykes v Midland Bank Executor Co* [1971] 1 QB 113, 124.

[41] See, for example, *Kendall Wilson Securities v Barraclough* [1986] 1 NZLR 576, 601 and *BBL v Eagle Star* [1995] 2 All ER 769, 791–6.

cause of loss is a 'pragmatic one based on common sense.'[41a] The question of reliance can be posed in various ways: (a) did the statement contribute to the decision to lend? (b) did it encourage the lender? (c) did it influence the lender's mind? It is a question of fact whether supervening events sufficiently weaken the causative potency of a valuation so as to render any initial reliance placed upon the valuation sufficiently insubstantial to negative causation.[42]

In property finance negligence cases, the passage of years between the loan and the issue of proceedings and eventual trial may well mean that the plaintiff cannot call any direct evidence that he relied upon the valuation in making the loan. An example of this difficulty is *Cavendish Funding Ltd v Henry Spencer and Sons Ltd*.[43] There the defendant stoutly argued that in the absence of direct oral evidence from a director of the plaintiff lender (directors being the only officers permitted to make lending decisions) as to what would have happened had the valuation been competently performed, the plaintiff's claim had to fail. The judge accepted that none of the plaintiff's documents were admissible under s 1(1) of the Civil Evidence Act 1968 as evidence to establish the necessary causal link. However he found the necessary reliance as a 'natural inference' that could be drawn from the facts of the case, *viz* the receipt of a valuation which the defendants had been instructed by the plaintiffs to make of a security against which the plaintiffs then lent in accordance with its prescribed loan-to-value ratio:

> In making a loan on security the plaintiffs were plainly relying on a valuation of that security.[44]

The courts have shown themselves very willing to make such inferences.[45]

On the other hand there have been recent examples where close scrutiny of the evidence has led to judges refusing to find the necessary reliance. For example, in both *BBL v Eagle Star*[46] and *Nyckeln Finance Co Ltd v Edward Symmons*[47] it was held that the lenders had made the decision to lend prior to the receipt of the valuations produced by the defendants.

[41a]   25 March 1996, CA; [1996] PNLR 380. See also *Alexander v Cambridge Credit Corp* [1987] 9 NSWLR 310, 359.

[42]   See *Kenney v Hall Pain & Foster* (1976) 239 EG 355.

[43]   (1996) unreported, 26 March, Evans-Lombe J.

[44]   Transcript, p 11.

[45]   See, for example, *HIT Finance Ltd v Lewis & Tucker Ltd* [1993] 2 EGLR 231, 234; *Nyckeln Finance Co Ltd v Stumpbrook Continuation Ltd* [1994] 2 EGLR 143, 148; *Allen v Ellis & Co* [1990] 1 EGLR 170.

[46]   [1995] 2 All ER 769.

[47]   (1996) unreported.

2.4　The standard of care

2.4.1　Introduction

The valuer's liability will be determined by reference to the general principles applicable to the determination of the liability of professionals. Although he will enter into contractual relationships with his clients, the obligation of a valuer under contract, as in tort, is not to provide an absolutely correct valuation but to discharge the task of valuing the subject property with reasonable care and skill. In this respect, in the absence of special contractual provision, the obligation in contract will generally be breached only if negligence is proved.[48] In *Daisley v B S Hall & Co*,[49] Bristow J said that:

> The duty of a practitioner in any professional skill, which he undertakes to perform by accepting instructions from his client, is to see the things that the average skilled professional in that field would see, draw from what he sees the conclusions that the average skilled professional would draw, and take the action that the average skilled professional would take.

The standard is that of the ordinary skilled man exercising and professing to have that special skill: 'the Bolam test'.[50]

The valuer's general duty is, therefore, to take reasonable care to give a reliable and informed opinion of the open market value[51] of the land in question at the date of valuation.[52] To exercise this duty properly, the valuer is expected to have a reasonably accurate and up-to-date knowledge of the area in which the subject property is located, including the state of the market as it affects values in that area,[53] and to be knowledgable about recent developments in general which relate to his specialism.[54] The valuer does not warrant that the land would fetch on the open market the value he puts on it, just as the attorney does not undertake that 'at all events you shall gain your case, nor [the] surgeon undertake that he will perform a cure'.[55]

---

[48]　See *Stewart v H A Brechin & Co* 1959 SC 306, 307.
[49]　(1973) EGD 184, 191.
[50]　See *Bolam v Friern Hospital Management Committee* [1957] 1 WLR 582, 586.
[51]　Or whatever other basis of valuation he is instructed to utilise.
[52]　See per Sir Thomas Bingham MR, *BBL v Eagle Star* [1995] QB 375, 403–4; see also *UCB Home Loans Corp Ltd v Roger North & Associates* [1995] EGCS 149 where it was held that the valuer's duty was simply to make a careful appraisal of the property and to provide an informed valuation as at the date of valuation, applying standards normal to the profession so that the lender could judge whether it provided sufficient security for the loan.
[53]　See *Baxter v F W Gapp & Co Ltd* [1938] 4 All ER 457; *Singer & Friedlander v Wood (John D) & Co* (1977) 243 EG 212, 213.
[54]　See *Weedon v Hindwood Clarke and Esplin* (1974) 234 EG 121; *Hooberman v Salter Rex* [1985] 1 EGLR 144.
[55]　*Lanphier v Phipos* (1838) 8 C & P 475.

2.4.2   Different standards

The fact that a particular valuer has a greater reputation, longer experience and a higher degree of skill than an 'average' valuer, does not mean that any special standard of care is applied. Conversely, the standard will not be lower if the valuer is a person of shorter experience, or lesser qualifications.[56] In *Andrew Master Hones Ltd v Cruikshank & Fairweather*,[57] the judge spoke of 'an objective test referable to the notional member of the profession and not a subjective test referable to the particular professional man employed'.

However, when a particular valuer holds himself out as having a particular specialism (for example in valuing a particular type of commercial property) then the standard of care is different:

> ... a [professional] who professes to exercise a special skill must exercise the ordinary skill of his speciality.[58]

Even where the valuer does not explicitly hold himself as having such a specialism, if he undertakes a valuation of a specialised nature then the standard of care owed will be determined by reference to the standard which would be expected of a valuer within that specialism, rather than the standard of a general practitioner.[59]

A valuer will not be negligent if he acted in accordance with the practice of competent respected professional opinion. Where there is a difference of opinion in the profession, he is entitled to act in accordance with the practice accepted as proper by a substantial number of persons in his profession. The applicability of this principle to valuation cases has been recognised in a number of cases.[60]

2.4.3   Professional practices

The fact that a section of a profession considers a particular practice acceptable will not of itself immunise the professional who follows that practice against a finding of negligence. The determination of what constitutes negligence is ultimately a matter for the courts, not expert evidence.[61]

The point is illustrated by the Scottish case of *Peach v Ian G Chalmers*

---

[56]   *Freeman v Marshall & Co* (1966) 200 EG 777; *Kenney v Hall, Pain and Foster* (1976) 239 EG 355.

[57]   [1980] RPC 16.

[58]   See *Maynard v West Midlands Regional Health Authority* [1985] 1 All ER 635, HL—a medical negligence case.

[59]   *Mendelson & Round v Duncan & Weller Pty Ltd* (1988) Aust Tort Reps 67, 334.

[60]   See, for example, *Mount Banking Corporation Ltd v Brian Cooper & Co* [1992] 2 EGLR 142; *Zubaida v Hargreaves* [1993] 43 EG 111.

[61]   *F v R* [1983] 33 SASR 189, at 194. See also *Voli v Inglewood Shire Council* (1963) 110 CLR 74 and *Edward Wong Finance Co Ltd v Johnson, Stokes & Master* [1984] AC 296.

& *Co*.[62] The pursuers had purchased a property for £34,000 in reliance upon a valuation provided by the defenders in the same sum. It was alleged that the property was in fact worth much less because it was of defective construction, which the defenders should have noticed. Expert witnesses were called, who differed in their evidence as to the correct value of the property at the time of purchase. The defenders' expert valued the property at £32,000–£33,000 at the time of the valuation. It was argued by the defenders that if there was a divided body of expert opinion as to how the property should be valued then it could not be said that the defenders had been negligent in arriving at a value which was supported by a body of competent valuers. In support of this proposition, *Maynard*[63] was relied upon.

The judge, however, held that he was not precluded from rejecting one strand of expert opinion if grounds existed for doing so. The experts' valuations differed substantially and, as the judge said, both could not be right. The question which had to be determined was what value a reasonably competent valuer could have placed upon the property at the relevant time. This was ultimately a question of fact.

If the valuers' argument in *Peach* was correct, valuers would almost never be found negligent because, as the reported cases reveal, defendants will almost always be able to call expert evidence in support of the valuation which is sued upon. Unlike in medical negligence cases, where often there will be no right answer, the value of a property at a particular time is a question of fact, and the evidence of one expert will have to be accepted over that of another, subject, of course, to the bracket.

2.4.4 General comments

Certain matters are *not* relevant to the standard of care. Although the standard of care required of the valuer will depend upon the nature of the instructions he receives, he cannot escape liability on the basis that he was not paid to provide a superior service or that he was asked to produce his report quickly. In *Sinclair v Bowden, Son & Partners*[64] the plaintiff requested that the survey be done quickly and stated that he did not require a full structural valuation report. Whereas a full structural survey would have cost 37 guineas, a fee of only 7 guineas was charged. The judge nevertheless found that the defendant's failure to detect defects was negligent.

In *Brickhill v Cooke*[65] the court held that a discounted fee did not permit a valuer to adopt a 'discounted' level of professionalism, and

[62] [1992] 2 EGLR 135.
[63] [1985] 1 All ER 635.
[64] (1962) EGD 424.
[65] [1984] 3 NSWLR 396.

therefore the standard of care expected of the valuer remained the normal standard to be applied generally. The standard will be the same whether the valuer has acted for a fee or not, and whether the fee is high or low.[66] Similarly, even where the valuer lacks professional qualifications, or where he has limited experience in the area of expertise required by the particular circumstances of the valuation, the required standard of reasonable competence and prudence remains undiminished.[67]

2.5   Approaches to valuation

2.5.1   Introduction

The uniqueness of each piece of real property means that exactitude is impossible to achieve: instead, the valuer must do his best with the imperfect tools at his disposal to arrive at an opinion of value. There have been a number of important judicial statements concerning the nature of valuations, and the appropriate considerations in judging the standard of care to be expected of the valuer. In *Baxter v Gapp*,[68] Goddard LJ said:

> Valuation is very much a matter of opinion. We are liable to make mistakes, and a valuer is certainly not to be found guilty of negligence merely because his valuation turns out to be wrong. He may have taken too optimistic or pessimistic a view of a particular property. One has to bear in mind that, in matters of valuation, matters of opinion come very largely into account.

The case of *Singer & Friedlander v Wood (John D) & Co*[69] is often referred to. Watkins J said:

> The valuation of land by trained, competent and careful professional men is a task which rarely, if ever, admits of precise conclusion. Often beyond certain well-founded facts so many imponderables confront the valuer that he is obliged to proceed on assumptions. Therefore, he cannot be faulted for not achieving a result which does not admit of some degree of error. Thus two able and experienced men, each confronted with the same task, might come to different conclusions without any one being justified in saying that either of them has lacked competence and reasonable care ... in doing his work.

These *dicta* have dominated judicial attitudes in relation to the recent litigation against valuers. The courts have accepted that valuation is an

---

[66]   See *Roberts v J Hampson & Co* [1990] 1 WLR 94.
[67]   See *Kenney v Hall, Pain and Foster* (1976) 239 EG 355.
[68]   [1938] 4 All ER 457.
[69]   (1977) 248 EG 212, 213.

'art', not a 'science',[70] and such a distinction brings with it judicial acceptance that imprecision and inexactitude are, to some extent at least, inevitable. Moreover, as is frequently stated, an error made by a valuer or surveyor will not in itself necessitate a finding of negligence.[71]

2.5.2   Margins of error

This acceptance that valuation is an art has led the courts to develop the notion of a 'bracket' or range as a mechanism to provide the necessary degree of protection to valuers against the imposition of an impossibly high standard of care: if a valuation falls within this bracket then, whether or not errors have been made,[72] it will not be considered to be negligent. In *Singer & Friedlander* Watkins J said:

> Pinpoint accuracy is not ... to be expected by he who requests a valuation. There is, as I have said, the permissible margin of error, the 'bracket' as I have called it. What can properly be expected from a competent valuer using reasonable skill and care is that his valuation falls within this bracket ... The permissible margin of error is said ... to be generally 10 % either side of a figure which can be said to be the right figure, ie ... not a figure which later, with hindsight, proves to be right but which at the time of valuation is the figure which a competent, careful and experienced valuer arrives at after making all the necessary inquiries and paying proper regard to the then state of the market. In exceptional circumstances the permissible margin ... could be extended to about 15 %, or a little more. Any valuation falling outside what I shall call the 'bracket' brings into question the competence of the valuer and the sort of care he gave to the task of valuation.[73]

This concept of a bracket was subjected to detailed analysis in *Mount Banking Corporation Ltd v Brian Cooper & Co*[74] and has since become a key feature in judicial determinations of whether negligence has been established.

It was argued in *Mount Banking* that if it could be shown that the valuer, when coming to his valuation, had made errors in reaching the end figure, but that nonetheless the final valuation fell within the 'bracket', albeit at the top end, then the plaintiff could still succeed in his claim. This argument was rejected: so long as the end valuation

---

[70]   Though, as Jacob J said in *Platform Home Loans v Oyston Shipways Ltd* (1996) unreported, 29 July, it is not 'astrology'. The valuers in that case were described as 'star struck': transcript, p 15.

[71]   *Luxmoore-May v Messenger May Baverstock* [1990] 1 WLR 1009; *Hardy v Walmsley-Lewis* (1967) 203 EG 1039; *Fryer v Boswell* (1981) 262 EG 158; *Wolverhampton v Hurning Son & Daw plc* [1996] EGCS 137.

[72]   See *Beaumont v Humberts* [1990] 2 EGLR 166, 169.

[73]   *Ibid*, 213; see also *Carivan Hotel Ltd v Globe Estates Ltd* [1974] 6 WWR 707, 721.

[74]   [1992] 2 EGLR 142.

came within the 'bracket', then there could be no finding of negligence, despite the fact that the valuer had made overt errors of method and of calculation in the steps taken up to the valuation:

> If the valuation that has been reached cannot be impeached as a total, then, however erroneous the method or its application by which the valuation has been reached, no loss has been sustained, because … it was a proper valuation.[75]

For a valuation to be negligent it must be *outside* the bracket.

It was argued in the Court of Appeal in *Craneheath Securities v York Montague Ltd*[76] that if a court was satisfied that there were a sufficient number of errors in the way in which the defendant valuer had carried out his valuation, then it should infer that the final valuation was wrong and therefore make a finding of negligence. Indorsing the approach of *Mount Banking*, Balcombe LJ[77] held that it was not enough for a plaintiff to show errors committed by the valuer in the process of arriving at a final valuation if the plaintiff could not attack the final valuation as wrong as a figure.[78] However, the fact that errors have been made in the process of arriving at the end valuation will be powerful indicators of a negligently erroneous final figure.[79]

In *Mount Banking* the judge had posed the question of what was the correct application of a 'bracket' or 'margin of error' (expressed in percentage terms). He said:

> If the valuation is too high, is it too high by such a margin as to be categorised as negligent? The margin of error approach is … a useful tool, for in most straightforward cases it can reasonably be expected … that competent surveyors acting with proper skill and care, and thus acting on all relevant evidence, will come within a moderate bracket of each other … I think the judge must approach the question, first by asking where the proper valuation or bracket of valuation lies. Then, if the Defendant is more than the permitted margin outside that proper figure, the inference of negligence should be drawn … In my judgment therefore, I should avoid seeking a mean figure between valuations and applying a margin of error, even a broad margin of error, to that.[80]

This passage raises a number of difficulties. While it is no doubt true that competent surveyors, when valuing a particular property, will come within a moderate bracket of each other, the reality of litigation will be that one expert or set of experts, appearing as witnesses for one party, will disagree violently with another set, appearing for the other party.

---

[75]   At 145.
[76]   [1996] 07 EG 141.   [77]   At 142.
[78]   And see also *Private Bank & Trust Co Ltd v Sallmans (UK) Ltd* [1993] 1 EGLR 144.
[79]   See *Nykredit Mortgage Bank plc v Edward Erdman Group Ltd* [1996] 02 EG 110, and p 52 below.
[80]   At 145.

In those circumstances, the judge will be faced with the task of making a finding of fact as to what was the correct value of the property at the relevant time. It is envisaged in *Mount Banking* that the judge might first, prior to any application of the 'bracket' (in the sense of 'margin of error'), make a finding of the range of proper valuations. Thus if the judge finds that the range of proper valuations was £90,000 to £100,000, then he is thereafter entitled (or perhaps required) to impose a further bracket around both the highest and lowest value. If the bracket is 10 per cent then the problem arises as to whether the 10 per cent figure is a percentage of £90,000 or £100,000. Taking it as a percentage of £100,000, then the actual range of non-negligent valuations will be £80,000 to £110,000.

An illustration of the application of *Mount Banking* is *Axa Equity & Law Home Loans Ltd v Hirani Watson*.[81] The plaintiff lender lent £225,000 in reliance on a valuation dated 27 January 1989 which valued the secured property at £300,000. The borrower defaulted and the property was eventually sold in September 1991 for £137,000. The plaintiff alleged that the true open market value at the time of the valuation was £220,000 and that no mortgage would have been granted had the proper valuation been made. The judge put the question in the following terms:

> My conclusion from reading these cases [*Singer, Corisand*, and *Mount Banking*] and from listening to counsel is that for the Plaintiff to succeed on this primary issue [negligence] it must show on a balance of probabilities that the valuation of £300,000 was one that could not properly have been reached by a competent valuer using proper skill and care. In most cases a Plaintiff would seek to prove his case by demonstrating what the proper figure was, contrasting it with the Defendant's figure and showing that the latter fell sufficiently outside whatever is the acceptable margin of error so as to be unacceptable and therefore probative of negligence.

The judge discussed the difference in terminology between the judges in the *Singer* and *Mount Banking* cases, as between the margin either side of the 'right figure', and the permitted margin outside the 'proper valuation or *bracket of valuation*': in the judge's view, there was no material difference in these two approaches because:

> The proper figure may not be precisely measurable but may be within a moderate, relatively small, bracket.

In *Hirani* the property which was valued was a residential house and therefore the judge considered the relevant percentage margin to be 10 per cent. There were other valuations of the same property prepared both before and after the valuation which was impugned. These were consistent with the defendant's valuation and the judge accepted their probative relevance because the ultimate question was not whether

[81] [1994] EGCS 90.

the defendant had used the right approach but whether the figure he eventually reached was a figure at which a competent valuer could have arrived. In considering those comparables which did provide assistance and the other valuations of the property, the judge came to the view that the valuation of £300,000 was not negligent, without considering what the correct value was.

It is clear that for the 'bracket' to have any use as an indicator of negligence, the courts must be prepared to come to a conclusion as to what is the 'correct value' at the time of the valuation and then a conclusion as to the appropriate percentage margin of error. This was the approach employed in *BNP Mortgages Ltd v Goadsby & Harding Ltd*.[82] In that case the judge found 'a proper valuation carried out by an ordinary competent valuer [on the date of the valuation] was £180,000'. The judge went on to find that the permissible margin of error would be approximately 10 per cent: 'the highest non-negligent valuation was therefore just about £200,000.' In *Craneheath Securities Ltd v York Montague Ltd*[83] it was accepted that for the 'margin of error' approach to have any meaning the court had to arrive at a notional 'right' figure[84] and so for this approach to be workable the court had to have evidence of both this figure and the appropriate margin:

> The margin of error approach may well make sense when the property being valued has a number of good comparables (eg houses on an estate, forestry or farmland). Then one can in effect take an 'average' as the 'right' figure and look at the deviation from it ... But, as I say, the approach depends on evidence.

In that case there was insufficient evidence for the judge to make a finding as to what that notional figure was and the claim accordingly failed. It is submitted that the danger with certain of the *dicta* in *Mount Banking* (as quoted above) is that, by first calculating a range of values and then applying a bracket to that range, the allowable margin of error may become far too wide. While it may be true that the concept of a 'correct value' is, by the very nature of values, a false one, it is submitted that the margin of error is the appropriate mechanism by which the law takes account of the fundamental imprecision of valuations. There are two ways of applying the margin of error: either to use percentages (which necessitate a fixed figure) or simply to state as two figures a range within which valuations will not be negligent.

The notion of a 'correct valuation', around which there will be a range of valuations which a competent valuer might reasonably reach, was

---

[82] [1994] 2 EGLR 169.
[83] [1994] 1 EGLR 159.
[84] And in *Nyckeln Finance Co Ltd v Stumpbrook Continuation Ltd* [1994] 1 EGLR 143, at 149, the judge spoke of a 'mean figure' around which the percentage margin was to fall.

approved by the Court of Appeal in *Nykredit Mortgage Bank plc v Edward Erdman Group Ltd.*[85]

The question of what the bracket should be will, of course, be vitally important to the question of whether the valuer was negligent. Although the mere fact that the valuation falls outside the bracket will not, in itself, necessarily indicate negligence, it will permit such an inference to be drawn. In *Baxter v Gapp*,[86] Du Parq LJ said:

> It is, of course, quite clear that the mere fact that there is an overvaluation does not of itself show negligence. Gross overvaluation, unless explained, may be strong evidence either of negligence or of incompetence. I have no doubt that there was in this case gross overvaluation, and one looks to see whether or not there is any explanation for it, and whether or not it can be said that the Defendant had failed to take any steps ...

In practice, this is a very strong inference, and once an overvaluation outside the bracket is shown, the burden of disproving the inference of negligence will in effect shift to the defendant.

The width of the bracket will ultimately be a matter of expert evidence[87] and may fluctuate depending upon the type of property being valued and the circumstances in which it is valued. It may be as great as 15 per cent (as a percentage of the actual value found). The determining factors will be the uniformity or, conversely, the uniqueness of the subject property, and the state of the market at the time of the valuation. It has been suggested that, where the property is a standard estate house, the margin of error would as narrow as 5 per cent.[88] This was recognised by Forbes J in *GREA Real Property Investments Ltd v Williams*[89] where he said:

> It is a fundamental aspect of valuation that it proceeds by analogy. The valuer isolates those characteristics of the object to be valued which in his view affects the value and then seeks another of known or ascertainable value presenting some or all of these characteristics with which he may compare the object he is valuing. Where no directly comparable object exists, the valuer must make allowances of one kind or another interpolating or extrapolating from his given data. The less closely analogous the object chosen for a comparison the greater the allowances which have to be made and the greater the opportunity for error.

---

[85] [1996] 02 EG 110, per Peter Gibson LJ, 114; see also *BBL v Eagle Star* [1996] 3 WLR 87, 102.

[86] [1939] 2 All ER 752, 758.

[87] As recognised by the Court of Appeal in *Nykredit*, at 114, and see *McIntyre v Herring, Son & Daw* [1988] 1 EGLR 231, 233; *Singer & Friedlander v Wood (John D) & Co* (1977) 243 EG 212; *BNP Mortgages Ltd v Barton Cook & Sams* [1996] 1 EGLR 239.

[88] Suggested by the expert in *BNP Mortgages v Barton Cook & Sams* [1996] 1 EGLR 239, 241.

[89] (1979) 250 EG 651, 653.

In relation to commercial property valuations, in circumstances where the appropriate method of valuation is the investment method,[90] care should be taken in the application of the 'bracket'. Employing that method, there will in general be two figures which are used to give a capital value: the estimated yearly rental value of the property (calculated in terms of price per square foot) and the yield. Both these figures will be arrived at by consideration of comparables and prevailing market conditions. In *BBL v Eagle Star*[91] the defendant's expert, when giving evidence as to the highest value which in his view a competent valuer might have attributed to the subject property, took (1) the highest estimated rental value and (2) the lowest yield which the competent valuer could have attributed to the property. Phillips J found that this approach was wrong. A competent valuer would never value a property on the basis of a combination of both the most extravagant possible rental value and the keenest possible yield. He accepted the evidence of the plaintiff's expert that the competent valuer would strike a balance between the two uncertains of estimated rental value and yield. The same approach is equally applicable to other methods of valuation which involve the use of two or more variables.

Examples of the appropriate brackets used in recent cases include the following:[92]

(a) in *BBL* it was accepted by the experts that valuations based upon comparables might produce variations by as much as 20 per cent;

(b) in *Muldoon v Mays of Lilliput Ltd*[93] the plaintiff's expert suggested a range of 15–20 per cent because of the rapidly increasing state of the market in 1988;

(c) in *BNP Mortgages Ltd v Barton Cook & Sams*[94] the margin was held to be 15 per cent because of the uniqueness of the property (and hence the greater difficulty in obtaining relevant comparables). On the other hand the court considered that in valuing properties where there would be a wealth of almost exact comparables, as on an estate laid out in a uniform way, then the margin could decrease to as little as 5 per cent;

(d) in *Birmingham Midshires Building Society v Richard Pamplin & Co*[95] Newman J held that, having regard to the property's characteristics, the appropriate margin of error was 11 per cent; and

---

[90] For a full consideration of the investment method and the terms used see Appendix 1 below at p 206.

[91] [1994] 2 EGLR 108, 120 (not reported in the All ER report).

[92] See also *Beaumont v Humberts* [1990] 2 EGLR 166 and *Trade Credits Ltd v Baillieu Knight Frank (NSW) Pty Ltd* (1985) Aust Tort Rep 80–757.

[93] [1993] 1 EGLR 43.

[94] [1996] 1 EGLR 239.

[95] [1996] EGCS 3.

(e) in *Private Bank & Trust Co Ltd v Sallmans (UK) Ltd*[96] the judge
allowed the defendants a 15 per cent bracket around the valuation which was in itself a range of £100,000.

The potential danger of the 'bracket' approach is its tendency to
reduce the forensic process of assessing whether there has been negligence or not to a simple inquiry into the 'correct value' through the
adduction of expert evidence, followed by an application of the correct
bracket percentage. If the valuation which is sought to be impeached is
outside that bracket then a finding of negligence is made. This ignores
the need to investigate the way in which the valuation was arrived at.

2.5.3 Valuation investigation errors

In practice, plaintiffs often attack not only the valuation figure, but the
process by which the valuation was arrived at. The courts are influenced by 'investigation errors' when considering whether or not a valuer
was negligent and in determining what the actual value of the property was at the date of valuation. Thus, in *Nykredit Mortgage Bank plc v
Edward Erdman Group Ltd*[97] the Court of Appeal considered the various
errors made by the defendant as powerfully indicative that its valuation was negligently high. Therefore, although it is clear that a plaintiff
must adduce positive and cogent evidence as to the actual value of the
property at the date of the valuation, a detailed criticism of the process
by which the valuation was arrived at will also usually be necessary
and desirable. This was recognised by Gibson J in *Corisand Investments
Ltd v Druce & Co*:[98]

> The assertion by a valuer of acknowledged skill and experience that in his
> judgment a property was worth a particular sum on a particular date, will
> … not readily be shown to have been such an opinion as no competent
> valuer could hold by simple reliance upon the assertion of another valuer,
> also of acknowledged skill and experience, that in his judgment the proper
> valuation was a figure so much lower than the first that the first must be
> regarded as a valuation which no competent valuer could put forward.[99]

The nature of the errors which adversely affect the final conclusion
as to value varies from valuation to valuation. The following are examples of the errors which have been dealt with in the reported cases:

(a) failing to take account of the relevant comparables, or taking
into account comparables which are insufficiently proximate, or

---

[96] [1993] 1 EGLR 144.
[97] [1996] 02 EG 110.
[98] (1978) 248 EG 315, at 504.
[99] See also *United Bank of Kuwait v Prudential Property Services Ltd* [1995] EGCS 190.

misleading. This may well arise out of a valuer's failure to familiarise himself with the state of the local market;[100]

(b) failing to take account of recent sales of the subject property;[101]

(c) failing to verify assumptions or information gleaned from third parties which prove to be false or failing to warn the client that assumptions needed to be verified;[102]

(d) failing to inspect properly the property or to take detailed notes while inspecting.[103] The valuer will clearly be in a stronger position in defending a negligence claim if he can rely upon contemporaneous notes to justify his valuation;[104]

(e) failing to make a proper appraisal of the property, its location and amenities and failing to research properly the property's previous use and the existence of any planning permissions;[105]

(f) a mathematical error or a mistake in calculation;[106]

(g) failing to detect or properly to take into account defects in the property which had an impact on the value of the property. Such errors are often the subject of surveyors' negligence cases;[107]

(h) utilisation of an inappropriate method or basis of valuation;

(i) ignorance or failure properly to apply relevant legislation;[108]

(j) in commercial cases failing to conduct adequate research into local demand for purchasing or leasing the particular category or property;[109]

(k) failing to take into account current market conditions.[109a]

2.6   The 'correct method'

A mistake in methodology is generally a necessary but not a sufficient condition of a finding of liability against the valuer. Two points should be noted:

---

[100] See below at 2.7 and *Kenny v Hall, Pain and Foster* (1976) 239 EG 355; *Birmingham Midshires Building Society v Pamplin & Co* [1996] EGCS 3.

[101] See below at 2.6.

[102] See *Old Gate Estates Ltd v Toplis & Harding & Russell* [1939] 3 All ER 209. Contrast *P K Finans International (UK) Ltd v Andrew Downs & Co Ltd* [1992] 1 EGLR 172, where the valuer expressly qualified his report by stating that he had not verified certain assumptions made about planning permission.

[103] See below at 2.8 and *Roberts v J Hampson & Co* [1990] 1 WLR 94; *Stewart v Brechin & Co* (1959) SC 306.

[104] See, for example, *Mount Banking Corp Ltd v Cooper* [1992] 2 EGLR 142 and *Bere v Slades* [1989] 2 EGLR 160.

[105] See generally *Singer & Friedlander v Wood (John D) & Co* (1977) 243 EG 212.

[106] See, for example, *BT Australia v Raine & Horne Pty Ltd* [1983] 3 NSWLR 221.

[107] See generally Murdoch & Murrells, *Law of Surveys and Valuations* 1st edn (1995).

[108] See, for example, *Thomas Miller v Richard Saunders & Partners* [1989] 1 EGLR 267; *Corisand Investments Ltd v Druce & Co* (1978) 248 EG 315.

[109] *Nykredit Mortgage Bank plc v Edward Erdman Group Ltd* [1996] 1 EGLR 119.

[109a] *Bristol and West Building Society v Christie* [1996] EGCS 53.

(a) the valuer can afford to make a mistake in the computation of his valuation or in the methodology generally if he nevertheless manages to value the property 'within the bracket'. A correct overall result can make up for incorrect methodology; and

(b) it may be possible for the valuer to escape liability *even if* his valuation seems to be outside the bracket. If he can show that he made the right inquiries, assessed the right information and reached the appropriate calculations which any competent valuer, exercising due skill and care, would have done and gone through then the valuer will be able to say that he *cannot* have been negligent. The reason for this is that if the valuer can show that he acted as competently as the average valuer then it will be open to him to say that although his valuation might *appear* to be outside the bracket it cannot be so and the width of the bracket must be greater than at first appeared.

Any particular valuation will involve the consideration of specific facts and issues. It would be impossible to lay down all the required steps which the valuer should take when conducting a valuation. Indeed, these will differ according to the nature of the subject property. However in certain cases the judges have set out general propositions which have greater application than the facts of the case in question. So, in *Singer & Friedlander v Wood (John D) & Co,*[110] Watkins J said, in an often-quoted passage:

> The way in which a valuer should conduct himself so as to fulfill his duty to a merchant bank, or any other body or person, varies according to the complexity or otherwise of the task which confronts him. In some instances the necessary inquiries and other investigations preceding a valuation need only to be on a modest scale. In others a study of the problem needs to be in greater depth, involving much detailed and painstaking inquiries at many sources of information. In every case, the valuer, having gathered all the vital information, is expected to be sufficiently skilful so as to enable himself to interpret the facts, to make indispensable assumptions and to employ a well-practised professional method of reaching a conclusion; and it may be to check that conclusion with another reached as the result of the use of a second well-practised method. In every case the valuer must not only be versed in the value of land throughout the country in a general way, but he must inform himself adequately of the market trends and be very sensitive to them with particular regard for the locality in which the land he values lies.

In *Mount Banking*, where the subject property was an existing office building with planning permission, the judge stated that the factors which should be considered by the valuer were as follows:

---

[110] (1977) 243 EG 212, 213.

(a) the size, condition, tenure and location of the property;
(b) planning permission and permitted user;[110a]
(c) the value and use of adjoining and neighbouring premises;
(d) the value, particularly rental and capital, of other offices in the general locality, and the extent to which they are comparable, so that any necessary consequent adjustments can be made when applying that information to the subject property;
(e) the state of the property market at the time;
(f) the effect of increases in interest rates;
(g) the realism of the projected development and its costing; and
(h) the proposed purchase price of the property.

It is suggested that this list is of general application.

The last requirement, to take into account the purchase price, requires particular attention. In domestic loan cases, the difficulty has often been that the valuer is led into error by giving too much credence to the agreed price when an advance is made for the purposes of a purchase. In commercial cases, the problem has usually been the other way round. In such cases, there may be an agreed purchase price or, in the case of an investment loan, the property may have been acquired recently by the borrower.

In *Mount Banking*,[111] the purchaser had contracted to purchase the property which was proposed as security for the loan for an amount which was considerably less than the valuation. The judge suggested that it might be good sense for a valuer to establish the proposed purchase price as a relevant piece of evidence in ascertaining the open market value. However expert evidence in that case suggested that a body of competent valuers considered it proper to make a valuation without ever knowing the proposed purchase price. As a result the judge refused to make a finding of negligence against the defendant valuer for failing to establish what the purchase price was. The judge saw the logic of this practice:

> ... the point has some validity [because] ... the purchase price may not truly reflect the open market value. A developer may see potential that a vendor has not seen.[112]

In *BBL* the discrepancy between the purchase price and the valuations was marked. In that case, the same expert witness (who had given evidence in *Mount Banking* to the effect that it was standard practice among valuers not to appraise themselves of the sale price of properties to be

---

[110a] In *Allied Trust Bank v Edward Symmons and Partners* [1994] 1 EGLR 165 the judge held that the valuer was entitled to value the subject property taking into account the prospect of planning permission, ie to include an element of "hope value". See also *Mid Kent Water plc v Batchelor* [1993] EGCS 103.
[111] [1992] 2 EGLR 142.
[112] At 146.

valued) accepted in cross-examination that such information might well be very useful. Phillips J firmly agreed with this logic, saying:

> Absent … express instructions (to disregard a recent sale), a valuer who gives an open market valuation without considering the implications of a recent sale in the market of the property being valued is, in my judgment, negligent.[113]

The judge considered that a recent purchase price was the best evidence of value and so held that it was the obligation of the valuer to ascertain the purchase price of the property being valued and to discover how the property had been marketed in order to achieve that price. The proper approach was to seek to establish the maximum value which a competent valuer could have reached after giving due regard to the manner in which the property was marketed, the sale price achieved, the delay between achieving that price and the date of valuation and relevant comparable transactions.[114]

More recently, it has been said that the argument that the price recently paid for the subject property is 'wholly irrelevant' is 'just silly'.[115] It is interesting to note that Guidance Note 1 of the new *RICS Appraisal and Valuation Manual* (1996) reflects Phillips J's analysis, requiring the valuer to investigate recent sale prices and the marketing history which preceded any sales, as a precursor to considering comparables. It specifically accepts that a recent sale will provide *prima facie* the best evidence of value.[116]

In *Corisand Investments Ltd v Druce & Co*,[117] a case involving the valuation of a hotel for mortgage purposes, Gibson J set out a number of matters to which a valuer should have regard when preparing a valuation:

(a) the valuer should, by inspection and inquiry, learn enough about the property to be able to start upon the basic method of valuation which he will apply, and thereafter he should apply that method effectively by obtaining any further information he needs;[118]

(b) because the purpose of the valuer's work is to determine the price which the property would fetch if offered for sale at the relevant time and in the relevant circumstances, these concepts will require definition. Now that the RICS has given definitions

---

[113] At 791.
[114] See also *Nyckeln Finance Co Ltd v Stumpbrook Continuation Ltd* [1994] 2 EGLR 143, 149.
[115] *Platform Home Loans v Oyston Shipways* (1996) unreported, 29 July.
[116] See GN 1.13.2; GN 1 is at Appendix 2.
[117] (1978) 248 EG 315.
[118] The failure to inspect properly the property (or failure to inspect at all) was considered in *Old Gate Estates v Toplis & Harding & Russell* [1939] 3 All ER 209; *Singer & Friedlander v Wood (John D) & Co* (1977) 243 EG 212.

of bases of value, the use of the term 'open market value' will be
sufficient to define both 'relevant time' and 'relevant circumstances', though if the valuation uses a different basis of value,
then this should be defined; and

(c) when the valuer has sufficiently informed himself of the size,
    nature and condition of the property, he can select the various
    valuation methods by which he will guide and check his opin-
    ion. Whether a particular method was the appropriate one to
    use in relation to a particular property will be a matter for expert
    evidence.

2.7   Comparables

Making a proper inspection and appraisal of the property is a necessary precondition of coming to a proper valuation. But once the valuer
has a sound knowledge of the subject property, how does he come to
an opinion of value? Whatever method of valuation the valuer employs,
the use of comparables remains the cornerstone of the valuer's practice.[119] Valuation is ultimately a comparative activity: if value is determined by the prices at which buyers are willing to buy and sellers are
willing to sell, then the best, indeed the only, evidence of market mood
is the prices obtained in recent transactions. Therefore knowledge of
the market, and a large database of comparable transactions, are absolutely vital to the proper practice of valuation.[120] Most actions brought
against valuers involve detailed consideration of comparables, both
those explicitly relied upon by the valuer at the time of the valuation,
and those which expert evidence relies upon in seeking either to support the valuation or to show that it was negligently inflated.[121]

It need hardly be said that the evidential value of comparables, both
those relied upon by the original valuer and those relied upon by the
experts, can vary enormously according to their proximity in time to
the date of the valuation and the similarity in size, condition, type and
location of the comparable property to the subject property. The fewer
genuine comparables which exist, the more difficult will be the valuation task. The valuer will have to rely more heavily upon his general

---

[119] See Enever and Isaac, *The Valuation of Property Investments* 5th edn (1995), 66; see also
the detailed analysis of valuation by comparables in relation to commercial property
by Phillips J in *BBL v Eagle Star* [1995] 2 All ER 769, 787–9.

[120] In *Trade Credits v Ballieu Knight Frank (NSW)* [1985] Aust Tort Reps 80–757 the valuer's negligently erroneous valuation stemmed from his use of inappropriate
comparables and his failure to find and take into account more suitable comparables.
See also *Baxter v Gapp* [1938] 2 All ER 457 for a similar failure.

[121] For an example of a 'battle of the comparables' see *Axa Equity & Law Home Loans v
Goldsack & Freeman* [1994] 1 EGLR 175.

experience, his local knowledge and his feeling about the general state of the market. In practice, the courts have granted a wider margin of error to the valuer in such cases.[122] So in *Axa Equity & Law Home Loans v Goldsack & Freeman* the judge allowed a wide bracket, having regard to the fact, as he held, that a valuer could not have had access to any 'true comparables, so that a greater than usual element of informed estimation was required'.[123]

2.8 RICS and ISVA guidelines

The Royal Institute of Chartered Surveyors (RICS) and The Incorporated Society of Valuers and Auctioneers (ISVA) have published guidelines, designed to regulate and harmonise professional practice in the field of asset valuation.

When valuing for mortgage purposes the valuer should have regard to the *Statements of Asset Valuation Practice and Guidance Notes*[124] prepared by the RICS Assets Valuation Standards Committee (known as 'the Red Book'). The Red Book is made up of 27 Statements of Asset Valuation Practice ('SAVPs') and 14 Information Papers. This work is applicable to the valuation of all fixed assets including valuations for security purposes.[125] Compliance with its statements of practice is mandatory. Although the SAVPs were specifically intended to apply to all valuations which were to be, or might be, included or referred to in any public or published document (such as company accounts and other financial statements subject to audit), the general principles set out in the SAVPs have been held to be applicable to mortgage valuations of a 'private' nature.[126]

The second edition of the Red Book was published under the title *Guidance Notes on the Valuation of Assets*, and many of the recent cases concerning negligent valuations refer to the work under this title because the valuations in question were made prior to the publication of the third edition.

Alongside the Red Book the RICS published the *Manual of Valuation Guidance Notes*[127] ('the White Book'), which was intended to complement the Red Book. The White Book is principally concerned with the mechanics of practice and to:

---

[122] See, for example, *Axa Equity & Law v Hirani Watson* [1994] EGCS 90.
[123] [1994] 1 EGLR 175, 178. For a detailed analysis of the use of comparables in rent reviews, and the valuers duties when advising on rent reviews, see *CIL Securities Ltd v Briant Champion Long* [1993] 2 EGLR 164.
[124] 3rd edn (1990), as amended.
[125] Though note below SAVP 1.3(c) and (d), and the commentary.
[126] See *Allied Trust Bank Ltd v Edward Symmons & Partners* [1994] 1 EGLR 165.
[127] 3rd edn (1992).

> ... ensure that the Valuer is aware of the normal procedures which should
> be followed, the information that should be collected, and the investiga-
> tions that should be made in order to arrive at the valuation.[128]

In late 1995 the RICS published, in association with the ISVA and the
Institute of Revenues, Rating and Valuation, the *RICS Appraisal and Valuation Manual*, which was intended to be an amalgamation and updat-
ing of the Red and White Books and which is made up of 22 Practice
Statements (PSs) and 18 Guidance Notes (and Appendices). The
Appraisal and Valuation Manual ('the *Manual*') was the profession's
response[129] to the rising concern in its ranks which resulted from a general confusion over the proper principles to apply in the valuation of
assets and, to some extent, to the enormous increase of litigation against
valuers which occurred from 1991 onwards. The old Red and White
Books were withdrawn with effect from 31 December 1995 in respect of
valuations undertaken after that date. Therefore the Red and White
Books will continue to be relevant to actions brought against valuers
for some years to come.

The Statement of Asset Valuation Practice No 1 ('SAVP') of the Red
Book (3rd edn) states that the SAVPs and IPs (Information Papers) apply
to all valuations which will be, or may be, included or referred to in
any publication or published document. But they do *not* apply to
valuations undertaken only for the private information of the client.
Accordingly they do not apply in any of the following cases:

1.3 ...

(c)   valuations of domestic dwellings where the owner or prospec-
         tive owner of a dwelling is borrowing from a lender such as a
         bank, or similar organisation;

(d)   valuations for mortgages or loans secured on commercial prop-
         erty for the private purposes of the lender or borrower.

Most valuations relied upon by lenders will fall within exception
(d). However it is stated at paragraph 1.4:

> Notwithstanding the preceding paragraphs, where a Member states that
> a valuation has been carried out in accordance with the Statements of Asset
> Valuation Practice and Guidance Notes, it is mandatory upon that Mem-
> ber to have done so.

This is an important qualification, as many lenders will specify the
basis of valuation as being 'the Red Book open market value', and
require adherence to the Red Book's principles, and hence many

---

[128] Foreword to 3rd edn.
[129] Prompted by the Mallinson Report of March 1994.

valuations *will* expressly state that they have been carried out in accordance with the Red Book. For instance, the valuation which was the subject of *Craneheath Securities v York Montague*[130] expressly set out its terms of reference as being:

> ... to prepare a valuation of the Freehold Interest in the property described, on an open market basis, as at today's date, on a going concern basis, including the benefit of goodwill, trade fixtures, fittings and contents used in connection with the business. We have provided our Valuation on an open market basis, and strictly in accordance with the Guidance Notes relating to the valuation of Property Assets published by the RICS.

In *Allied Trust Bank Ltd v Edward Symmons & Partners*[131] where the valuation fell within 1.3(d), and where the plaintiff had not commissioned the valuation and no specific instructions as to methodology had been given by the commissioning client, the judge said:

> I would not regard SAVP 1, although in terms inapplicable, as irrelevant. I reach this superficially paradoxical conclusion, because, in my judgment, a valuer, who, lacking specific instructions to the contrary, adopted in respect of a wholly private transaction a method of valuation prescribed for valuations which were to be made public could not justifiably be criticised for having acted in accordance with the guidance provided by the SAVP. The effect of the ... SAVP [No. 1], which reflected developing practice, was to permit a wider latitude in respect of private valuations than that applicable to valuations which might be made public and to confine the mandatory application of the guidance notes (in so far as guidance notes are mandatory) to the latter. That does not, however, in my opinion, mean that the standard for 'public valuations' lost all relevance.

The courts will give consideration to these guidance notes and practice statements when deciding what standard of care was required of the valuer and whether it was adhered to: however they are not finally determinative of 'non-negligent' practice, so that the valuer cannot, without more, refer to his compliance with the practice set out as an absolute defence. Conversely, simple failure to comply with published guidelines will not in itself constitute negligence. Sir Michael Ogden QC said in *PK Finans International (UK) Ltd v Andrew Downs & Co Ltd:* [132]

> ... these Guidance Notes [the Red Book, 2nd edn] are not to be regarded as a statute. I suspect that they are as much for the protection of surveyors as anything else, in that they set out various recommendations which, if followed, it is hoped will protect the surveyor from the unpleasantness of being sued. In any event, mere failure to comply with the Guidance Notes

---

[130] [1994] 1 EGLR 159; [1996] 1 EGLR 130, CA.
[131] [1994] 1 EGLR 165.
[132] [1992] 1 EGLR 172.

does not necessarily constitute negligence ...

Both the old Red and White Books and the new *Manual* give detailed guidance to valuers as to the proper performance of their duties. PS 8 of the *Manual* and VGN 12 of the White Book deal specifically with the valuation of commercial land and buildings for secured lending purposes; while PS 9 of the *Manual* and VGN 2 of the White Book deal specifically with the valuation of residential property for secured lending purposes. GN 3 of the *Manual* provides further guidance concerning residential mortgage valuations. The RICS/ISVA has produced a Specification for the Valuation and Inspection of Residential Property for Mortgage Purposes, which is to be found at Annex A to PS 9 of the *Manual* (applicable to valuations after 1 January 1996) and at VGN 2A of the White Book. These by and large reproduce the leaflet *Mortgage Valuation Guidance for Valuers* (1992), and provide important guidance concerning the proper approach to residential mortgage valuations. Further, the RICS and the British Bankers' Association have jointly produced 'Model Conditions of Engagement for the Valuation of Commercial Land and Buildings for Secured Lending Purposes'. These are to be found at the Appendix to PS 8 of the *Manual* and at the Annex to VGN 12 of the White Book.[133] Reference should be made to these documents for detailed analysis of the proper conduct of valuations in both the residential and commercial fields. More general guidance concerning valuation practice is to be found at GN 1 of the *Manual* and at VGN 1 of the White Book. However the relevant obligations, which will largely inform the nature and ambit of the legal standard of care placed upon the valuer, may be summarised as follows:

(a) VGN 2A of the White Book/PS 9, Annex A of the *Manual* (which relate to residential properties) state, at 1.1, that the valuer must have 'knowledge of and experience in the valuation of the residential property in the particular locality;[134]

(b) an inspection/reinspection should always be carried out to the extent necessary to produce a valuation: *Manual*, PS 6.1; VGN 2A/PS 9, Annex A2. The valuer must determine precisely what is the subject matter of the valuation, having regard to the RICS/ISVA *Code of Measuring Practice*: VGN 1, 6.2 and Background Notes; appendix to PS 8/Annex to VGN 12, at 2.1; GN 1.8.1 and GN 3.2 of the *Manual*;

(c) the valuer should take into account the characteristics of the locality, the availability of communications and facilities affecting value; the age, construction, use and state of repair of the property: *Manual*, PS 6.2.1; appendix to SAVP 1; VGN 1, 6.2(e)

---

[133] PS8, PS9 and the Annex to PS9 are reproduced at Appendix 2.
[134] See also the Commentary to VGN 2A and *Baxter v Gapp* [1938] 4 All ER 457, 459.

and Background Notes; VGN 2A/PS 9, Annex A, at 4.2;

(d) the valuer should analyse details of comparable market transactions and other valuation evidence; if it can be obtained, any price recently realised for the subject property; and market conditions and trends generally: PS 6.2.5 of the *Manual*; VGN 1, 6.2(e); GN 1.13 of the *Manual*.

2.9   Open Market Value and related bases of valuation

Open Market Value ('OMV') is a term defined in SAVP No 2 (Red Book 3rd edn) in the following terms:

> 1.1 Open Market Value means the best price at which the sale of an interest in property might reasonably be expected to have been completed unconditionally for cash consideration on the date of valuation, assuming:
>
> (a)   a willing seller;
> (b)   that, prior to the date of valuation, there had been a reasonable period (having regard to the nature of the property and the state of the market) for the proper marketing of the interest, for the agreement of price and terms and for the completion of the sale;
> (c)   that the state of the market, level of values and other circumstances were, on any earlier assumed date of exchange of contracts, the same as on the date of valuation; and
> (d)   that no account is taken of any additional bid by a purchaser with a special interest.
>
> 1.2 The use of the expression 'Open Market Value', not qualified by any reference to Existing Use or Alternative Use, implies the value for any use to the extent to which that value is reflected in the price obtainable in the open market.[135]

There are Guidance Notes to this Statement, explaining and giving detailed commentary on this definition: these notes, and the commentary to the new definition of 'OMV' contained in the *Manual* are reproduced in full in Appendix 2 of this book.

OMV should be distinguished from the other important basis of valuation which is relevant for lenders, the *forced sale value* basis.[136] Most valuations for mortgage purposes will be expressed to be of the 'open market value' (OMV) of the property. Indeed, GN 18 of the Red Book

---

[135] The *RICS Appraisal and Valuation Manual* (1996) adopts the same definition but in place of the words 'might reasonably be expected to' reads 'would'; and adds a fifth assumption, that is 'that both parties to the transaction had acted knowledgably, prudently and without compulsion'. The relevant parts of PS 4, which sets out the new OMV, is reproduced at Appendix 2.

[136] Defined at SAVP 2, para 4.1 as the OMV 'with the proviso that the vendor has imposed a time limit for completion which cannot be regarded as a "reasonable period" '.

(2nd edn) stated (at para 4) that, when a property was valued for security purposes (whether a mortgage or debenture) the basis of valuation should be OMV, and that, moreover, it was not normally appropriate to value property to be used as a security at forced sale value. This is repeated in PS 3 of the *Manual* as regards domestic mortgages.

In relation to commercial mortgages, the new *Manual* introduces two new bases of valuation, the Estimated Realisation Price ('ERP') and the Estimated Restricted Realisation Price ('ERRP'): OMV, ERP and ERRP are recognised as being potentially appropriate to the valuation of commercial property which is to be security for lending purposes. ERP is defined at PS 4.5.1 as:

> An opinion as to the amount of cash consideration before deduction of costs of sale which the Valuer considers, on the date of valuation, can reasonably be expected to be obtained on future completion of an unconditional sale of the interest in the subject property assuming:
>
> (a) a willing seller;
> (b) that completion will take place on a future date specified by the Valuer to allow a reasonable period for proper marketing (having regard to the nature of the property and the state of the market);
> (c) that no account is taken of any additional bid by a prospective purchaser with a special interest; and
> (d) that both parties to the transaction will act knowledgably, prudently and without compulsion.

The ERRP is defined by PS 4.6.1 in exactly the same terms, except that the assumed completion date does *not* allow a reasonable period for proper marketing of the property. The ERRP basis is designed to replace the forced sale basis.

The OMV basis of value rests upon the assumption that values will remain static. The valuer must assume a sale at the date of valuation, and so must not allow predictions as to future market movements, or the possibility of a collapse in property prices, to influence his valuation. On the other hand current values are solely a function of market mood and if there is, at the time of the valuation, a belief amongst buyers and sellers that prices are likely to move upwards or downwards, then that view may have an impact on current value, in which case it should influence an OMV valuation.[137] It should also be borne in mind that the OMV basis requires the valuer to give his opinion of the 'best price' for which the property would be likely to sell, not an 'average' or 'fair' price.

---

[137] See *BBL v Eagle Star* [1995] QB 375, 404, per Sir Thomas Bingham MR: the judge went on to state that ultimately, the valuer's 'concern is with current value only. He is not asked to predict what will happen in future'. See also *Lusograin Comercio Internacional de Cereas Limitada v Bunge AG* [1986] 2 Lloyd's Rep 654, 663 and *Nykredit Mortgage Bank plc v Edward Erdman Group Ltd* [1996] 1 EGLR 119, 121, CA.

The vital difference between OMV and ERP is that, while OMV assumes a sale as at the date of the valuation (so that marketing of the property, negotiations and the conveyancing process are assumed to have already taken place) ERP postulates a *future* sale, and so requires the valuer to take into account the predicted future movement of the market, interest rates and other variables. Thus the OMV value may well be different from the ERP value. The ERP was introduced as a way of bringing a greater degree of realism to the valuing of loan security property (where, assuming borrower default, the lender will only ever sell the property at a future date) and, at least as a happy by-product, to reduce the valuer's exposure to negligence claims.[138]

Although OMV (and increasingly ERP and ERRP) will generally be the basis on which a valuation is undertaken, nonetheless the appropriate valuation basis should be specifically agreed between the valuer and the client prior to the undertaking of the valuation.[139] Of course, the instructions given to a valuer may require a valuation upon an unorthodox basis. In *Predeth v Castle Phillips Finance Co Ltd*[140] the valuer was instructed to carry out a 'crash sale valuation'. Allegedly in reliance upon the valuation of the third party valuer, the defendant, a mortgagee in possession, sold the property to a purchaser who then sold at a substantial profit. The valuer's evidence was that he took the phrase 'crash sale' as meaning a sale which was even more rapid than a forced sale, assuming a four-week exposure to the market, and that, on this basis, had he been asked to give a forced sale valuation the value he gave the property would have been higher, and still higher on the open market value basis. The Court of Appeal accepted that although the phrase 'crash sale' was not a term in general use, it clearly implied a sense of urgency which could only relate to a very limited period of exposure to the market prior to exchange of contracts. Such assumed conditions would necessarily involve a much lower valuation than one conducted on an OMV basis, where a much longer period of exposure to the market prior to exchange is assumed (in this case, three months was judged to be the appropriate period).

In *Predeth* the lender argued that, irrespective of the instructions given to the valuer, he nonetheless owed a duty to the lender to advise it of the 'true market value' of the property. The statement of Watkins J in *Singer & Friedlander*[141] was relied upon, to the effect that:

> ... a valuation must reflect the honest opinion of the valuer of the true

---

[138] Indeed it has been suggested that the *Appraisal and Valuation Manual*, and particularly the ERP, go some way to eliminating the prospect of negligence actions: lecture to PNBA by Mr J E S Hewetson ARICS, 19 June 1996.

[139] As is specifically required by PS 3.1.1(a) of the *Appraisal and Valuation Manual*.

[140] [1986] 2 EGLR 144.

[141] At 213.

market value of the land at the relevant time, no matter why or by whom it is required, be it by merchant bank, land developer or prospective builder.

The Court of Appeal rejected this argument: the valuer had been instructed to give a valuation upon a particular basis, namely assuming a very quick sale, and therefore had no duty to advise the lender of the open market value, 'the true market value', as Watkins J put it. The case is important in that it refuses the invitation to impose upon valuers an overriding duty to state the open market value unless instructed to do so. It is a valuable warning to those who commission valuations to make it clear to valuers the nature of the valuation they seek.

2.10   'For mortgage purposes'

In *Allied Trust Bank Ltd v Edward Symmons & Partners*[142] a valuation was provided the basis of which was expressed to be of the 'open market value for mortgage purposes'. The judge considered the question whether the words 'for mortgage purposes' modified the meaning of OMV. He held that these words did not make any significant difference to the generally accepted idea of OMV:

> The purpose of the valuation does not *prima facie* alter the 'open market value' ... I accept that upon this analysis the words 'for mortgage purposes' add little to 'open market value' other than to invite a degree of conservatism in valuation having regard to the fact that the valuation is to be used for security purposes.[143]

This view echoes that of Watkins J in *Singer & Friedlander*:

> Whatever conclusion is reached, it must be without consideration for the purposes for which it is required. By this I mean that the valuation must reflect the honest opinion of the valuer of the true market value of the land at the relevant time, no matter why or by whom it is required, be it by merchant bank, land developer or prospective builder.[144]

In *Craneheath Securities Ltd v York Montague Ltd*,[145] Jacob J likewise rejected the argument that the valuer should proceed more 'cautiously' when valuing for mortgage purposes. He said:

> While [the valuer] ought to have exercised all proper skills in carrying out his valuation I reject the suggestion that he should have arrived at a lower figure simply because the valuation was for mortgage purposes. The practical effect of the RICS guidelines is to put any need to take extra caution where the property is to be a security upon the lender, not the valuer.

[142]   [1994] 1 EGLR 165.
[143]   At 119.
[144]   At 213.
[145]   [1994] 1 EGLR 159.

In *Corisand Investments Ltd v Druce & Co*[146] the relevant valuation was made in September 1973, before the publication of the RICS *Guidance Notes* (first published in 1976), and just prior to a collapse in the property market. It was argued by the plaintiff that where a valuation is being conducted for mortgage purposes, the valuer must take account of the fact that, in the event that the mortgagee has to realise his security, then it will have to realise the asset by means of a forced sale in unadvantageous circumstances, and the valuation must therefore make allowance for that consideration. This is effectively the argument that the appropriate basis of value when valuing for mortgage purposes is the forced sale basis. Moreover, it was argued, the fact that the mortgagee would only (if at all) be enforcing its security at some date in the future, the valuation had to take account of likely future fluctuations in the property market. Against this, the defendant valuer argued that it was essential to value in accordance with market conditions at the date of valuation. In *Corisand* the valuer valued a hotel (which was to be security for a second mortgage) at £275,000 on 28 September 1973. The valuation was based on the valuer's opinion that the market was still in boom, with purchasers eager to pay more for such an hotel than any ordinary calculation of investment return could justify. The figure therefore reflected what the valuer judged could at that time be immediately realised at auction on that hotel with full vacant possession. No deduction fell to be made to allow for the fact that the valuation was for mortgage purposes, and would therefore be sold at some time in the future when the market was likely to have declined.

Gibson J rejected this approach. He said:

> The sale price which the valuer must try to estimate for the guidance of the intending lender is that sale price which the property is likely to fetch—as the valuer can judge—at the time relevant to the possible realisation of the security and in the circumstances then relevant.[147]

Therefore, in the circumstances of *Corisand*, where the market was, in September 1973, artificially high, the valuer was required either to exclude such content of the market price as was added by the high state of the market at that time (what Gibson J described as the 'speculative content'), or else to identify that part of the value which precariously depends on the immediate state of the market. Gibson J continued:

> … if the current market price which the valuer judges would be realized at auction at the time of valuation is based upon a market which the valuer knows to be 'high' and supported by speculative buyers apparently willing

---

[146] (1978) 248 EG 315.
[147] At 322.

> to pay prices not justified by ordinary principles of investment return, then such content of the market price so estimated as depends upon the market being in that state (which I shall call the 'speculative content') should either not be included in a valuation for mortgage purposes, or should be identified as such, and as so included, for the guidance of the lender, if at the time of valuation there is substantial ground for the valuer to know that the speculative content of his estimated market price will not or may well not be maintained in future, or may well not be readily realisable on the forced sale of the property ... a mortgage valuation must look for a certain period into the future ... The valuer can reasonably be required to consider what the position of the property may well be in circumstances of forced sale within 6 to 12 months of his valuation.

It is plain that Gibson J proceeded on the basis that an open market valuation and 'a mortgage valuation' were different concepts, the latter involving a percentage reduction from the former.

In *BBL v Eagle Star*,[148] the plaintiff lender invited Phillips J to apply the passage in relation to a valuation expressly stated to be given at 'open market value'. Phillips J declined this invitation, saying:

> The basis of valuation being described by Gibson J in this passage is a forced sale valuation. His comments must not be applied to an open market valuation. Where a property market is booming it is inevitable that the current market price will be affected by the entry into the market of property speculators hoping to make capital gains. No discount falls to be made from the open market valuation on this account ... [a valuer should not] allow personal optimism or pessimism as to the future to affect his valuation.[149]

Gibson J's remarks arose out of the expert evidence given during the trial of the action. In so far as he indicates that a valuer should, when valuing a property 'for mortgage purposes' make a deduction from the open market value of that element of the value which relates to what the valuer considers to be an artificially inflated market, and allow predictions as to future property price fluctuations (whether upward or downward tending) then these *dicta* should not be followed. This is primarily because the definition of OMV now specifically envisages that the valuer must value the property as at the moment of the valuation.

In *Craneheath Securities v York Montague*,[150] Jacob J expressed surprise that the open market value was the basis of valuation when the property was to be used as a security:

> ... where, as here, the valuation is heavily dependent on the turnover or profitability of the business conducted from the property. If he has to resort

---

[148]   [1995] 2 All ER 769.
[149]   At 786.
[150]   [1994] 1 EGLR 159, 161.

to his security, the lender is unlikely in practice to be trying to realize it when the business is running smoothly. It is much more likely that the business has collapsed wholly or at least partially. So the obvious implications of this method of valuation for a lender is that realisation of the security will not reach the valuation.

The position appears to be that where, as in the cases of *Corisand* and *Craneheath Securities*, the security is dependent on the turnover of a business operating from the property, then the valuer's duty should be to value the property on the assumption that the business being run from the property has ceased. However where a valuer uses the 'open market value' as his valuation basis when valuing property for mortgage purposes, he will not be negligent, and, furthermore, he will not be required to deduct what Gibson J called 'speculation value'.

2.11 The type of inspection and the standard of care

The type of valuation which the valuer is instructed to undertake will influence the standard of care imposed on him. Most valuations which are carried out for building societies, although paid for by the borrower, will be commissioned by and directed to the lender, and then passed by the lender to the borrower. The lender usually gives the borrower a choice of obtaining one of three types of valuation:

(a) the mortgage inspection and valuation;
(b) a house/flat buyer's report and valuation; or
(c) a full structural survey and valuation.

The fee payable differs according to the type of report chosen by the borrower. In general the borrower contents himself with the mortgage inspection and valuation which will therefore be, for domestic mortgages, the document on which the lender relies. In *Roberts v J Hampson & Co*[151] the judge considered what was involved in undertaking a standard building society valuation:

> It is a valuation and not a survey, but any valuation is necessarily governed by condition. The inspection is, of necessity, a limited one. Both the expert surveyors ... agreed that with a house of this size they would allow about half an hour for their inspection of the site. That time does not admit of moving furniture, of lifting carpets, especially where they are nailed down ...

However this general statement was qualified. The valuation was nonetheless an appraisal by a skilled professional man:

[151] [1990] 1 WLR 94.

It is inherent in any standard fee work that some cases will colloquially be 'winners' and others 'losers' from the professional man's point of view. The fact that in an individual case he may need to spend two or three times as long as he would have expected, or as the fee structure would have contemplated, is something he must accept. His duty to take reasonable care in providing a valuation remains the root of his obligation.[152]

Commenting on the same type of valuation, Auld J said in *Whalley v Robert & Roberts*:[153]

The defendants were not instructed to undertake a structural survey of the detail called for in the standard form of the RICS *House Buyer's Report and Valuation* inspection. They were instructed to inspect and to provide a mortgage valuation report. It is common ground that this involved them in making a brief and reasonably careful visual inspection to enable them, in the terms of the bank report form, to provide a valuation and general guide as to the condition of the property. I am satisfied on the evidence before me that this would not normally involve the use of a spirit-level unless the lack of level in the property became evident on a visual inspection so as to call for further investigation.[154]

However, even where the nature of the inspection has been strictly defined by the contract, or where the limitations of any inspection have been noted in the report itself, the courts have shown themselves willing to hold a surveyor or valuer negligent in not following up or warning the recipient of the report of any signs of structural problems etc which a visual inspection should have indicated.[155] As was said in one case, 'if you do not look, you must warn'.[156]

---

[152] At 101.
[153] [1990] 1 EGLR 164.
[154] At 168; in *Smith v Bush* [1990] 1 AC 831, 858, Lord Griffiths had said that it was only defects which were observable 'by a careful visual examination' which had to be taken into account.
[155] See, for example, *Matto v Rodney Broom Associates* [1994] 2 EGLR 163; *Heatley v William H Brown Ltd* [1992] 1 EGLR 289; *Cross v David Martin Mortimer* [1989] 1 EGLR 154 (all domestic survey cases). Contrast *Sutcliffe v Sayer* [1987] 1 EGLR 155.
[156] Per Judge Carter QC in *Hill v Debenham, Tewson & Chinnocks* (1958) 171 EG 835, 837; see also *Lloyd v Butler* [1990] 47 EG 56.

3 Damages

3.1 Introduction

In a property finance negligence case the plaintiff lender will be seeking compensation for the losses which he has suffered by making the advance. The lender will have paid out the advance plus various costs of recovery. In most cases the lender will have received some repayments from the borrower and some net proceeds of the sale of the property. In addition, it will have lost interest on the sum advanced. The lender's total loss is, therefore, likely to be: the sum advanced plus costs and interest minus payments and recoveries. The question examined in the cases is how much of this loss is recoverable from a negligent professional.

A central issue, is the extent to which professionals could be held liable for losses which, they contended, 'would have happened anyway' as a result of the property market collapse. In *BBL v Eagle Star*,[1] Phillips J held that the bank could not recover that part of its loss which was attributable to the fall in the property market. This decision was followed in a number of first instance cases.[2] It was, however, overruled by the Court of Appeal[3] who held that, where the lender would not, but for the negligent valuation, have made the loan, he could recover all the net loss he had sustained as a result of having done so. The fall in the property market was not to be treated as a new intervening cause breaking the link between negligence and loss. The appeal against this decision was, however, allowed by the House of Lords,[4] not on the grounds favoured by Phillips J but on the basis that damages were to be limited to 'the consequences of the valuation being wrong'.

The result of this decision is that a plaintiff lender is entitled to recover all losses which are:

(a) effectively caused by the breach of duty; and

---

[1]   [1995] 2 All ER 769.
[2]   *Nyckeln Finance v Stumpbrook Continuation* [1994] 2 EGLR 143; *Mortgage Express Ltd v Bowerman & Partners* [1994] 2 EGLR 156; *BNP Mortgages v Goadsby & Harding* [1994] 2 EGLR 169.
[3]   [1995] QB 375.
[4]   [1996] 3 WLR 87.

   (b) not too remote a consequence of it; and

   (c) not the result of his own failure to mitigate his loss; and

   (d) within the scope of the duty owed by the defendant to the plaintiff.

In this chapter we will consider the quantification of damages claims by lenders under three heads: causation and the calculation of total loss; mitigation; and the scope of the duty. We will then consider the application of these principles to valuer and solicitor cases respectively. Finally, there are two additional issues which require separate treatment: allowances for the proceeds of mortgage indemnity policies and claims for equitable compensation. Claims for interest are considered in the next chapter.

3.2   Causation and the calculation of total loss

3.2.1   Introduction

The purpose of damages for breach of contract is to place the plaintiff in the position in which he would have been had the contract been properly performed.[4a] In tort, the fundamental aim is to award:

> ... that sum of money which will put the party who has been injured, or who has suffered, in the same position as he would have been in if he had not sustained the wrong for which he is now getting his compensation or reparation.[5]

The law takes a 'pragmatic and commonsensical' approach to questions of causation.[6] In particular, if a breach of duty does no more than provide the occasion for loss, it is not regard as causative. [7]

3.2.2   'No transaction' and 'successful transaction' cases

For a number of years the courts assessed loss by dividing property finance cases into two categories: 'no transaction' and 'successful transaction' cases.[8] A 'no transaction' case is one in which, if the professional adviser had not been negligent, there would have been no loan transaction. A 'successful transaction' case is one in which, if the professional adviser had not been negligent, there would have been a transaction on different terms—most commonly the lender would have

---

[4a] See *Robinson v Harman* (1848) 1 Exch 850, 855.

[5] Per Lord Blackburn, *Livingston v Rawyards Coal Co* (1880) 5 App Cas 25, 39.

[6] See, generally, *BBL v Eagle Star* [1995] QB 375, 406.

[7] See *Galoo v Bright Grahame Murray* [1994] 1 WLR 1360.

[8] The terminology was first used in *Hayes v James & Charles Dodd* [1990] 2 All ER 815, 818–19.

still have made a loan but in a reduced sum.

In *BBL v Eagle Star*,[9] Lord Hoffmann states that although the distinction 'has a certain pragmatic truth', it is not based on principle and should be abandoned. This is because:

> Every transaction induced by a negligent valuation is a 'no transaction' case in the sense that ex hypothesi the transaction which actually happened would not have happened. A 'successful transaction'… is only the most common example of a case in which the court finds that, on the balance of probability, some other transaction would have happened instead.

In other words, the objection to the distinction is that it is unduly restrictive, being based on the erroneous assumption that, if the professional had not given negligent advice, there are only two possible events which would otherwise have occurred: a 'no transaction' outcome or a 'successful transaction' outcome. In fact, as Lord Hoffmann makes clear, there are at least four possible eventualities:

(a) the lender would have done something more advantageous with his money: an 'alternative loan' case;

(b) the lender would have used the money in some different but equally disastrous venture: a 'disastrous loan' case;

(c) the lender would not have made the loan but would have kept the money on deposit or would not have borrowed the money from a third party source: a 'no loan' case (this is the old 'no transaction' case); or

(d) the lender would have made a lesser loan on the security of the valued property: a 'lesser loan' case (this is the old 'successful transaction' case).

It is important to be clear that the effect of the decision of the House of Lords in *BBL* is not to preclude recovery of losses on the basis that but for the defendant's negligence the lender would not have lent at all. In all three of the cases dealt with in the appeal itself, the damages had been calculated on a standard 'no transaction' basis.[10] These calculations were not criticised by Lord Hoffmann and in *SAAMCO v York Montague*[11] the award of the full 'no transaction' loss (less an allowance for contributory negligence) was upheld. Although, in the other two cases, it was held that damages should be reduced this was not because of any criticism of the 'no transaction' calculation but because part of the total loss fell outside the scope of the valuer's duty.

The continuing applicability of the basic 'no transaction' calculation is confirmed by the decision of Jacob J in the post-*BBL* case of *Platform*

---

[9]   [1996] 3 WLR 87, 99D–F.
[10] For the cases, see below, section 3.2.4.
[11] The lead appeal in *BBL*, on appeal from May J [1995] 2 EGLR 219.

Home Loans v Oyston Shipways.[12] In that case the loss was calculated on the basis that, if the valuers had stated the true value of the property, no loan would have been made. This gave a full 'no transaction' loss, including interest and allowing for contributory negligence, of £585,000. The judge held that all this loss fell within the scope of the valuer's duty.

3.2.3   Assessment of loss

If the plaintiff can establish an 'alternative loan', then its capital loss will be calculated on a no-loan basis and it will also be entitled to recover contractual interest calculated on the basis of the interest it would have received from the alternative transaction.[13] Conversely, if the defendant can establish a 'disastrous loan' then plainly this will have the effect of reducing (or entirely wiping out) the plaintiff's claim to damages. In practice, it seems unlikely that 'alternative loans' or 'disastrous loans' will be established.[14]

The burden of proof is on the plaintiff to establish loss and if he cannot show that the defendant's negligence would have made any difference he will not succeed in recovering substantial damages.[15] In other words, the plaintiff must lead evidence to show that the case is an 'alternative loan', a 'no loan' or a 'lesser loan' case. The two most common situations are 'no loan' and 'lesser loan' and they are considered in the next two sections.

3.2.4   'No loan' cases

In a 'no loan' case, had the professional not been negligent no loan would have been made. This could have been either because the lender would not have lent or because the borrower would not have borrowed at all. If the lender can establish a 'no loan' case, a restitutionary approach to the calculation of loss is adopted:

> ... by awarding the [lender] all he has paid out less what (acting reasonably to cut his losses, including selling the property) he has recovered.[16]

Difficult questions arise in relation to the burden of proof. In general, before damages will be assessed on this basis, the court will have to make a specific finding of fact that, absent the professional's breach of

---

[12]   (1996) unreported, 29 July.
[13]   See *Swingcastle v Gibson* [1991] 2 AC 223, 239.
[14]   There appear to be no reported cases in which the loss has been assessed on either basis.
[15]   Unless special rules apply in misrepresentation cases: see 3.2.4 below.
[16]   Per Sir Thomas Bingham MR in *BBL* in the Court of Appeal, at 419; subject to the extent of the scope of the duty owed by the defendant: see below at 3.4.

duty, no money would have been lent. The onus will be on the lender to establish that no money would have been lent had it known the truth.[17] This is likely to be a highly contentious issue as most plaintiffs will seek damages on a no-loan basis, simply because the damages award-able will be much higher than on a lesser loan basis. But in making such a claim the plaintiff should pay careful attention to the evidence required: evidence should, if possible, be obtained from the underwriter who made the decision.

However, this general rule may not apply in cases where the profes-sional has made a misrepresentation to the lender. In *Downs v Chappell*,[18] Hobhouse LJ (with whom Butler-Sloss and Roch LJJ agreed) pointed out that where the professional was guilty of a misrepresentation:

> In general, it is irrelevant to inquire what the representee would have done if some different representation had been made to him or what other trans-action he might have entered into if he had not entered into the transac-tion in question. Such matters are irrelevant speculations.[19]

In other words, where a claim is for negligent misrepresentation, it appears that reliance is the only relevant concept: if the lender has relied on the misrepresentation, the question as to what he would have done if a true representation had been made is irrelevant. In *Bristol & West Building Society v Mothew*[20] the majority of the Court of Appeal took the view that they were bound to apply this approach.[21]

It seems that it is necessary to distinguish two kinds of cases:[22]
(1) *Where a lender sues a professional for negligently failing to give the proper advice*: In such a case, the lender must show what advice should have been given and that:

> ... if such advice had been given he would not have entered into the relevant transaction [that is, a 'no loan' case] or would not have entered into it on the terms he did [that is, a 'lesser loan' case]. The same applies where the client's complaint is that the solicitor failed in his duty to give him material information.[23]

(2) *Where a lender sues a professional for negligently giving incorrect advice or information*: In such a case, it is sufficient for the lender to prove that he relied on the advice on information:

---

17 See, for example, *Mount Banking Corporation Ltd v Brian Cooper & Co* [1992] 2 EGLR 142.
18 [1996] 3 All ER 344.
19 At 359c, by way of example, he referred to the Privy Council case of *United Motor Finance v Addison* [1937] 1 All ER 425, 429.
20 (1996) unreported, 24 July, CA.
21 See, per Millett LJ, 9–14; and per Staughton LJ at 42–3 who made it clear that he would have preferred the same approach as in negligent omission cases; Otton LJ did not refer to *Downs v Chappell* but does not apply it when setting out his approach.
22 Per Millett LJ, *ibid*, 11–12.
23 *Ibid*, 11.

It is not necessary for him to prove that he would not have acted as he did if he had been given the proper advice or the correct information.[24]

This distinction is contrary to the way in which the question of causation is approached in the professional negligence authorities. It is also likely to be difficult to apply in practice. Lenders will be drawn into pleading cases on the basis of implied representations in order to be in a position to argue that their case is within the second category.

Furthermore, the approach is inconsistent with that of the House of Lords in *BBL*. It is clear that Hobhouse LJ believed that the principle he outlined applied to all misrepresentation cases. There is no sensible distinction to be drawn between a solicitor who gives negligent advice on compliance with standard conditions and a valuer who gives negligent advice as to value. If Hobhouse LJ was right, all that a plaintiff in a negligent valuation case would have to show was that he relied on the valuation: he could then claim his full loss insofar as it falls within the scope of the duty. This is not consistent with Lord Hoffmann's approach to the distinction between 'successful transaction' and 'no transaction' cases.[24a] Lord Hoffmann as stated above, specifically envisages the possibility of defendants leading evidence that the lender would have lent, absent negligence, on some altogether different but equally disastrous venture and of lenders giving evidence of a successful alternative loan. According to Hobhouse LJ such speculations are 'irrelevant'.[24b] Lord Hoffmann does not appear to have appreciated the difficulties with *Downs v Chappell* when he referred to it in the course of his speech in *BBL*. The House of Lords did not hear oral argument on this case and the written submissions on the case were directed only to the 'cap' point.

It is submitted that the principle in *Downs v Chappell* should be applied only to classical misrepresentation cases: ones in which the plaintiff has entered into a contract in reliance on a misrepresentation by the other party to the contract which is actually[25] or 'deemed' to be fraudulent.[26] The burden should be on the plaintiff in all types of 'professional negligence' to prove that the incorrect advice caused him loss.

If the lender can establish that his is a 'no loan' case, the lender's total loss is calculated by taking:

The sum of:

(a) the sum advanced;

(b) the lender's interest claim;[27]

---

[24]   *Ibid*, 12.

[24a]   See *BBL v Eagle Star* [1996] 3 WLR 87, at 99C.

[24b]   See also Simpson (1996) 140 SJ 997.

[25]   As was the case in *United Motor Finance v Addison* [1937] 1 All ER 425.

[26]   As it would be under s 2(1) of the Misrepresentation Act 1967.

[27]   See Chapter 4.

(c) the cost of repossessing the land and realising the security; this may include the expenses of abortive sales, insurance premiums, builder's fees for upkeep of the property, lender's expenses and disbursements and the estate agent's fees/commission for selling the property, including advertising.[28]

Less:

(a) any sums received from the borrower by way of repayments of interest or capital;
(b) sums received on realisation of the security;
(c) any other sums received by the lender between date of possession and date of sale (for example rent from the property).

Depending on the way in which interest is dealt with, this total loss can be calculated either at the date of realisation of the security or at the date of trial. If the former date is taken, it will then be necessary to add statutory interest to the date of trial.[29]

3.2.5   Lesser loan cases

In many situations, the professional's mistakes will have been such that, even if the correct advice or information had been given, the lender would still have made a loan, albeit in a lower sum. This will often be the situation in valuer's negligence cases where no property purchase is involved.

In lesser loan cases the general measure of damages is the difference between the sum the lender advanced in reliance on the negligent valuation or advice and the sum it would have advanced had it been told the true value of the security, or the true facts.[30]

In *London & South of England Building Society v Stone*[31] it was agreed by counsel, and that agreement was indorsed by Stephenson LJ, that:

> ... the true measure of damages for the breach of a defendant surveyor's duty to value a property mortgaged to a plaintiff building society is the difference between the sum the building society actually advanced on the false valuation, which the surveyor carelessly and unskilfully put on the property, and the sum the building society would have advanced on the true valuation, which a careful and skilful surveyor would have put on it.

It is submitted that this analysis remains correct when the total loss

---

[28] See Goddard LJ's judgment at first instance in *Baxter v Gapp* [1938] 4 All ER 457, 465; and Phillips J in *BBL v Eagle Star* at 818.

[29] As was done in *Platform Home Loans v Oyston Shipways* (1996) unreported, 29 July.

[30] *London & South of England Building Society v Stone* [1983] 1 WLR 1242, 1260, per Stephenson LJ; *Corisand Investments v Druce* (1978) 248 EG 315; *Singer & Friedlander v Wood (John D) & Co* (1977) 243 EG 212; *Allied Trust Bank Ltd v Edward Symmons & Partners* [1994] 1 EGLR 165.

[31] [1983] 1 WLR 1242, per Stephenson LJ, at 1262.

is being calculated.

A number of points should be noted relating to lesser loan cases:

(a) the figure for the actual value at the time of valuation should be the *true value* (so far as it is possible to assess it), not the highest non-negligent valuation which could have been given;[32]

(b) any interest repayments made by a borrower will be taken into account in reducing the lender's damages, even though such payments would probably have been made had the lender lent at the lower level;[33] and

(c) the incidental costs of realising the security, taking proceedings, etc, will not be recoverable, as they would have been incurred in any event.[34]

3.3   Mitigation of loss

3.3.1   Introduction

The general rule is that a plaintiff must take all reasonable steps to mitigate the loss to him consequent upon and flowing from the defendant's wrong, whether tortious or contractual. The plaintiff:

> ... cannot recover for any such loss which he could thus have avoided but has failed, through unreasonable action, or inaction, to avoid. Put shortly, the plaintiff cannot recover for avoidable loss.[35]

The general principle of mitigation has three aspects:

(a) a plaintiff cannot recover for losses which he could reasonably have avoided;

(b) a plaintiff cannot recover for losses which he, in fact, has avoided;

(c) a defendant is entitled to be credited for all positive benefits which the plaintiff has received as a result of steps taken to mitigate.

The plaintiff's 'total loss' is therefore reduced by any losses which fall under these three heads.

It is submitted that such losses must be deducted from the total loss claimed before the court considers whether the loss 'falls within the scope of the defendant's duty'. This is because losses which should have been avoided are not treated as losses which were caused by the

---

[32]   *Scotlife Homeloans (No 2) Ltd v Kenneth James & Co* [1995] EGCS 70; *BBL v Eagle Star* [1996] 3 WLR 87, 102B–F.

[33]   *Corisand v Druce* (1978) 248 EG 315; *Assured Advances Ltd v Ashbee & Co* [1994] EGCS 169—though in neither case was this point the subject of a reasoned analysis and it is questionable that it is correct.

[34]   See *Corisand*, at 506.

[35]   *McGregor on Damages* 15th edn (1988), 168, and see generally Chapter 7.

defendant. It appears that this was the approach favoured by Jacob J in *Platform Home Loans v Oyston Shipways*.[36]

Like any other plaintiff a lender is, therefore, under a duty to take reasonable steps to reduce its loss. The burden of proving a failure to mitigate is on the defendant.[37] Two contentions are commonly made: that the plaintiff has failed to take reasonable steps to realise the security and/or that that plaintiff has failed to enforce the borrower's covenant to repay. These are considered in the next two sections.

3.3.2   Failure to take reasonable steps to realise the security

Any damages entitlement flowing from the professional's breach of duty will, of course, be reduced by sums received from the sale of the security. The contention is often made that lenders have been dilatory in obtaining possession and selling the property causing a loss of interest and a decline in the capital value of the property.

In *Nyckeln Finance Co Ltd v Stumpbrook Continuation Ltd*,[38] it was held that where the market was falling, the lender should have sought repossession in order to sell the property after the borrower's default earlier than it did. In that case the judge limited the lender's damages by accepting the valuer's submission that the security could have been sold at a higher price at an earlier time. This had the result of capping the primary capital measure of damages and the period of time over which the lender could claim damages for loss of use of the sum lent.

However the judge accepted the lender's submission that the well-known passage from Lord Macmillan's speech in *Banco da Portugal v Waterlow*[39] set out the proper approach to take in relation to property finance negligence cases:

> Where the sufferer from a breach of contract finds himself in consequence of that breach placed in a position of embarrassment the measures which he may be driven to adopt in order to extricate himself ought not to be weighed in nice scales at the instance of the party whose breach of contract has occasioned the difficulty. It is often easy after an emergency has passed to criticize the steps which have been taken to meet it, but such criticism does not come well from those who have themselves created the emergency. The law is satisfied if the party placed in a difficult situation by reason of the breach of a duty owed to him has acted reasonably in the adoption of remedial measures, and he will not be held disentitled to recover the cost of such measures merely because the party in breach can suggest other measures less burdensome to him might have been taken.

---

[36]   (1996) unreported, 29 July.
[37]   *Roper v Johnson* (1873) LR 8 CP 167; *Garnac Grain v Faure & Fairclough* [1968] AC 1130, 1140.
[38]   [1994] 2 EGLR 143.
[39]   [1932] AC 452 at 506.

However, loss which results from action or inaction by the plaintiff while attempting to mitigate its loss must be shown to have been caused by the defendant's breach if it is to be recoverable from the defendant.[40]

Thus, although in *Nyckeln* the judge found, on the facts, that there had been a failure to mitigate loss, a lender will not normally be expected to take possession of the security and seek a swift sale immediately the borrower defaults on payments under the loan. In *Nyckeln* itself the judge accepted that a prudent bank would give a borrower six months to sort out its problems. But conversely a prudent bank cannot reasonably give a borrower too great a period of time to seek refinancing or to pay off its borrowing. Lord Lowry commented in *Swingcastle v Gibson*:[41]

> I do not overlook the fact that, *once the borrower had well and truly defaulted*, the lenders had access to their remedy and thereby to their money (emphasis added).

The question whether a lender has failed to realise its security timeously, or has failed to make reasonable attempts to do so, will depend on the facts of each case, but it is suggested that matters the court is likely to take into account will include:

(a) the perceived capability of the borrower to remedy any payment default and stabilise itself;

(b) whether the market is on a downward turn or not and so whether the lender reasonably considers that it should delay the marketing of the security until prices have increased; and

(c) whether the lender has marketed the property properly.

There is a substantial body of law dealing with the duty of the mortgagee to the mortgagor after it has taken possession of the secured property.[42] Although the lender has no 'duty' to the defendant professional to sell at a proper price, it is suggested that the mortgagee's duty to the mortgagor in practice as exemplified in the various cases[43] can properly inform a consideration of whether the lender has mitigated its loss.[44]

3.3.3   Failure to take steps to enforce the borrower's personal covenant to repay

It will usually be the case that the borrower's default triggers the process

---

[40] *The Elena d'Amico* [1980] 1 Lloyds Rep 75, 89, a principle applied in *Cavendish Funding Ltd v Henry Spencer* (1996) unreported, 21 March.

[41] [1991] 2 AC 223, 237B.

[42] See, generally, *Fisher and Lightwood's Law of Mortgages* 10th edn (1987), 388.

[43] *Cuckmere Brick Co Ltd v Mutual Finance Ltd* [1971] Ch 949; *Palk v Mortgage Services Funding plc* [1993] 2 WLR 415.

[44] Goddard LJ in *Baxter v Gapp* [1938] 4 All ER 457 considered that this body of law (as it then stood) was relevant.

of possession, sale and discovery of the facts that give rise to an action in negligence. Of course, even if the security proves deficient to meet the principal sum and accrued interest, the borrower still has a contractual obligation to pay the sums due. What if the lender decides not to pursue the borrower for the deficiency, and looks only to the professional? The question was posed in *London & South of England Building Society v Stone*:[45]

> Can ... [the defendant] claim credit for what the borrower has not repaid if the lender could have insisted on repayment in full or in part and could, if the borrower refused, have sued him with a reasonable prospect of success?

Clearly if the borrower is evidently lacking in funds then the lender will have no obligation to issue proceedings against him and will not be penalised by any reduction in damages for such failure.[46] In practice this will usually be the case.

In *Eagle Star Insurance Co Ltd v Gale & Power*[47] it was held that the borrower's covenant to repay had to be taken into account in assessing damages against the defendant valuers. In that case the plaintiff had lent £3,015 on a valuation of £3,350. At the date of trial the borrower had not actually defaulted but it was held by Devlin J that the property had actually been worth £1,600. The borrower had, unusually, aside from other (unspecified) covenants, covenanted to pay the future sum of £1,500. The judge gave judgment in the sum of £100 'to indemnify the plaintiff against the possibility of their not being able to recover their monies from [the borrower]'. The case arose out of peculiar facts and, it is suggested, is confined to them.

However, in so far as *Eagle Star v Gale & Power* established a principle that the negligent professional can in all circumstances take advantage of the value of the borrower's covenant (if the covenant can realistically be ascribed a value) then this principle is no longer good law. In *London & South of England Building Society v Stone* the plaintiff sought damages against the valuer, after having spent a large sum of money repairing the property. Under the terms of the mortgage, the borrower was liable to indemnify the plaintiff for this expenditure. The borrower sold the property and repaid the principal sum. He did not however, indemnify the plaintiff for all sums spent on repairing the property. The plaintiff made a decision not to pursue the borrower on the ground that the plaintiff felt 'morally responsible' for the loss of the borrower's home. In addition, the plaintiff believed that the enforcement of the covenant to pay would injure public relations. O'Connor LJ held that

---

[45]   [1983] 1 WLR 1242, per Stephenson LJ, at 1262.
[46]   See *Pilkington v Wood* [1953] Ch 770.
[47]   (1955) 166 EG 37.

Eagle Star v Gale & Power was wrongly decided. Stephenson LJ said[48] that a court would only be justified in reducing a lender's damages for its failure to pursue the borrower:

> ... if it was reasonable for the [plaintiff] to enforce the borrower's covenant to pay; for what the borrower might pay could only be take into account in mitigation of the lender's damages if the lender ought to have miti-gated that loss and damage by enforcing the borrower's covenant.

The wrongdoer must show that:

> ... the wronged party's reasoned choice to waive his contractual rights against the third party is unreasonable in the ordinary course of events in the particular field of commercial business and in all the circumstances, it may be some special, of the particular case ... the lender's conduct in not taking steps to reduce the loss will not be weighed in nice scales at the instance of the party who has occasioned the loss.[49]

It is to be noted that Stephenson LJ places the burden of showing that the lender *should* have pursued the borrower upon the defendant. In the *Stone* case the Court of Appeal decided that the lender had acted reasonably in not enforcing the borrower's covenant and accordingly refused to reduce the damages awardable to the plaintiff on the ground of failure to mitigate.

It is possible that statutory interest could be disallowed for a period if the court considers that the plaintiff should have instituted proceedings earlier.

3.4   The scope of the duty

3.4.1   The decision of the House of Lords in BBL

The question as to what sums are recoverable by lenders in property finance cases has, generally, been treated as being about 'measure of damages'. However, in *BBL v Eagle Star*, the House of Lords said that this was the wrong point of departure. The first question to be asked was not 'what is the correct measure of damages for the loss suffered by the lender?', but rather 'what is the nature and scope of the duty owed by the valuer?' The scope of the duty has to be determined by reference to the kind of damage from which the valuer had to take care to render the lender harmless.[50] As a result, the real question in such cases is whether the loss was 'the kind of loss in respect of which the duty was owed'.

---

[48]   *Ibid*, 1262.
[49]   *Ibid*, 1262.
[50]   *Caparo Industries plc v Dickman* [1990] 2 AC 605 at 627.

Lord Hoffmann (who gave the only speech) said:

> The scope of the duty, in the sense of the consequences for which the valuer is responsible, is that which the law regards as best giving effect to the express obligations assumed by the valuer, neither cutting them down so that the lender obtains less than he was reasonably entitled to expect, nor extending them so as to impose on the valuer a liability greater than he could reasonably have thought he was undertaking.[51]

A rule to the effect that a wrongdoer should be responsible for all the consequences of his wrongful conduct would be 'exceptional' because the law usually limits liability to the consequences which are 'attributable to that which made the act wrongful'. This means that, in a case where the defendant is liable for providing inaccurate information, that liability is limited to the damage suffered as a consequence of the information being inaccurate.[52]

Lord Hoffmann considered that the principle adopted by the Court of Appeal made the wrongdoer responsible for consequences which, though in general terms foreseeable, did not appear to have any sufficient causal connection with the subject matter of the duty. He stated a different principle in the following terms:

> … a person under a duty to take reasonable care to provide information on which someone else will decide upon a course of action is, if negligent, not generally regarded as responsible for all the consequences of that course of action. He is responsible only for the consequences of the information being wrong. A duty of care which imposes upon the informant responsibility for losses which would have occurred even if the information which he gave had been correct is not in my view fair and reasonable as between the parties. It is therefore inappropriate either as an implied term of a contract or as a tortious duty arising from the relationship between them.[53]

This approach distinguishes between a duty to *provide* information and a duty to *advise* someone as to what course of action to take. Only in the latter case will the adviser be responsible for all foreseeable loss resulting from the course of action being taken.[54]

Lord Hoffmann's reasoning closely follows Professor Dugdale's suggested 'purposive' approach to the assessment of damages which was discussed in detail in the argument. In an article on the Court of Appeal decision[55] Professor Dugdale said:

> The purpose of V's [the valuer's] valuation is not to persuade L [the lender] to make a loan. It is to protect L from having inadequate security provision

51 [1996] 3 WLR 87, at 93G–H.
52 At 94E.
53 At 95D–E.
54 See 95E–G.
55 'A Purposive Analysis of Professional Advice: Reflections on the *BBL* Decision' [1995] JBL 533, 545–6.

if it decides to make the loan; to provide L with a valuation on the basis of which it can make adequate security provision as at the date of the loan. ... The basis of the valuer's liability is failure to take care. The extent of his liability is calculated by asking what has been lost in the light of the purpose of the duty of care. The purpose was to enable the lender to make adequate security provision and the loss must be limited to the inadequacy of the security.

The result of this analysis is that damages are limited to the 'consequences of the valuation being wrong'. In practice, this means that the lender's damages will be limited to the difference between the valuation and the actual value at the time of the valuation. It will be seen that the application of this principle has the effect of linking the defendant's potential liability to the extent to which he has been negligent: put simply, the greater the professional's fault, the greater the damages recoverable. The theory that the lender should be entitled to recover the whole of his loss, subject to a 'cap' limiting his recovery to the amount of the overvaulation:

> ... will ordinarily produce the same result as the requirement that loss should be a consequence of the valuation being wrong, because the usual such consequence is that the lender makes an advance which he thinks is secured to a correspondingly greater extent.[56]

But Lord Hoffmann refused to rule out the possibility that other kinds of loss might flow from the valuation being wrong. He pointed out that the appearance of a 'cap' is the result of the plaintiff having to satisfy two separate requirements:[57]

(a) he must prove that he has suffered loss; and
(b) he must establish that the loss fell within the scope of the duty which was owed.

This is the approach which must be applied to the assessment of damages in all professional negligence cases.

3.4.2   The application of the decision

The application of the decision can be illustrated by facts of the three appeals. In *SAAMCO v York Montague*,[58] the lenders advanced £11 million on the basis of a valuation of £15 million. The judge found that the actual value of the property was only £5 million. He assessed the plaintiff's loss, on a no transaction basis (including costs of funds), at £9.7 million and then made a reduction for contributory negligence of 25 per cent. Lord Hoffmann analysed the position in this way:

---

56   *Ibid*, 100F.
57   *Ibid*, 100G.
58   [1995] 2 EGLR 219.

The consequence of the valuation being wrong was that the plaintiff had £10 million less security than they thought. The whole loss was within the scope of the defendant's duty.[59]

As a result, the plaintiff was entitled to recover its full loss, and the valuer's appeal was dismissed.

In *UBK v Prudential*[60] the lender advanced £1.75 million on the security of a property which the defendants valued at £2.5 million. The judge found that the correct value was between £1.8 million and £1.85 million. The total loss suffered by the lender was £1.3 million, assessed on a no transaction basis. According to Lord Hoffmann:

> ... the damages should have been limited to the consequences of the valuation being wrong, which were that the lender had £700,000 or £650,000 less security than he thought.

As a result, the appeal was allowed and the damages were reduced to the difference between the valuation and the correct value.

Finally, in *Nykredit v Edward Erdman*[61] the lenders advanced £2.45 million on the security of a property valued at £3.5 million. The actual value of the property was said by the judge to be £2 million, or at most £2.375 million. The lender's total 'no transaction' loss was quantified at £3.058 million and judgment was given in this sum. The appeal was allowed and the House of Lords substituted for the judge's award of damages 'a figure equal to the difference between £3.5 million and the true value of the property at the date of valuation'.[62]

It is important to note that the decision of the House of Lords does not involve a return to the approach of Phillips J at first instance. The defendant is not relieved of the losses consequent upon a fall in the property market: he can be liable for such losses provided that they were within the 'scope of his duty'. Furthermore, the approach is not the same as that advanced by Hobhouse LJ in *Downs v Chappell*.[63] He suggested that a 'cap' on damages could be imposed in the following way:

> ... compare the loss consequent upon entering into the transaction with what would have been the position had the represented, or supposed, state of affairs actually existed. Assume that there had been no tort because the represented, or supposed facts were true: if on this hypothesis the claimant would have been no better off than in fact he was, this will suggest that the proposed award will lead to an overcompensation.[64]

---

[59] At 102G.
[60] [1994] 2 EGLR 100.
[61] (1993) unreported, 1 October, HHJ Byrt QC.
[62] At 104C.
[63] [1996] 3 All ER 344.
[64] *Ibid*, at 362a–b.

If the 'check' does show an 'overcompensation' then the damages can be reduced accordingly.

Lord Hoffmann suggests that this is what he conceives to be 'in accordance with the normal principle of liability for wrongful acts'.[65] In fact, such a principle does not give the same result as Lord Hoffmann's own approach. The *'Downs v Chappell* cap' will give a lower figure than Lord Hoffmann's approach because it 'factors out' all the loss 'attributable' to the fall in the property market. To put it another way, taking 'the extent of the overvaluation' at the date of the advance makes no allowance for a subsequent fall in the true value: if there was a valuation of £1 million and a true value of £500,000, the lender 'thought he had security of £1 million' but, in a situation where the market fell 40 per cent and the property sold for £300,000, the lender would, in any event, have found himself with security worth only £600,000. On this basis it could be said that the 'extent of the overvaluation' was £300,000 rather than the £500,000 which Lord Hoffmann treats as being the correct figure.

The position can be illustrated by using the example which Sir Thomas Bingham MR suggested in *BBL v Eagle Star* in the Court of Appeal:

> (1) A valuer (V) negligently advises a lender (L) that the value of a property is £1m. (2) L's policy is to lend 80 % of valuation on mortgage. (3) So L lends the borrower (B) £800,000 in reliance on the valuation ... (4) In fact the market value of the property at the date of valuation was £500,000. (5) Had V so advised no loan would have been made. (6) B defaults in repayment and L repossesses and sells the land. (7) By this time there had been a sharp fall in the property market. (8) L sells for the best available price: £300,000.[66]

The Court of Appeal held that the appropriate measure of damages was £500,000 (£800,000 minus £300,000) plus the costs of realisation, of reasonable interest, etc. There are three other possibilities:[67]

(1) *Phillips J*: The damages would be the sum advanced (£800,000) minus the true value of the property at the date of the advance (£500,000) equals £300,000 plus costs of realisation and interest.

(2) *Hobhouse LJ*: The basic measure would be the sum advanced (£800,000) minus the realisations (£300,000) equals £500,000 plus the costs of realisation and interest. However, if the representation had been true the value of the property would have been £1 million, the fall in the market would have been the same (£500,000 to £300,000, that is, 40 per cent)

---

[65]   *BBL v Eagle Star*, at 97A.
[66]   [1995] QB 375, 403.
[67]   Not taking into account what are, possibly, different treatments of interest and costs of realisation: see below.

thus the sum realised on sale would have been £600,000. As a result, the total loss would have been £200,000, being the sum advanced (£800,000) less the sum realised (£600,000) plus the costs of realisation and interest. As a result, the damages should be 'capped' at £200,000 plus the costs of realisation and interest.

(3) *Lord Hoffmann*: The consequence of the information supplied by the valuer being wrong was that the lender would have £500,000 'less security than he thought'. As a result, the damages should be limited to £500,000.

3.4.3   Cases in which the defendant will be liable for all the consequences of the wrongful act

In *BBL v Eagle Star*, the House of Lords point to two categories of case in which a defendant may be liable for all the consequences of his wrongful act.

(1) *'Fraud' cases*: Lord Hoffmann points out that fraud is generally thought to be an exception to the principle that a person providing information upon which another will rely in choosing a course of action is responsible only for the consequences of the information being wrong.[68] He notes however that, in *Downs v Chappell*,[69] Hobhouse LJ seemed to have expressed the contrary view. In *Slough Estates v Welwyn Hatfield DC* [69a] May J considered the application of *BBL* to fraud damages. He rejected the argument that he was bound to follow *Downs v Chappell* and held that, the effect of *BBL* was that fraud was an exception to the general principle: liability for fraud does extend to all losses suffered as a consequence of entering into the transaction.

(2) *'Decision advice' cases*: Lord Hoffmann says that when a defendant is under a duty to advise whether or not a course of action should be taken he will be liable for all the foreseeable loss which is the consequence of that course being taken.[70] These cases can be called 'decision advice' cases. It seems unlikely that such cases will often occur in property finance claims. It would be highly unusual for a lender to seek the advice of a valuer or a solicitor as to whether or not a loan should be made. This is a commercial decision for the lender.

   In addition, it is submitted that there are some cases in which the 'scope of the duty' is such that it covers all the foreseeable consequences of the information being wrong.[71]

---

[68]   At 96E.
[69]   [1996] 3 All ER 344, 359.
[69a]   (1996) unreported, 11 July.
[70]   *Ibid*, 95F.
[71]   This point is discussed further in section 3.6 below.

3.4.4   Issues arising from BBL

The decision of the House of Lords gives rise to at least three areas of difficulty:

(a) At what stage is a reduction for contributory negligence to be made? Should this be deducted from the 'total loss' or only from the 'loss falling within the scope of the duty'?

(b) How is the analysis to be applied in solicitor cases where the breach of duty involves something more complex than a failure to provide accurate information?

(c) How is 'interest' to be taken into account?

The first two questions are dealt with elsewhere in this chapter.[72]

The question of interest was not dealt with by the House of Lords but was adjourned *sine die*. There are at least three possibilities:

(a) that the loss should be limited to the extent of the overvaluation without any allowance for interest (save for the interest included in the total 'capped' loss);

(b) that interest should be added to the loss within the scope of the duty from the date of the realisation of the security;

(c) that interest should be added to the scope of the duty from the date of the overvaluation.

The first possibility appears, at first sight, to represent the position taken by Lord Hoffmann in the *UBK* and *Nykredit* cases[73]—in stating the award of damages to be substituted for that made by the judge in each case under appeal no allowance was made for interest. The second possibility appears to be most consistent with the logic of the decision. An award of interest would be made on this basis on the ground that, if the lender had had the security which he thought, he would have obtained interest on proceeds of realisation from the date of realisation.[74] There are also general 'policy' arguments in favour of this approach: if no award of interest were made there would be a strong incentive for defendants to delay judgment as long as possible.

The third possibility was, however, adopted by Jacob J in *Platform Home Loans v Oyston Shipways*.[75] In that case all three alternatives were advanced in argument (although it appears that neither defendant advanced the first with much enthusiasm). The judge held that the correct approach was to add interest to the amount of the overvaluation from the date of the valuation to the date of the trial. He appears to have accepted the argument that because the defendants were, in effect, prepared to concede that some interest must be payable, then 'logically

---

[72] For contributory negligence, see 4.4.5 and for solicitor cases see 3.6.

[73] See 3.4.2 above.

[74] This is the view of Halpern and Peacocke in their article, (1996) 146 NLJ 1157.

[75] (1996) unreported, 29 July.

the only point you can add it from is the point at which that prima facie measure of loss occurs, which is the date of valuation'.[76] This had the effect of widening the 'scope of the duty' from the date of valuation to the date of judgment 'as at date of judgement', all the lender's actual loss fall within this broader scope.

It is submitted that this approach is incorrect in principle: interest is not added to 'measure of loss' but to 'any part of the debt or damages … for all or any part of the period between the date when the cause of action arose' and payment or judgment.[77] The lender's loss is only crystallised on realisation. Furthermore, the cause of action may not have arisen on the date of the advance[78] in which case there would be no power to award interest.[79] For these reasons, it is suggested that interest should be added to the loss suffered within the scope of duty from the date of sale of the property at the statutory rate.

3.5   Assessing damages in valuers' negligence cases

The decision in *BBL* is easiest to apply in valuers' negligence cases. If a valuer is shown to have been negligent, the assessment of damages proceeds by looking at the following four questions:

(a)   What would have happened if the valuer had reported the true value of the property?

(b)   What 'total loss' has the lender suffered?

(c)   What was the amount of the 'overvaluation'?

(d)   Is the 'total loss' suffered within the scope of the valuer's duty of care?

The first two questions have already been considered.[80] The lender must show that the case is a 'no loan', 'lesser loan' or 'alternative loan' case.

The third question is dealt with by assessing the 'extent of the overvaluation'. This is the difference between the figure which was stated in the valuation and the 'correct value' at the date of the valuation. This figure is the 'mean' of the range of non-negligent values, not the 'highest non-negligent value'.[81]

The fourth question is answered by considering whether or not the total loss is greater than the 'overvaluation'. If so, the damages recoverable are limited to the amount of the overvaluation.

In short, the valuer's liability is limited to that tranche of security

[76]   See transcript, pp 39–40, per Mr Patten QC.
[77]   See s 35A(1) of the Supreme Court Act 1981.
[78]   See Chapter 5 below.
[79]   See Chapter 4 below for interest generally.
[80]   See 3.2 above.
[81]   See *BBL v Eagle Star*, 102B–F.

which the lender mistakenly thinks he has by reason of the overvaluation: the extent of the overvaluation is, in effect, a 'cap' on the lender's loss.

3.6   Assessing damages in solicitors' negligence cases

The general analysis set out above concerning the measure of damages in valuer's negligence cases is equally applicable to solicitors' negligence cases in so far as they relate to the quantification of the prima facie amount of loss which the lender is potentially entitled to recover from the solicitor.

Although solicitors' cases were not expressly considered by the House of Lords[82] it is clear that the general principles in that case must also be applied. The court must decide whether or not the loss suffered was 'within the scope of the solicitor's duty'. As a result, in so far as the solicitor is in breach of a duty to take reasonable care to provide accurate information for the purpose of enabling a lender to decide upon a course of action, the lender's loss should be limited to 'the consequences of the information being wrong'. A number of different categories of case can be considered.

(1) *Inaccurate report on title*: The only 'solicitor cases' to which Lord Hoffmann's analysis can be directly applied are those involving straightforward 'title reporting errors' as a consequence of which the lender has 'less security than he thought'. This would include cases such as the following:

- where there are title defects in the property which have the effect of reducing its value;
- where the solicitor provides other inaccurate information to the lender, for example concerning the existence of planning permission, building regulation approval or an NHBC certificate, the absence of which means that the value of the property is reduced.

In such cases, the maximum amount of the damages recoverable will be the amount by which the value of the security was less than it would have been if the information provided by the solicitor had been correct: the difference between the value which the property would have had if the report on title had been correct and its true value.

(2) *Failure to provide information relevant to the value of the security:* In *BBL*, Lord Hoffmann dealt only with cases in which a defendant *in fact*

---

[82]   There being no appeal in *Mortgage Express Ltd v Bowerman & Partners*, the only 'solicitor's case' considered by the Court of Appeal in *BBL v Eagle Star*. See however the analysis of *McElroy Milne v Commercial Electronics Ltd* [1993] 1 NZLR 39, 994.

provided incorrect information. However, it is submitted that the same analysis can be applied where there has been a *failure to provide* information relevant to the value of the security. This would mean that, for example, when a solicitor fails to provide information which would have led a lender to realise that a valuation was incorrect, the damages would be limited to the difference between the correct value of the property (which would have come to light if the solicitor had passed on the information) and the reported value. On the basis of this approach, the damages appeal in *Mortgage Express Ltd v Bowerman & Partners* would have been dealt with in the same way as the valuer appeals: the damages would have been reduced to the figure representing the difference between the value stated by the valuers and the true value of the property.[83]

(3) *Providing inaccurate information relevant to the borrower's ability to repay*: It has been suggested that the *BBL* analysis can also be applied in cases where the solicitor has failed to draw the lender's attention to information which is relevant to the borrower's ability to make the repayments due. In *Bristol & West Building Society v Mothew*[84] in breach of an express instruction, the solicitor had failed to report the fact that purchasers had arranged a second mortgage at the time of the purchase. In remitting the case to the judge for the assessment of damages, Millett LJ remarked that the plaintiff had to prove that the loss fell within the scope of the defendant's duty to inform it of the arrangements which the purchasers had made with the bank (the second mortgagee). He went on to say:

> The Society was told that [the borrowers] had no other indebtedness and that no second charge was contemplated. The existence of the second charge did not affect the Society's security. The absence of any indebtedness to the bank would not have put money in the purchaser's pocket; it would merely have reduced their liabilities. Whether their liability to the bank affected their ability to make mortgage repayments to the Society has yet to be established, but given the smallness of the liability its effect on the purchaser's ability to meet their obligations to the Society may have been negligible. It may even be, for example, that the purchasers made no payments at all to the bank at the relevant time, and if so it is difficult so see how any part of the loss suffered by the Society can be attributable to the information supplied to it by the Defendant. It would have occurred even if the information had been correct.[85]

The Court of Appeal did not hear argument about the application of

---

[83] Professor Dugdale believed that his 'purposive approach' would have this effect: see [1995] JBL 533, 549.
[84] (1996) unreported, 24 July, CA.
[85] *Ibid*, transcript, pp 14–15.

BBL to the facts of the case in *Mothew* and these comments are in any event *obiter*. The difficulty with this approach is that it leaves out of account the reason why the lender wanted to know about the second charge in the first place. This information is relevant to the borrower's overall financial position: the fact that the borrower is only able to finance the purchase with the benefit of a second charge means that he is incurring additional financial burdens which will affect his ability to repay. It is suggested that on a proper application of the *BBL* decision, the court must in each case, compare what the lender in fact obtained with what he believed he was obtaining as a result of the solicitor's advice. This means that, in a *Mothew* type case, the court will have to consider what conclusions the lender would have drawn about the borrower's ability to repay if the solicitor had provided the correct information. If the lender would have concluded on a reasonable investigation that the borrower was unlikely to be able to repay then the 'consequence of the information being wrong' is that the lender has entered into a transaction which is not viable. In other words, all the loss suffered by the lender will fall within the scope of the solicitor's duty. As a result, it is submitted the lender can recover all the loss suffered as a result of entering into that transaction

(4) *Information tending to reveal borrower fraud*: When an honest but negligent solicitor fails to provide information tending to reveal borrower fraud,[86] the 'consequence of the information being wrong' (or rather, of the information not being supplied) is that the lender has become the victim of a fraud. What the lender 'thought he had' was the covenant of an honest and solvent borrower; the 'consequence of the information not being supplied' is that the lender in fact had was the covenant of a fraudster. As a result, the whole of the loss suffered is within the scope of the solicitor's duty.[87]

(5) *'Risk advice' cases*: In another class of case, the solicitor's breach of duty may go beyond the simple provision of information relating to the transaction. The solicitor may be in breach of a duty to advise his client as to the potentially adverse consequences of a particular course of action. For example, if a lease contains a particularly onerous covenant, a solicitor's duty may extend beyond simply drawing the clause to the lender's attention. He may be obliged to warn the lender of the potentially adverse consequences of taking a lease containing such a covenant as security. In a complex commercial property loan, the solicitor is likely to be under a duty to draw a number of matters to the

---

[86]   See Chapter 1.
[87]   For a different view see Halpern and Peacocke (1996) 146 NLJ 1157, 1158—in which they suggest that 'the courts will have to evolve ways of applying *BBL*' in such situations, without suggesting how this might be done.

lender's attention and to warn of the risks that result from them making a loan.

As has been seen, Lord Hoffmann draws a distinction between 'information' and 'advice' cases. In the latter category he places cases in which a defendant is under a duty to advise whether or not a course of action should be taken ('decision advice' cases). It is submitted that 'risk advice' cases fall between these extreme poles. The professional has a duty to advise, going beyond the mere 'provision of information', but not as far as advising on whether or not a loan should be made. It is submitted that in such cases that the adviser should be liable for all the foreseeable loss which is a consequence of his breach of duty.

(6) *'Decision advice' cases:* It is clear that, in cases where the defendant has advised on the lending decision itself, he is liable for the foreseeable consequences of the loan having been made. It is unlikely that there will be many cases against solicitors which fall under this head.

3.7   Mortgage Indemnity Guarantees

In a number of cases, negligent professionals have attempted to take the benefit of Mortgage Indemnity Guarantee (MIG) policies taken out by lenders. In a typical case, if a proposed loan exceeds the lender's maximum 'loan-to-value' ratio, the lender will require the borrower to pay the premium for a MIG policy to provide cover for the difference between the amount advanced and the lender's normal advance. The premium is generally deducted from the advance. The contract of insurance will be expressed to be with and for the benefit of the lender. Payment will be triggered by any shortfall in recovery on realisation of the security on the borrower's default.

The general rule is that when damages are assessed, the proceeds of any policy of insurance are disregarded. This principle is known as *res inter alios acta*. It was described by Phillips J as requiring:

> ... the court to disregard an indemnity received by the plaintiff from a third party in respect of the loss caused by the defendant ... The law disregards the (extraneous) intervention so that the plaintiff remains entitled to recover from the defendant the full amount of the loss or damage initially suffered.[88]

As long ago as 1874 Bramwell B had expressed 'dismay' at the contrary proposition.[89]

---

[88]   *BBL v Eagle Star* [1995] 2 All ER 769, 802. See also *Parry v Cleaver* [1970] AC 1.
[89]   *Bradburn v Great Western Railway Co* (1874) 10 LR Ex 1.

In the *BBL* case Phillips J[90] held the valuers could not claim credit, when the lender's damages came to be assessed, for recoveries made by the lender from Eagle Star under the MIGs, because such recoveries fell 'fairly and squarely' within the doctrine of *res inter alios acta*. In that case the premiums had been paid by the borrower.

However, defendants in property finance negligence cases have not been deterred by this judgment. The argument has also been run by borrowers who are being pursued on their personal covenants. The point has arisen in a number of cases over the past three years, with varying results.

In *Alliance & Leicester Building Society v Edgestop*[91] it was a term of the advance to the borrower that the premium for the MIG should be paid out of the advance. Knox J, who was not referred to Phillips J's judgment, held that he was not satisfied that the insurance payments could be accurately described as *res inter alios acta*:

> On the contrary the indications are that it was a term of the fraudulently induced (loan) transactions that the insurance should be effected and on that basis it seems to me more like *res inter eosdem facta* ...

Knox J held that the policy was part of the overall bargain between the parties and therefore the mortgagee should give credit for insurance monies, just as it gave credit for payments from the borrowers and receipts from the sale of the property.

However, in *Portman Building Society v A B & Co*,[92] Ian Kennedy J came to the opposite conclusion on very similar facts. In that case, the premium for the MIG was added to the advance (and hence would in due course be paid by the borrower). The defendant solicitor argued that receipts pursuant to the MIG policy should enure to its benefit. Ian Kennedy J said that:

> ... the ordinary approach to policies of indemnity is that they are to be ignored since the insurer by relieving the insured of his loss acquires by subrogation the right to pursue any claims available to the insured.

This was also the approach of Mr Wadsworth QC in *MTI Funding (Berkeley) Ltd v Greenslade Hunt*,[93] where the judge declined to follow Knox J's reasoning in *Edgestop* and instead followed *BBL*. The same analysis has been adopted in a number of other first instance cases. These were considered in *Europe Mortgage Company Ltd v Halifax Estate Agencies*[94] in which May J said that the critical questions were whether the MIG was effected for the benefit of the valuer and whether the

---

[90] In an interlocutory judgment on 8 March 1993, unreported, the *ratio* of which is repeated in the final judgment.
[91] (1994) unreported, 13 June, LEXIS.
[92] (1995) unreported, 25 May.
[93] (1995) unreported, 10 March.
[94] (1996) *The Times*, 23 May.

insurer had rights of subrogation against the valuers. He held that there was no basis for asserting that the insurance was effective for the benefit of the valuers and struck out a paragraph in the defence seeking credit for the value of receipts under the policy.

The judge in *Edgestop* relied heavily upon the fact that the borrower had paid the premiums by addition to the advance. However, in *The Yasin*,[95] Lloyd J held that in an action by subrogated insurers it was irrelevant that the premiums had not been paid by the plaintiff. No sensible distinction could be drawn between cases where the premium is paid by a plaintiff, by a third party or even by the defendant paying the premium. What was important was that the contract of insurance was for the benefit of the plaintiff and was not expressed to enure for the benefit of the defendant.[96]

The defendants may seek to argue that the MIG is a contract of suretyship rather than insurance, in which case they can take the benefit of it. However, to show a contract of surety the defendant must show that the insurer has contracted to undertake the same obligations as the borrower and that the insurer is not undertaking a commercial speculation for a consideration. This will rarely be the case. The point was considered in *Bristol & West Building Society v Freeman and Pollard*.[97] The judge followed the reasoning of Phillips J.

More recently, in *Woolwich Building Society v Brown*[98] an action by the subrogated insurer (in the name of the lender) against the borrower on his personal covenant after sale of the property, it was argued by the borrower that the benefit of a MIG taken out by the lender should enure for his benefit. Such an argument entailed that the very fact of the borrower's default (which triggered the insurance payout) resulted in the extinction of his liability under his personal covenant. Not surprisingly this argument was rejected by Waller J. The MIG enured for the sole benefit of the lender, and indeed it was difficult to conceive of a policy payable on the eventuality of non-payment enuring to the benefit of the nonpayer. Waller J relied upon Staughton LJ's statement in *Mortgage Corporation v McNicholas*,[99] a case involving similar facts, in response to an argument that the MIG enured to the benefit of the borrower:

> I do not think that can be right for two reasons. First, the policy is at pains to say that the insured is the Mortgage Corporation not, I would point out, the mortgagor. Secondly, it seems to me inconceivable that any insurance company would be stupid enough to provide insurance in favour of

---

[95] [1979] 2 Lloyd's Rep 45, 56.
[96] See by contrast *Mark Rowlands Ltd v Berni Inns Ltd* [1986] QB 211.
[97] (1996) unreported, 20 February.
[98] (1995) unreported, 13 December, Waller J.
[99] (1992) unreported, 22 September.

individuals in the event of their not paying their debts.

It is suggested that the view expressed by Phillips J will be upheld. Two central arguments appear to support this approach:

(a) the logic of the *Woolwich* case is difficult to resist. If the mortgagor cannot obtain the benefit of a MIG payment, then it follows that such reasoning applies *a fortiori* to cases where the defendant is a professional;

(b) the *Edgestop* approach strikes at the heart of the long-established and fundamental right of an insurer to be subrogated to the assured's rights. If Knox J was correct then in the normal case the insurer will not be in a position to be subrogated to the assured lender's loss. There is no issue of double recovery because any damages recovered by the assured lender for which an insurance payment has been received would be received on resulting trust for the insurer.

In most cases, where the issue is whether the loss should lie on the lender's insurer or the professional's insurer, it is 'clear beyond argument' that the loss should fall upon the latter.

3.8   Equitable compensation

Where a beneficiary under a trust establishes that the trustee has acted in breach of trust the court has jurisdiction, in addition to the other equitable remedies available to it, to compensate the beneficiary for monetary loss arising out of the breach of trust by awarding what is known as 'equitable compensation'. The court can also make an award of equitable compensation against a fiduciary who is in breach of his fiduciary duty.[100] The basic rule is that:

> ... a trustee in breach of trust must restore or pay to the trust estate either the assets which have been lost to the estate by reason of the breach or compensation for such loss. Courts of Equity did not award damages, but acting in personam, ordered the defaulting trustee to restore the trust estate [101] ... If specific restitution of the trust property is not possible, then the liability of the trustee is to pay sufficient compensation to the trust estate to put it back to what it would have been had the breach not been committed[102] ... Even if the immediate cause of the loss is the dishonesty or failure of a third party, such loss would not have occurred.[103]

---

[100] See Meagher, Gummow and Lehane, *Equity: Doctrines and Remedies* 3rd edn (1992), para 552.

[101] See *Nocton v Lord Ashburton* [1914] AC 932, at 952, 958, per Lord Haldane.

[102] See *Caffrey v Darby* (1801) 6 Ves 488; *Clough v Bond* (1838) 3 My & Cr 490.

[103] Per Lord Browne-Wilkinson, *Target Holdings Ltd v Redferns* [1996] 1 AC 421, 434.

This statement of the law most clearly relates to 'traditional trusts' where the trust is still subsisting and the beneficiary has an interest in having the trust fund reconstituted. In such circumstances the appropriate order will be the reconstitution of the trust fund. However, where the trusts have come to an end by the time an action for breach of trust comes to trial, and the beneficiaries have become absolutely entitled to the trust property then the appropriate order is that the defaulting trustee compensates plaintiff beneficiaries directly. In both cases the 'measure of compensation' is the same: the difference between what the beneficiary has in fact received and the amount he would have received but for the breach of trust.[104]

The jurisdiction to award equitable compensation is separate from the jurisdiction to award damages at common law. But to what extent do the principles of remoteness and causation, as developed at common law, also apply to the assessment of equitable compensation? Although these rules do not apply directly in the assessment of equitable compensation,[105] nonetheless the principles underlying both systems are the same.[106] Lord Browne-Wilkinson said the two fundamental principles of the law of damages:

(i)   that the defendant's wrongful act must cause the damage complained of; and

(ii) that the plaintiff is to be put 'in the same position as he would have been in if he had not sustained the wrong for which he is now getting his compensation'

applied as much in equity as in common law.[107]

In *Target Holdings* the plaintiff lender had retained the defendant solicitor, who was also retained by the borrower. The advance monies were remitted to the solicitor to pay over to the borrower when the purchase had been completed and the mortgage deed executed on the property. The solicitors paid over the advance monies prior to completion and the execution of the mortgage documentation, and it was common ground between the parties that this was a breach of trust. However some days later the borrower's purchase was completed and a valid mortgage executed in favour of the lender. The lender sought summary judgment for the whole sum on the basis that once the breach of trust had occurred the solicitors came under an immediate obligation to restore the trust fund. The fact that the lender obtained precisely what it would have obtained had no breach occurred was irrelevant.

This argument succeeded in the Court of Appeal. However, the House of Lords held that the fact that a trustee, if he commits a breach of trust

---

[104] *Ibid*, at 435B.
[105] *Ibid*, at 434F.
[106] *Ibid*, at 432H.
[107] *Ibid*, at 432E–F.

by the payment away of trust monies to a stranger, comes under an immediate obligation to remedy that breach did not mean that the quantum of equitable compensation payable 'is ultimately fixed as at the date when the breach occurred'. On the contrary:

> The quantum is fixed at the date of judgment, at which date, according to the circumstances then pertaining, the compensation is assessed at the figure then necessary to put the trust estate or the beneficiary back in the position it would have been in had there been no breach.[108]

In that case it was not possible at the summary stage to determine whether, absent the solicitor's breach of trust, the lender would not have proceeded with the transaction or would have lent in any event.

Nonetheless there remain important differences between the jurisdiction to award damages at common law and compensation in equity:

> The basis of the fiduciary obligation and the rationale for equitable compensation are distinct from the tort of negligence and contract. In negligence and contact the parties are taken to be independent and equal actors, concerned primarily with their own self-interest. Consequently the law seeks a balance between enforcing obligations by awarding compensation and preserving optimum freedom for those involved in the relationship in question, communal or otherwise. The essence of a fiduciary relationship, by contrast, is that one party pledges herself to act in the best interest of the other. The fiduciary relationship has trust, not self-interest, as its core, and when breach occurs, the balance favours the person wronged. The freedom of the fiduciary is diminished by the nature of the obligation he or she has undertaken —and obligation which 'betokens loyalty, good faith and an avoidance of a conflict of duty and self interest': *Can Aero v O'Malley*.[109] In short, equity is concerned not only to compensate the plaintiff but to enforce the trust which is at its heart.[110]

Under this 'protective jurisdiction' equitable compensation can be assessed more stringently against the defendant than are damages in tort and contract. Thus, the concepts of foreseeability and remoteness (as developed in contract and tort) do not, strictly speaking, apply to the assessment of equitable compensation and cannot be relied upon to reduce the compensation to which the plaintiff is entitled.[111] Nevertheless, the overriding principle is that:

> Equitable compensation for breach of trust is designed to achieve exactly what the word compensation suggests: to make good a loss suffered by

---

[108]   *Ibid*, at 437D–E; applying *Re Dawson (decd)* [1966] 2 NSWR 211 and *Canson Enterprises Ltd v Boughton & Co* (1991) 85 DLR (4th) 129, per McLachlin J, at 160–3.

[109]   [1974] SCR 592 at 606.

[110]   *Canson Enterprises Ltd v Boughton & Co* (1991) 85 DLR (4th) 129, per McLachlin J, at 154.

[111]   *Ibid*, at 163.

the beneficiaries and which, using hindsight and common sense, can be seen to have been caused by the breach.[112]

However, where equitable compensation is awarded for breach of an equitable duty of skill and care (as opposed to a fiduciary duty):

> There is no reason in principle why the common law rules of causation, remoteness of damage and measure of damages should not be applied by analogy in such a case.[113]

Strictly speaking, the defence of contributory negligence does not apply to claims founded on breach of trust or fiduciary duty. There may, however, be an equitable jurisdiction which allows the court to make a reduction in compensation which has the same effect.[114]

After the decision of the Court of Appeal in *Target Holdings*, a number of actions by lenders against solicitors were reformulated as claims for breach of trust or breach of fiduciary duty. However the availability of such claims was considerably restricted by the the decision of the Court of Appeal in *Bristol & West Building Society v Mothew*[115] and such claims are unlikely to be of such importance in the future.

---

[112] Per Lord Browne-Wilkinson in *Target Holdings*, at 365.
[113] Per Millett LJ, *Bristol & West Building Society v Mothew* (1996) unreported, 24 July.
[114] See *Day v Mead* [1987] 2 NZLR 43 and Chapter 4, p 143 below.
[115] (1996) unreported, 24 July: for which see generally Chapter 1 at section 1.5 and 1.6 above.

4 Interest

4.1 Introduction

In a property loan transaction the lender agrees a rate of interest with the borrower. This rate may be fixed or variable: its level will be determined by the strength of the borrower's covenant, prevailing interest rates and the margin required by the lender. In general, the higher the credit risk, the greater the interest rate. If the borrower is unable to repay the advance and the security proves inadequate the lender will not recover the full sum of the advance plus contractual interest. In a property finance negligence action the lender will try to recoup as much of his loss as possible. In many cases, the claim for 'interest losses' will be a substantial component of the claim.

The result of the House of Lords decision in *Swingcastle v Alastair Gibson*[1] is that the plaintiff in a property finance negligence case is not entitled to recover from the defendant the interest which the borrower agreed to pay to the lender. This is because the professional is not to be taken as warranting the borrower's covenant. The lender will, however, be entitled to recover some 'lost interest ' as damages.

In a property finance negligence case the essence of the plaintiff's complaint is that because of the negligence of the professional, more money was advanced to the borrower than otherwise would have been. As well as his capital loss the lender will therefore suffer a loss in the cost to himself of funding the extra advance (if he borrowed it to lend it on) or in the opportunity cost—the loss of the benefit which the money could have brought if invested elsewhere.

In this chapter we consider the legal background to the award of interest and look in detail at the way interest can be awarded to a plaintiff in a property finance negligence case. In particular, we discuss the leading case of *Swingcastle v Alastair Gibson*[2] and its consequences, and we consider the position in relation to the recovery of interest on a compounded basis.

---

[1]   [1991] 2 AC 223.
[2]   *Ibid.*

4.2   General principles

4.2.1   Interest at common law

The English law was long reluctant to award interest at all. This attitude has often been explained on the basis that claims to interest smacked of usury. At common law, therefore, there is no general power to award interest by way of general damages.[3] In *London, Chatham & Dover Railway v S E Railway*,[4] for instance, an account was taken and a sum of money found payable by the defendant to the plaintiff for a period from a certain date. The House of Lords held that interest could not be awarded to compensate the plaintiff for being deprived of the use of that sum from the accrual of the cause of action until judgment.

This principle, however, does not apply to a claim for interest as 'special damages'. Thus, in *Wadsworth v Lydall*[5] the defendant failed, in breach of contract, to pay money to the plaintiff on a certain date. The plaintiff had contracted to purchase a property in anticipation of the receipt of that money. He therefore had to borrow from a third party in order to complete the purchase of the property. The plaintiff claimed the interest payments made to the third party as damages. The Court of Appeal held that the plaintiff was entitled to be compensated by the defendant for those payments, as special damages within the second limb of *Hadley v Baxendale*.[6] This case was accepted as being correct by the House of Lords in *The President of India v La Pintada Compania Navigacion*.[7]

The principle established in *Wadsworth* has significantly limited the impact of the common law rule as stated in *London, Chatham & Dover Railway*. This is of particular importance in property finance negligence cases, where the cost of borrowing money to replace money paid away, or opportunity costs, incurred as a result of the defendant's breach of contract, constitute an 'integral' element of the plaintiff's loss.[8]

Disputes about the recovery of interest in property finance negligence cases generally involve claims for awards of interest *as* damages— claims for interest as one item of consequential loss flowing from the defendant's breach of duty—rather than interest *on* damages.

---

[3]   This is subject to some special exceptions: see generally *McGregor on Damages* 15th edn (1988), para 576 *ff*.
[4]   [1893] AC 429.
[5]   [1981] 1 WLR 598; applying *Trans Trust SPRL v Danubian Trading Co Ltd* [1952] 2 QB 297.
[6]   (1854) 9 Exch 341: ie 'the damages should be ... such as may reasonably be supposed to have been in the contemplation of both parties at the time they made the contract as the probable result of the breach', at 354, per Alderson B.
[7]   [1985] AC 104, 129.
[8]   See *Hungerfords v Walker* (1989) 84 ALR 119, 129: see also *Atlantic Salvage Ltd v City of Halifax* (1978) 94 DLR (3d) 513; *Sanrod Pty Ltd v Dainford Ltd* (1984) 54 ALR 179.

The clearest analysis of this distinction is to be found in the Australian case of *Hungerfords v Walker*[9] where it was stated:

> There is, in our view, a critical distinction between an order that interest be paid upon an award of damages and an actual award of damages which represents compensation for a wrongfully caused loss of the use of money and which is assessed wholly or partly by reference to the interest which would have been earned by safe investment of the money or which was in fact paid upon borrowings which otherwise would have been unnecessary or retired. On the one hand, there is no common law power to make an order for the payment of interest to compensate for the delay in obtaining payment of what the court assesses to be the appropriate measure of damages for a wrongful act. If such interest is to be awarded at common law, it must be pursuant to statutory authority. On the other hand, there is no acceptable reason why the ordinary principles governing the recovery of common law damages should not, in an appropriate case, apply to entitle a plaintiff to an actual award of damages as compensation for a wrongfully and foreseeably caused loss of the use of money.

Although in *Wadsworth* the exception to the general common law was stated to apply only to 'special damages' claims, it is not clear why a distinction should have been made between special and general damages, and it is submitted that a plaintiff should be entitled, subject to being able to prove his loss within the second limb of the *Hadley v Baxendale* rule, to interest for loss of use of a sum of money, whether claimed as general or special damages.[10]

4.2.2 Interest under statute

The unsatisfactory position at common law has produced statutory intervention. The court is given a discretionary jurisdiction to award simple interest by s 35A of the Supreme Court Act 1981 'at such rate as the court thinks fit or as rules of court may provide'.

Section 35A envisages that interest will generally be awardable from the 'date when the cause of action arose'[11] until the date of judgment, though the court is specifically empowered to award interest in relation only to a part of the period between those two dates. Thus, for instance, if a defendant pays over to the plaintiff the full amount of the plaintiff's claim after proceedings have been commenced, the plaintiff is entitled to proceed with his claim in relation to the interest element between the accrual of the cause of action and the date of payment.[12]

However, where the full amount of the plaintiff's claim (less any

---

[9]   (1989) 84 ALR 119, at 135, per Brennan and Deane JJ.
[10] As suggested in *Hungerfords v Walker* (1989) 84 ALR 119, 127.
[11] Section 35A(1).
[12] Section 35A(1)(*a*).

interest element) is paid over prior to the institution of proceedings, the plaintiff cannot maintain an action for that interest element, ie for the plaintiff having been kept out of its money between the date when the cause of action accrued and the date of payment.[13] This is a serious *lacuna* in the law (as the House of Lords recognised), but, although the Law Commission has recommended statutory intervention,[14] Parliament has taken no action.

4.3 Interest in property finance cases

4.3.1 The 'Swingcastle' case

The leading case relating to interest in property finance negligence cases is *Swingcastle Ltd v Alastair Gibson*. This was a 'no transaction' case in which the plaintiff lender had lent £10,000 to a borrower against security which had been negligently overvalued at £18,000. On the borrower's default the lender sold the security for £12,000. Despite the fact that it had therefore recovered more than its capital the lender brought an action against the valuer for the balance of the sum outstanding from the borrower. The Court of Appeal dismissed an appeal by the valuer from the first instance judge's award of that sum to the lender, on the basis that it was bound by *Baxter v Gapp*.[15] Neill LJ, giving the leading judgment, clearly considered that *Baxter* was an unattractive authority, and digressed to review the possible approaches which the court could take to compensate a lender for the loss of use of the amount of money lent:

> A number of approaches are possible, including the following. (a) The lender could be awarded the unpaid interest owed by the borrower at the date when the security was realised. This was the method adopted in *Baxter v Gapp*.[15a] But to award damages on this basis is in effect to treat the valuer as the guarantor of the contract of loan. In the absence of authority I would for my part reject this solution. (b) The lender could be awarded a sum equivalent to the amount he would have earned by way of interest on another loan if he had had the money available for this purpose. In my view, however, such an award should not be made in the absence of evidence that the money lent would have been used for another transaction. This evidence would have to be directed to proving an unsatisfied demand for loans and I anticipate that such evidence might seldom be forthcoming. Moreover even if evidence of a lost transaction were available, I see no reason why the interest should be at the default rate rather than at the

---

[13] *The President of India v La Pintada Compania Navigacion* [1985] AC 104.
[14] Cmnd 7229 (1978) (Law Com No 88).
[15] [1939] 2 KB 271.
[15a] *Ibid*.

ordinary rate provided for in a standard contract for this type of business. (c) The lender could be awarded a sum equivalent to the interest which it would have been earned if the sum had been placed on deposit. (d) The lender could be awarded a sum to represent the loss of the opportunity to invest the money elsewhere. This was the solution adopted by the Supreme Court of British Columbia in *Seeway Mortgage Investment Corporation v First Citizens Financial Corporation*,[15b] where it was said, at 101: 'what the plaintiff lost then was the opportunity to invest its $50,000 in a security which had the same risks except that the appraisal would be accurate.' I do not propose to express any concluded view about these methods of assessment. I do not consider that any one of the last three methods of assessment would be right to suit all cases. It would depend on the evidence.

The Court of Appeal was reluctant to follow *Baxter*, especially as the principle point in issue in *Swingcastle*—whether interest recoverable from a professional should be based on the contractual obligation of the borrower or the actual cost to the lender of advancing more than he would otherwise have done—had not been argued in that case, either at first instance or on appeal.[16]

The House of Lords allowed the valuer's appeal. Basing himself on the principle that the lender is entitled to be put into the position he would have been in if the negligence had not occurred and he had received a competent valuation report, Lord Lowry said that the recoverable loss is the loss of the use of the principal while it is locked in the loan, plus disbursements. This is because the relevant loss is the loss caused by the *valuer*, not the loss caused by the borrower's default, that is being compensated by the valuer. Valuers should not be expected effectively to warrant the borrower's obligations.

In so far as *Baxter v Gapp* was authority for the proposition that a lender could be awarded interest on the contractual basis it was overruled. Lord Lowry said:[17]

> *Baxter v Gapp* is not an attractive precedent. For one thing, it does not clearly exemplify the proposition contended for by the lenders, even if that proposition can be teased out of it; secondly, the dispute was about all the plaintiff's consequential damage and the pecuniary effect of the difference in interest rates ... was relatively insignificant; and thirdly, and most importantly, the approach, if carefully scrutinized, seems contrary to principle: the aggrieved party was entitled to be placed in the same position as if the wrong had not occurred, and not to receive from the wrongdoer compensation for lost interest at the rate which the borrower had contracted to

---

[15b]   (1983) 45 BCLR 87.
[16]   [1990] 1 WLR 1223 per Farquharson LJ, 1234.
[17]   [1991] 2 AC 223, 236–7.

observe … The approach of the valuer in this case and the analysis of Neill LJ … seems to me to be correct. What the lenders lost, in addition to their other damages, was the use of the £10,000 while it was perforce locked up in the loan.

Given that this was a 'no transaction' case the true loss of the lender was therefore to be measured by the following formula:
(a) the principal sum advanced to the borrower; plus
(b) disbursements in connection with the advance; plus
(c) interest on the principal sum advanced at a standard commercial rate; plus
(d) the legal costs of possession proceedings; plus
(e) estate agents' costs in connection with the forced sale; minus
(f) the sale price of the property, recovered; and
(g) any repayment by the borrowers.

In that case the 'standard commercial rate' was used because, the lender not appearing in the appeal, there was no evidence as to how the loan was financed and what would have happened if it had not been made.

What is interesting about the judgments of both the Court of Appeal and the House of Lords in *Swingcastle* is that it would appear to have been accepted by all the parties as well as by both the courts that interest could be awarded as damages on the lender's capital loss without resort to s 35A of the Supreme Court Act 1981. Given that in *Swingcastle* the property was realised for more than the amount of the loan, the lender's claim was confined to its loss of use of the loan amount for the period between the date of advance and the date of realisation of the security. Had that claim been classified as a pure 'interest' claim then it would have fallen foul of the House of Lords' decision in the *President of India* case.[18] As Phillips J said in *BBL v Eagle Star*:[19]

> … the House of Lords [in *Swingcastle*] held that the plaintiffs were entitled to recover *by way of damages*, not contractual interest, but interest at such rate as was appropriate to compensate them for the loss of use of their money from the date of the advance to the date when the security should have been realised (emphasis added).

Although the case was not mentioned in any of their Lordships' judgments, it would appear that the jurisdiction to make such an award was accepted as being founded upon the exception to the general common law rule as stated in *Wadsworth v Lydall*. That component of a damages award which is made to compensate the lender for the loss of use of the sum advanced is made under the second limb of the principle in *Hadley v Baxendale*: on the basis of 'special knowledge' as to the results

[18] [1985] AC 104.
[19] [1995] 2 All ER 769, 817.

of the lender having made an advance in reliance on negligent advice.

4.3.2   Compound interest

In the limited class of cases in which interest could be recovered at common law, the courts would award only simple interest. The 'giving of interest upon interest'[20] was avoided. Similarly, under s 35A of the Supreme Court Act 1981 only simple interest can be recovered. On the other hand, the courts of equity have traditionally been prepared to award compound interest 'when they thought that justice so demanded, that is to say in cases where money had been obtained and retained by fraud, or where it had been withheld or misapplied by a trustee or anyone else in a fiduciary position'.[21]

It was suggested in *Westdeutsche Landesbank Girozentrale v Islington Borough Council*[22] that equity should extend its jurisdiction to award compound interest to common law actions in certain circumstances. In that case the plaintiff bank had paid money over to the defendant council under a void 'swaps' contract. It was awarded that sum as money had and received, and its claim for compound interest on the sum from the date on which it was paid over was accepted both at first instance and by the Court of Appeal. A majority of the House of Lords rejected this argument, confining the equitable jurisdiction to those situations identified by Lord Brandon in *The President of India*. It was held that the court had no power to award compound interest either at common law or under statute, and the jurisdiction in equity to award compound interest extended only to actions against trustees or other fiduciaries where the award was in lieu of an account of profits improperly made by the trustee.

However it is submitted that this decision has no direct bearing on interest claims by lenders in property finance claims. The bank's claim for compound interest in *Westdeutsche Landesbank* was a claim in the nature of interest in the strict sense (ie it was claimed as interest, not damages). The speeches of the majority did not cast doubt on the principle that compound interest could be recovered as special damages in an appropriate case.[23] In an appropriate case, therefore, there seems no reason for interest when claimed as damages rather than when claimed on damages to be compounded.

Indeed, *Swingcastle* would appear to have opened the door to a plaintiff obtaining compound interest as part of a damages award. In *BBL v*

[20]   *Bushwall Properties Ltd v Vortex Properties Ltd* [1975] 1 WLR 1649.
[21]   Per Lord Brandon in *The President of India*, at 116, and see *Wallersteiner v Moir* (No 2) [1974] 1 WLR 341.
[22]   [1996] 2 WLR 802.
[23]   The only mention of *Wadsworth v Lydall* was by Lord Woolf, one of the minority, at 854B–855C.

Eagle Star, Phillips J also seemed to indicate that the plaintiff's claim could legitimately have included interest by way of special damages on a compound basis.[24] As can be seen below (at 4.3.3) there are circumstances, such as where the lender can show that, absent the negligent act, it would have kept the funds lent on deposit, which would have effectively borne compound interest in the sense that the interest generated (whether monthly, quarterly or annually) would be added to the capital sum, which increased sum would then have provided the capital sum for the next interest calculation. In this situation, as was recognised in *Hungerfords v Walker*,[25] a simple interest award would undercompensate the plaintiff for its true loss.[26]

It is submitted that lenders who have borrowed the loaned funds from third party sources should also be entitled to compound interest as damages. It is foreseeable at the time of the loan transaction that the lender might have to go to the market to obtain the necessary funds itself. As a result, the interest payable on these sums falls within the second limb of *Hadley v Baxendale*.[27] Compound interest was awarded on this basis in *SAAMCO v York Montague*.[28]

4.3.3   The bases on which interest can be recovered

As a result of *Swingcastle*, it is now clear that interest can be recovered from valuers or solicitors on one of five bases in which the lender could be awarded:

(1) *A sum equivalent to the amount he would have earned by way of interest on another loan if he had had the money available for this purpose*: This would involve the lender revealing the average rate of return on the average loan made at or around the time of the loan made in the particular case. As this would involve revealing the percentage of loans which ended in losses for any particular period (which might reduce recoverable damages to zero, if the defendant is able to argue that the only result of the plaintiff not making the loan would have been that, in all probability, an equally disastrous loan would have been made)[29] it is assumed that lenders would be reluctant to claim interest on this basis. In addition, the lender would have to show that the demand for loans exceeded the supply—which is unlikely, having regard to the profligate nature

---

[24]   At 817; although in *Alliance & Leicester Building Society v Edgestop* ((1994) unreported, 13 June, Knox J) compound interest on an interim damages award was refused, without any reasons being given.

[25]   At 133.

[26]   See also Bowles and Whelan 'Judgment Awards and Simple Interest Rates' (1981) 1 *International Review of Law and Economics* 111.

[27]   (1854) 9 Exch 341.

[28]   [1995] 2 EGLR 219—although it appears that the point was conceded by the defendant.

[29]   See Chapter 3.

of the lending at the time which is relevant to most property finance negligence claims.[30] If a claim is to succeed on this basis, the lender will also have to adduce evidence that the money lent would have been used for another transaction, for example by proving an unsatisfied demand for loans at the time of making the advance.

In *HIT Finance Ltd v Lewis & Tucker Ltd*[31] Wright J commented that there was no evidence before him as to how the money would have been employed if it had not been lent. Furthermore, there was no evidence that the plaintiff would have been able to make a further loan in the same or some lesser sum at the same or a later date. There appears to be no case where the plaintiff has succeeded in claiming interest on this basis.

However this basis potentially allows a lender, subject to evidence, to circumvent the actual decision in *Swingcastle* and recover a sum which, albeit not the contractual interest payable by the borrower concerned, reflects the contractual sum payable by another borrower. There would, of course, be likely to be little difference between the two. Further, such sum would effectively be a compounded sum. It should be remembered that, because such the claim is for special damages and falls to be proven within the second limb of *Hadley v Baxendale*, the fact that the plaintiff had, at the time of entering into the loan, an alternative transaction which would have involved payment by the 'alternative borrower' of a much higher interest rate, the plaintiff could not claim to be reimbursed for the loss of that higher rate, because it would be, unless the defendant was aware at the time of breach of the alternative loan, too remote.[32]

(2) *A sum equivalent to the interest which would have been earned if the sum had been placed on deposit*: On this basis, the lender must provide evidence of prevailing interest rates at the time of lending. It is often claimed on the basis of three-month London Interbank Offered Rate (LIBOR). The advantage to this approach is that, if a lender can show that the money would have been placed on a deposit earning compound interest (which will almost always be the case), he can potentially recover such interest as damages.

(3) *A sum to represent the loss of the opportunity to invest the money elsewhere*: It is difficult to see how, in an ordinary lending situation, the lender could present evidence in relation to this basis which was not evidence in support of the first or second basis. There appears to be no reported case in which such an award has been made.

---

[30]   See the Introduction and Chapter 6.
[31]   [1993] 2 EGLR 231.
[32]   Compare *Victoria Laundry (Windsor) Ltd v Newman Industries Ltd* [1949] 2 KB 528.

(4) *A sum to represent the cost of borrowing the money from a third party source*: On this basis, the plaintiff should lead evidence of the actual cost of borrowing the money lent on. This basis will be appropriate where the plaintiff is a lender which borrows the sums which are loaned from third party sources which it then lends on to the borrower.

So, in *Nykredit Mortgage Bank plc v Edward Erdman Group Ltd*[33] the plaintiff, who was a secondary lender, had borrowed the monies lent on to the borrower from a third party source, at a rate of LIBOR + 0.4/0.25 per cent. The plaintiff was awarded interest at that rate (to reflect the actual cost of borrowing the capital amount for the particular plaintiff) rather than at the higher rate which interest under statute would have achieved. It is clear from the transcript of *Nykredit* that the interest element of the damages was calculated on a non-compounded rate. However it is suggested that a lender should be entitled to any compound interest rate which he has become liable to pay by reason of borrowing funds to lend on in reliance upon the act of negligence.

In *Hungerfords v Walker*[34] the plaintiff partnership had, by reason of the defendant accountants' negligence, paid over more tax than in fact they were liable to pay over a number of years. The plaintiffs sued the defendants for the amount overpaid and further claimed damages for loss of the use of the monies overpaid. It was alleged that had the plaintiffs retained the monies paid over in tax, they would have used them to discharge certain loans which the plaintiffs had taken out and on which they were paying compounded interest. The High Court of Australia awarded compounded interest, based on the actual interest rate which the plaintiffs were liable to pay during the relevant period. This is an example of compound interest being awarded as special damages.

(5) *Statutory interest under s 35A of the Supreme Court Act 1981*: If no other rate is appropriate, the rate of interest awarded by way of statutory interest could apply to an award for interest as damages under that section and if no other rate is calculable the judgment debt rate can be used.[35] The difficulty with this basis from the lender's point of view is that, under s 35A, the courts can award only simple interest. On the other hand the statutory basis might actually overcompensate a plaintiff, as was conceded in *Nykredit Mortgage Bank plc v Edward Erdman Group Ltd*.

After *Swingcastle*, the courts are suspicious of attempts by lenders to recover a sum equivalent to a contractual rate of interest in the guise of awarding the lenders' opportunity costs. The court will look at the

---

[33] (1993) unreported, 1 October, Judge Byrt QC.
[34] (1989) 84 ALR 119.
[35] *Pinnock v Wilkins & Sons* (1990), *The Times*, 29 January, CA.

substance of the transaction, rather than the form. This is illustrated by the case of *HIT Finance Ltd v Lewis & Tucker Ltd*[36] in which the plaintiff was a company with £100 issued share capital owned jointly by two parent companies (A and B). Its finance was provided by A and B as and when it agreed to make an advance to a borrower in accordance with the loan facilities provided by A and B which provided for a high rate of interest. The plaintiff claimed interest on the basis of the cost of borrowing the advance monies from A and B.

Wright J rejected this argument on the basis that the court had to look at the commercial reality of the situation. The plaintiff was simply the cypher of A and B, who were in reality the parties who had suffered the loss. As a result, it was ultimately A and B who were to be compensated and, even though no evidence had been adduced on this point to this effect, the court took into account that both A and B were:

> ... owned and controlled by major public limited companies, so that any money that they might have surplus to requirement and not taken up by loans to the plaintiff company in the present case would be put to the best available use.[37]

As a result, Wright J awarded, under the 'loss of use' head of damage, simple interest calculated at 1 per cent above base rate from the date of loan to date of judgment.

4.3.4   Commercial Court practice

In *BBL v Eagle Star*[38] Phillips J awarded interest on the basis that:

> BBL [the lender] are entitled to recover damages by way of interest on the premise that [the valuer's] negligence caused them to lose the use of the whole of the sums that they advanced from the dates of the advance to the dates when the properties securing the loans were sold.

He awarded interest on the capital lent at base rate plus 1 per cent, applying the practice in the Commercial Court:

> In the Commercial Court, in the absence of evidence to the contrary, the court proceeds on the presumption that base rate plus 1% fairly compensates a plaintiff for being deprived of the use of money: see *Shearson Lehman Hutton Inc v Maclain Watson* [1990] 3 All ER 723.[39]

The plaintiff's claim in *BBL* and Phillips J's judgment proceeded on the basis of a distinction between a 'loss of use' interest award from (1) date of loan to date of sale of property and (2) from date of sale to date

---

36   [1993] 2 EGLR 231.
37   *Ibid*, at 238.
38   [1995] 2 All ER 769, 817.
39   At pp 817–18.

of judgment. The plaintiff claimed 'interest as damages' on period (1) and interest (albeit at the same rate) pursuant to s 35A of the Supreme Court Act 1981 for period (2). It is not clear why this distinction was made, and it is suggested that the plaintiff can perfectly legitimately claim 'interest as damages' for the whole period from date of loan to date of judgment (with the appropriate reduction of the capital amount on which the interest runs after sale). Such a distinction was not made in *HIT Finance Ltd v Lewis & Tucker Ltd*.[40]

The other peculiarity of the use of the Commercial Court practice in property finance negligence cases is that there appears to be a confusion between the notion of 'loss of use' and 'cost of borrowing'. The distinction between these two concepts reflects the existence of the two types of lender: that is, between the building societies and clearing banks, who have the funds available to make loans in any event, and secondary lenders, who will generally borrow from a third party source to lend on, their profit being the differential between the two interest rates which are contracted for.

In the first case 'interest damages' should, in the absence of specific evidence as to other loans which would have been made, be ascertained on the assumption that, in a 'no loan' case, the lender would have placed the money on the money markets or placed it on deposit. However, having made this the basis for an award for loss of use, Phillips J then uses the *Shearson Lehman* principle which explicitly uses the base rate plus 1 per cent formula as a presumption (which is rebuttable) of the cost of *borrowing*. Bristow J said in *Miliangos v George Frank (Textiles) (No 2)*:[41]

> The court fixes a rate applicable for plaintiffs in general … by applying its judicial knowledge of what is from time to time the bank rate or minimum lending rate, and its judicial knowledge of the fact that, in practice, by and large, it costs about one per cent more than that to borrow money … The Court is not concerned with the actual cost of borrowing to the individual concerned in the individual case. Depending on many variables, some people can borrow more cheaply than others. The court fixes a rate applicable for plaintiffs in general.[42]

On the other hand in *Tate & Lyle Food and Distribution v Greater London Council*[43] Forbes J advocated a less restrictive approach:

> I feel satisfied that in commercial cases the interest is intended to reflect the rate at which the plaintiff would have had to borrow money to supply

---

[40] [1993] 2 EGLR 231. However the application of Lord Hoffmann's 'scope of duty' principle may *de facto* result in such a distinction: see above at 3.4.

[41] [1977] QB 487, at 496.

[42] See further *BP Exploration Co (Libya) v Hunt (No 2)* [1979] 1 WLR 783 and *Polish SS Co v Atlantic Maritime Co* [1985] QB 41.

[43] [1982] 1 WLR 149.

the place of that which was withheld. I am also satisfied that one should not look at any special position in which the plaintiff may have been: one should disregard, for instance, the fact that a particular plaintiff, because of his personal situation, could only borrow money at a very high rate, or, on the other hand, was able to borrow at specially favourable rates. The correct thing to do is to take the rate at which plaintiffs in general could borrow money. This does not however, to my mind, mean that you exclude entirely all attributes of the plaintiff other than that he is a plaintiff. There is evidence here that large public companies of the size and prestige of these plaintiffs could expect to borrow at 1% over Minimum Lending Rate [now base rate], while for smaller and less prestigious concerns the rate might be as high as 3%. I think it would always be right to look at the rate at which plaintiffs with the general attributes of the actual plaintiff in the case (though not, of course, with any special or peculiar attribute) could borrow money as a guide to the appropriate interest rate. If commercial rates are appropriate I would take 1% over MLR as the proper figure for interest in this case … I should add, perhaps that the proper question is: at which rate could the plaintiff borrow the required sum and not what return could the plaintiff have expected if he had invested it.[44]

This passage indicates how the Commercial Court practice is often inappropriate for the assessment of interest in property finance negligence cases. The last sentence recognises the difference between a 'cost of borrowing' and a 'return on investment/deposit'. Further, in a case where the cost of borrowing basis was specifically used, then the judge's award was tailored to the reality of the situation.[45]

4.3.5 Credit for receipts

In most cases, the borrower will have made interest and/or capital repayments. In the *BBL* case the lender received sums by way of contractual interest, agency fees and, latterly, rental income from the secured properties. The lender gave credit for these receipts by simply totalling them up and deducting the amount achieved from the total of the 'loss of use' damages claim. It was argued by the valuer that credit should be given for receipts as and when received on a running account basis, so that early receipts would reduce the capital sum then outstanding (and thus reduce the 'loss of use' claim *pro rata* from the date of receipt). This approach was rejected by Phillips J,[46] although he indicated that had the lender been claiming loss of use interest on a compounded basis, the valuer's argument might have succeeded.

[44] At 154–5.
[45] See *Nykredit Mortgage Bank plc v Edward Erdman Group Ltd* (1993) unreported, 1 October, HHJ Byrt QC.
[46] *Ibid*, at 818.

A similar approach was taken by Ralph Gibson J in *Corisand v Druce*, where the judge simply totted up the receipts and deducted them from the capital damages sum, awarding interest from the date of loan on the capital sum. It is difficult to understand the logic of Phillips J's or Gibson J's approach and it is respectfully suggested that the correct approach would be to take account of payments at the time when they are made.

5 Limitation

5.1 Introduction

Claims against the professionals who advised the lender at the time at which an advance was made will not usually be considered until the borrower defaults. This can happen a considerable time after the loan is made. The lender will then need to consider the solicitors' file and obtain a retrospective valuation. This means that a lender may not be aware of a claim until years after the professional advice was given. As a result there is often considerable scope for defendants to argue that the limitation periods laid down by the Limitation Act 1980 ('the 1980 Act') have expired.

In each case, the vital question for both lenders and professionals is: when does the limitation period expire? The answer depends upon when the cause of action accrued. Most property finance negligence cases are pleaded in both contract and tort. The different causes of action give rise to different analyses of the date upon which the cause of action accrued.[1]

5.2 Claims in contract

Any action 'founded on simple contract' must be brought within six years of 'the date on which the cause of action accrued.'[2] In a contract claim the 'cause of action accrues' at the date on which the breach of contract takes place.[3] The cause of action founded on contract is made out simply by proof of breach: that alone will entitle the plaintiff to nominal damages. Actual damage need not be pleaded or proved. Knowledge of the fact that there has been a breach is similarly irrelevant. As a result, plaintiffs may lose their right to proceed on a cause of action before they know that it has accrued. The only provision (other than where the plaintiff is under a disability) which will prevent time

---

[1]   Much of the litigation relating to the question of whether a defendant owes concurrent obligations in tort and contract has been generated by limitation issues: see generally *Henderson v Merrett Syndicates Ltd* [1995] 2 AC 145.
[2]   Section 5 of the 1980 Act.
[3]   See *Gibbs v Guild* (1882) 9 QBD 259; *Lynn v Bamber* [1930] 2 KB 72.

from running from the moment of breach is s 32 of the 1980 Act, which concerns cases involving fraud, concealment or mistake.[4]

The position is more complicated where the breach consists of a failure to act.[5] In *Midland Bank Trust Co Ltd v Hett, Stubbs & Kemp*[6] it was held that in the case of a continuing duty to act the breach occurred only at the time when fulfilment of that duty became impossible. However, this case was distinguished by the Court of Appeal in *Bell v Peter Browne & Co*[7] in which the 'continuing duty' argument was rejected. It was held that the breach occurred after the defendant had had a reasonable time in which to act but had failed to do so. This means that, in most cases of a failure by a solicitor to act, the breach of contract will take place a short time after the solicitor has been instructed to carry out a particular task.

In cases against valuers the date of breach will not, in general, be the date of the misleading valuation report. The breach occurs not when the relevant report is made, but when it is received by the lender (so that if it is written and sent on the fourth of the month and received on the seventh, then the cause of action accrues on the latter date). This is because the relevant contractual obligation will be not simply to make a valuation of a property, but to submit such a valuation to the party who has commissioned it.

In claims against solicitors the position will be less clear cut. The latest possible date for breach of 'reporting and investigation obligations' would be the date of completion of the advance. In the case of a failure to carry out some post-completion obligation, by analogy with *Bell*, time will begin to run as soon as the solicitor has had a reasonable time to carry out the obligation. This means that if a solicitor fails to apply for registration of a legal charge, the limitation period will start to run after the expiry of a reasonable time from the date of completion.

The 'latent damage' provisions in s 14A of the 1980 Act[8] do not apply to claims for breach of contract even where the breach of contract alleged involves or is founded upon an allegation of careless or negligent conduct.[9]

5.3 Claims in tort

In general, an action founded on tort 'shall not be brought after the expiration of six years from the date on which the cause of action

---

[4] See generally, McGee, *Limitation Periods*, 2nd edn (1994), Chapter 20.
[5] See generally, Evans, *Lawyers' Liabilities* (1996), pp 189–91.
[6] [1979] Ch 384.
[7] [1990] 2 QB 495.
[8] See below, section 5.5.
[9] See *Iron Trades Mutual Insurance Co Ltd v J K Buckenham* [1990] 1 All ER 808; and *Re Eras EIL Actions* [1992] 2 All ER 82.

accrued'.[10] In order to establish a cause of action in negligence, the plaintiff must show that he has suffered damage. In other words, the cause of action only accrues once:

(a) the defendant has committed a breach of the duty of care; and

(b) the plaintiff has actually suffered legally recognised damage.

As a result, the limitation period in tort does not start running until damage is incurred.[11] This is often much later than the date of the breach of duty. Difficult questions arise as to when damage is incurred for the purpose of constituting the cause of action in negligence.

The leading case is *Forster v Outred & Co*.[12] An action was brought against solicitors by a plaintiff who had entered into a mortgage whereby she charged her property to secure a loan to her son. He subsequently defaulted and the mortgagees called in the loan. The plaintiff alleged that the defendants should have advised her as to the nature of the transaction. The issue arose as to whether a writ issued seven years after the date of the mortgage deed and five years after the demand for repayment by the mortgagees was statute-barred. The plaintiff argued that until the formal demand for payment she was subject to only a 'contingent liability'. The defendants argued that by entering into the mortgage she sustained immediate economic loss. Her freehold became encumbered with a charge: she merely had an equity of redemption.

The Court of Appeal held that although the plaintiff came under no actual liability to pay the sums lent until formally demanded, by entering into the mortgage she suffered actual damage, that is damage 'capable of assessment in money terms',[13] or 'capable of quantification in terms of money'[14] for which she could have been compensated as at the date of the mortgage deed.[15]

The principle that emerges from *Forster* is therefore that where, by reason of the solicitor's negligence, the plaintiff enters into a transaction whereby he exposes himself to a future loss, the damage may be deemed to have been sustained on the entering into the transaction because, depending on the circumstances of the case:

(a) the value of the plaintiff's property is thereby impaired, and if the property were to be sold at that time, the damage would be capable of evaluation; or

(b) there is an increase in the plaintiff's obligations; or

---

[10] Section 2 of the 1980 Act.

[11] The fact that the damage is only discoverable at some later date is irrelevant: *Cartledge v E Jopling & Co* [1963] AC 759; *Pirelli General Cable Works v Oscar Faber & Partners* [1983] 2 AC 1.

[12] [1982] 1 WLR 86.

[13] At 94.

[14] At 99.

[15] Reliance was placed on the case of *Howell v Young* (1826) 5 B & C 259. This case and the reliance on it in *Forster* is criticised in McGee, *ibid*, 76.

(c) the plaintiff has not secured the rights which should have been secured.[16]

However, just because it can be shown that, as at a certain date, damage will, as a matter of probability or inevitability, occur at some future date, 'actual damage' will not be treated as having been suffered at the earlier date, because the damage remains to be incurred in the future.[16a]

The fact that the risk might never arise, as in *Forster*, where there was at least a possibility at the moment when the mortgage was entered into that the plaintiff's son would repay the mortgage, will not prevent the court from viewing the market's ascription of a value to the risk of the contingency occurring as a discount on the asset's present value, so as to constitute damage to it.[17] It has been suggested that the English decisions have proceeded according to the view that:

> ... where the plaintiff is induced by a negligent misstatement to enter into a contract and the contract, as a result of the negligence, yields property or contractual rights of lesser value, the plaintiff first suffers financial loss on entry into the contract, notwithstanding that the full extent of the plaintiff's financial loss may be incapable of ascertainment until some later date. In part, the English approach appears to have been influenced by the general principle stated in *Darley Main Colliery Co v Mitchell* (1886) 11 App Cas 127 that damages in respect of a cause of action are awarded on a once and for all basis.[18]

It is explicitly recognised in *Forster* that the court could assess the damages awardable when the transaction is entered into, based upon a consideration of the risk of default (or the happening of the contingency in any particular case). Such an exercise would, in *Forster*, have undercompensated the plaintiff. A court determining damages immediately following the plaintiff's entry into the transaction would have had to reduce any award to take into account the possibility that the son would continue to make payments under the loan agreement. On the other hand, had the son in fact paid off the loan in full, the plaintiff in *Forster* would have received a windfall.

The *Forster* principle was refined in *D W Moore & Co v Ferrier*[19] where Bingham LJ suggested that the following test could be used to determine whether 'loss' was sustained at the date of entering into the relevant transaction:

---

[16] See *Hopkins v McKenzie* [1995] 6 Med LR 26, 30.

[16a] *Ibid*, p 30.

[17] See further *Melton v Walker & Stanger* (1981) 125 SJ 861; *Costa v Georghiou* (1985) 1 PN 201; *Baker v Ollard & Bentley* (1982) 126 SJ 593. In all these cases, the court held that the plaintiff was 'actually', not 'potentially' worse off immediately the transaction was entered into: per Mustill LJ in *Bell v Peter Browne* [1990] 2 QB 495, 513.

[18] Per Mason CJ, *State of Western Australia v Wardley Australia Ltd* (1992) 109 ALR 247, 259.

[19] [1988] 1 WLR 267. An argument that *Forster* had been implicitly overruled by the House of Lords decision in *Pirelli General Cable Works Ltd v Oscar Faber & Partners* [1983] 2 AC 1 was rejected in *Aikman v Hallett & Co* (1987) unreported, 23 March.

If the plaintiff were to have discovered the negligence immediately on entering into the transaction, would he have recovered more than merely nominal damages?[20]

The facts of *D W Moore* show the difficulties which are inherent in the *Forster* approach. In *D W Moore* the defendant solicitors had drawn up an agreement between the plaintiff insurance broker and a third party, F, whereby F became a director and shareholder of the plaintiff company. The agreement provided that if F ceased to be a shareholder of the plaintiff, then he could not trade as an insurance broker within fifteen miles of the plaintiff. Five years after the agreement, F commenced trading within that distance. Because he remained a shareholder, the restrictive covenant, as it was drawn, was unenforceable. It was alleged that the covenant had therefore been negligently prepared by the solicitors. The writ was issued five years after this event, and therefore ten years after the agreement. The Court held that the plaintiff's claim was statute-barred. The agreement was worth less to the plaintiff the moment it was entered into by reason of its defective wording. The plaintiff therefore sustained legally recognised damage the moment the agreement became binding and could have obtained more than nominal damages from that date.

It is suggested that this reasoning is difficult to apply and leads to artificial results. The Court of Appeal's decision in effect requires a plaintiff to launch proceedings and proceed to trial whether or not the event which makes the loss actual rather than contingent has happened. In *D W Moore*, had the trial occurred prior to F's departure to set up in competition, the court would have had to assess the chances of such a step being taken (by a non-party to the litigation). The result is that the assessment and proper compensation of loss is very seriously hampered in some types of case by the application of the *Forster* principle.

Of course, there may be cases in which the plaintiff's loss *can* be calculated:

... when it is claimed a contract was made as a result of negligent advice and at the time it is possible to quantify the loss which the plaintiff has sustained or at least part of it, the cause of action may be said to arise at the time the contract was entered into but this is dependent upon a factual decision that the loss is quantifiable.[21]

It is submitted that the correct approach (which coincides with *dicta* in *Forster*) is that the loss must be capable of quantification in monetary terms before it can be regarded as having been sustained. It is suggested

---

[20]   Applied in *Islander Trucking Ltd v Robinson & Gardner Mountain (Marine)* [1990] 1 All ER 826; and by Nicholls LJ in *Bell v Peter Browne & Co* [1990] 2 QB 495; see also *Mathew v Maughold Life Assurance Co Ltd* (1985) 1 PN 142.

[21]   *BCNZ v Progeni International Ltd* [1990] 1 NZLR 109, 113. The judge relied upon *UBAF v European American Banking* [1984] 2 All ER 226, for which see below.

that its application to the facts of a case like *D W Moore* would lead to a finding that the cause of action only accrued on F actually setting up a business in competition to the plaintiff's. Any attempt to properly quantify damage prior to that event occurring would have been impossible.

The decision in *Forster v Outred* has been considered in a number of Commonwealth jurisdictions. In Australia, misgivings have been expressed about the perceived harshness of the principle.[22] The point has been made that 'in truth and reality' the plaintiff in *Forster* did not, when she entered into the loan, lose anything. 'Only when the son defaulted and became bankrupt was the plaintiff bound to repay his indebtedness to the company'.[23] On this view the plaintiff's loss arose, not at the time of entry into the mortgage, but at the time of the son's default.[24]

Most recently, in *State of Western Australia v Wardley Australia Ltd*[25] the High Court of Australia considered the situation where, as a result of the defendant's negligence, a plaintiff enters into a contract which exposes him to a contingent liability. In that case the plaintiff had, in reliance upon the representation of the defendant, entered into a deed of indemnity with a bank, indemnifying the bank against the default of a borrower. The question arose as to when the plaintiff suffered loss: on entering into the indemnity, or when the bank called upon the plaintiff for payments under it on the default of the borrower. It was held that the assumption of an executory and contingent liability was *not* recognisable loss:

> In our opinion, in such a case, the Plaintiff sustains no actual damage until the contingency is fulfilled and the loss becomes actual; until that happens the loss is prospective and may never be incurred.[26]

Forster was distinguished on the basis that in that case the plaintiff had sustained immediate actual loss by incumbering the equity of her property by a mortgage. In so far as *Forster* decided otherwise, it was held that it should not be followed.

The extent to which *Forster* could be explained on the narrow basis suggested in *Wardley* was considered in *Lewis v Osborne*.[27] A child was injured in a road accident because of a driver's negligence. The parent

---

[22] See however, the Canadian case of *Central Bank Co v Rafuse* (1987) 31 DLR (4th) 481, where *Forster* was accepted as correct, though in that case the plaintiff could take advantage of the 'discoverability rule' (the equivalent of s 14A of the 1980 Act).

[23] *Magman International Pty Ltd v Westpac Banking Corporation* (1991) 104 ALR 575, 577.

[24] See also *Hawkins v Clayton Utz* (1988) 164 CLR 539.

[25] (1991) 102 ALR 213 (FCA); (1992) 109 ALR 247.

[26] Per Mason CJ, Dawson, Gaudron and McHugh JJ, at 258: see also Brennan J at 261–2, Deane J at 265, and Toohey J at 276–8. See also *SWF Hoists and Industrial Equipment Pty Ltd v State Government Insurance Commission* (1990) ATPR 41-045; *City of Kamloops v Nielson* (1984) 10 DLR (4th) 641, 684–5.

[27] (1995) unreported, 28 November, Dyson J.

of the child had been advised by solicitors to agree, on behalf of the child, to the acceptance of a settlement with the driver's insurers and to enter into a parent's indemnity with the driver and his insurers against any later claim brought by the child. Thirteen years later the child brought proceedings against the driver, who issued third party proceedings under the indemnity against the parent. The parent issued fourth party proceedings against the solicitors. The question arose whether those fourth party proceedings were statute-barred. This question depended on whether the parent's cause of action against the solicitors arose when the parent entered into the indemnity or when the driver issued the third party notice against him, claiming to be indemnified under the indemnity.

The judge refused to distinguish *Forster* and held that that case (and the later English cases which had applied it) had explicitly recognised that a contingent liability could cause the plaintiff immediate actual damage, although:

> It is a question of fact in each case whether actual damage has been established.[28]

He agreed with the defendant's argument that the cause of action arose on the earlier date, and that quantification of loss depended on an assessment of the likelihood that the driver would claim on the indemnity (which in turn depended, although the judge did not explicitly state this, on an assessment of the likelihood that the child would bring proceedings against the driver).

As a result, the judge held that *Wardley* did not represent the English law in so far as it decided that contingent loss could not amount to 'actual damage' for the purpose of the commencement of the Limitation Act. It is submitted that this reasoning is wrong. It is noteworthy that in *First National Bank plc v Humberts*[29] the *Wardley* case was referred to with approval by both Saville and Neill LJJ. On the facts of *Lewis*, the decision that the cause of action accrued at the moment at which the parent entered into the indemnity must have involved an implicit acceptance that the chances of the child claiming against the other driver were capable of proper assessment and quantification at that moment (that is, when the child was aged two). It is difficult to see how the judge could have come to such a conclusion without clear evidence.

The *Forster* treatment of damage has been applied in cases where a plaintiff has, in reliance upon a negligently prepared valuation report or survey, purchased or leased a property. This follows from the fact that the normal rule for assessing damages in surveyors' negligence

---

[28] Per Neill LJ in *D W Moore v Ferrier* [1988] 1 WLR 267, 278.

[29] [1995] 2 All ER 673. The appeal in this case was heard by the House of Lords but was settled before judgment was given.

cases is that the measure of damages, assessed as at the time of breach, is the difference between the amount paid for the asset in question and its true value at the date of purchase.[30] Thus, in *Secretary of State for the Environment v Essex, Goodman & Suggit*[31] the plaintiff acquired a lease in reliance upon the defendant surveyor's allegedly negligent survey of the building. After the lease was completed it became apparent that the property had defects which had not been detected in the survey. It was held that the plaintiff suffered loss, and therefore its cause of action in negligence accrued at the moment when it entered into the lease, because the lease was worth less than had been paid for it.

This analysis applies *a fortiori* to the usual action brought by the purchaser of property who has relied upon an allegedly negligent survey in entering into the transaction. It is clear that the loss is sustained at the moment of purchase. The application of *Forster* in such cases presents no difficulty because the plaintiff's loss is not dependent on the occurrence of an event which is outside the plaintiff's control.

5.4 Property finance tort claims

5.4.1 The possible 'accrual dates'

The *Forster* treatment of damage has been applied without difficulty in property negligence cases[32] involving the acquisition of a lease or the purchase of property. However, in cases in which lenders are plaintiffs the courts have not applied the *Forster* analysis uniformly. There are at least five possible dates on which the lender suffers damage:

(a) the date on which the advance is made;
(b) the date on which the value of the security becomes less than the value of the lender's claim;
(c) the date on which the borrower defaults;
(d) the date on which the rights acquired by the lender are worth less than the lender's claim; or
(e) the date on which the security is realised.

Some support for all these possibilities can be found in the cases.

5.4.2 Date of the advance

The first possible date for the accrual of the cause of action is the date of the advance. In support of this possibility, it can be argued that the

---

[30] See *Watts v Morrow* [1991] 1 WLR 1421.
[31] [1985] 2 EGLR 168.
[32] See, for example, *Melton v Walker & Stanger* (1981) 125 SJ 861; *Secretary of State for the Environment v Essex, Goodman & Suggit* [1985] 2 EGLR 168; *Costa v Georghiou* (1985) 1 PN 201; *Baker v Ollard & Bentley* (1982) 126 SJ 593; *Kitney v Jones Lang Wootton* [1988] 1 EGLR 145; and *Lee v Thompson* [1989] 2 EGLR 152.

lender, at the moment at which the money is advanced, obtains an asset (that is, a charge secured on property) which is worth less than it should be. This is the pure application of the *Forster* analysis. The rationale for its application is that even before the borrower defaults, the transaction is riskier by reason of the decreased (or entirely non-existent) cushion between the amount of the loan and the value of the security and the mortgage security would be worth less were it to be assigned.

This approach has the advantage of certainty.[33] However, being a pure application of *Forster*, it has to involve treating a potential loss as an actual loss a discount being applied to reflect the fact that the full loss might not, in fact, be incurred. Furthermore, it can lead to injustice as a lender will not, ordinarily, be aware of negligence by solicitors or valuers until the realisation of the security. In domestic cases in particular, this may be many years after the date of the advance.

This possibility is also inconsistent with the decision of the Court of Appeal in *First National Commercial Bank plc v Humberts*.[34] The defendants were valuers who had valued a property at £4.4 million, in reliance upon which the plaintiff lenders advanced £2.6 million in and after July 1983. The lenders alleged that the actual value at the time of the loan was in fact £2.7 million. The writ was issued in March 1990. Therefore if the cause of action arose prior to March 1984 the claim in tort would be statute-barred.

The court approached the question in terms of that posed in *Forster*: that is by asking 'When did the plaintiff sustain legally recognised loss or damage capable of assessment in money terms from the assumed breach of duty?' The defendants argued that the cause of action in tort accrued at the date of the loan because at that moment the lenders obtained a security worth substantially less than that stated by the valuers.

This argument was accepted by the judge at first instance[35] but was rejected by the Court of Appeal. Although the lenders would not have lent at all had they known the actual value of the property, the cause of action did not arise at the date of the loan because until after March 1984, the lender's outlay, plus the cost of borrowing, was less than the value of the security which it held. The court held that that date was the *earliest* date on which the cause of action could have arisen:

> As at July 1983 and until after March 1984 the plaintiffs would, in my judgment, have been quite unable to establish that they had lost the whole or any part of their advance, since, as they have themselves demonstrated,

[33] See Evans, *ibid*, 184–6.
[34] [1995] 2 All ER 673. Moreover its rejection would appear to be implicit in Lord Hoffmann's speech in *BBL v Eagle Star* [1996] WLR 87 where he rejected Mr Sumption QC's argument that the court should assess a lender's damages by an estimation of the value of the rights which the lender received at the date of advance (at 100–1).
[35] (1993) 10 Const LJ 141.

the security they had exceeded the advances.[36]

It appears that the Court of Appeal in *Humberts* thought that the appropriate 'value' of the security which had to be considered was the 'open market value', rather than the forced sale value.[36a]

It seems, therefore, that, applying the *Moore v Ferrier* test, had the bank sued prior to March 1984 they would have obtained only nominal damages (for breach of contract) because up to that date the entirety of their loan was secure. Moreover, precisely because the lenders would not have lent on a non-negligent valuation they would never have lost the difference between a security worth £4.4 million and a security worth (on the assumed facts before the court) £1.7 million less.

In addition, it was argued by the defendants in *Humberts* that the plaintiffs suffered immediate loss at the time of the loan because they then incurred legal and administrative costs in transacting the loan. This argument was rejected by Saville LJ:

> To my mind it would be wrong simply to take the debit side of the deal and to describe it as loss or damage flowing from the breach of duty without taking into account the credit side of the deal.[37]

The reason for this was that, at the time of the advance, the lenders were not 'out of pocket': they had incurred expenditure but they had also received benefit.[38] It was recognised in *D W Moore v Ferrier*[39] that the proper application of *Forster* did not necessitate that damage will always be considered to be suffered when a plaintiff enters into a transaction as a result of negligent advice.

5.4.3 Date on which the security is worth less than the loan

The second possibility is that the cause of action accrues on the date on which the security is worth less than the loan. On this analysis, the date on which the primary limitation period in tort begins to run depends on a consideration of the amount outstanding under the mortgage and the value of the security. Time begins to run only when the former is greater than the latter.

In *Humberts*, the issue was whether the cause of action had arisen before 20 March 1984. It was accepted that, at that date, the value of the security was greater than the value of the lender's claim. The Court of Appeal held that the cause of action did not accrue during the period prior to 20 March 1984. The court did not decide that the cause of action *did* accrue when the latter became greater than the former, nor did it need to. For the plaintiff's appeal to succeed all that needed to be

---

[36] [1995] 2 All ER 673, 678d–e.
[36a] *Ibid*, at 676d, 678d. It is arguable whether the OMV is appropriate.
[37] *Ibid*, at 677b.
[38] *Ibid*.
[39] [1988] 1 WLR 267, 278.

established was that the defendant had not shown on the balance of probabilities that the cause of action had accrued prior to March 1984:[40] the court did not need to decide, in order to determine the appeal, precisely when 'actual damage' had been sustained.

The court, accordingly, did not lay down any rule of general application in valuers' cases that actual damage would always be sustained at the moment when the value of the security became less than the amount outstanding under the loan. As a result, the *ratio* of *Humberts* is a narrow one: that the cause of action does not accrue as long as the security is worth more than the lender's claim.

It is submitted that the argument that the cause of action accrues at the date on which the security is worth less than the lender's claim is unsatisfactory for at least three reasons.

Firstly, the approach is based on the assumption that the 'contingent risk' of borrower default gives rise to an actual loss. However, loss in fact depends on two factors: inadequate security *and* borrower default. As the Court of Appeal said in *BBL v Eagle Star*:[41]

> ... even assuming an excessive advance made on a negligent overvaluation the lender may suffer no actual loss on making the loan or at any other time since the borrower may repay the loan with interest in accordance with the terms of the transaction.

When a lender enters into a loan on the basis of inadequate security, 'in truth and reality' he does not lose anything. Such loss occurs only on default.[42] Moreover this approach in effect involves ascribing a nil value to the borrower's covenant. It is based on the assumption that, on a 'benefit and burden' approach, the only benefit which the lender receives is the value of the property. This assumption is inconsistent with the approach of the Court of Appeal with *UBAF v European American Banking*[43] and with the commercial reality of a loan transaction.

Secondly, the practical application of this approach is not straightforward. Although the amount outstanding under the loan is capable of ascertainment on any given day, the value of the security is much more difficult to work out. The latter figure will usually require expert valuation and may well be a matter of dispute. The correct figure can only be decided at trial in the light of the final finding as to the correct valuation. As the property market fluctuates and the amount outstanding changes (for example because the borrower makes payments off the arrears), the date on which the cause of action arises may be very difficult to ascertain.

In valuer cases where limitation issues arise, each party's contentions

---

[40]   Per Saville LJ at 678j.
[41]   [1995] QB 375, 419E.
[42]   See *Magman International Pty Ltd v Westpac Banking Corporation* (1991) 104 ALR 575, 577.
[43]   [1984] 2 All ER 226; see below.

on liability and on limitation will often be diametrically opposed: on liability a valuer will wish to argue for the highest possible value, on limitation he will wish to argue for the lowest. More importantly, a prudent and swift acting plaintiff may find at trial that his action was premature, that his retrospective valuation evidence was too pessimistic and, as at the date of the writ, the value of the security was, in fact, greater than the sum outstanding. As there was no cause of action on the date of issue, the action would fail.

Thirdly, this approach gives rise to serious problems in the assessment of damages if the borrower does not default. A lender who discovers that there has been an overvaluation but whose borrower has not defaulted is placed in a difficult position. The borrower could, of course, default in the future. If the lender does not bring proceedings he risks a claim becoming statute-barred. If the lender does bring proceedings then what is his loss? It cannot be the 'diminution in value of the security' because there is no market in individual mortgages.[44] The court will have to 'guess' the chances of the borrower defaulting.[45] This was in fact done in *Eagle Star v Gale and Power*[46] where Devlin J awarded damages taking into account the continuing value of the borrower's covenant. The obviously arbitrary nature of the figure chosen demonstrates the difficulties of this approach, which, in addition to involving an assessment of the security at a particular time, require the court to ascribe a value, at any given time, to the borrower's covenant.

5.4.4 Date of borrower default

The third possibility is that the cause of action accrues only when the borrower defaults. The argument is that the lender suffers actual loss only at the date of borrower default: only then can he take steps to sell the security and only then is he exposed to the risk that the security will be inadequate to pay off the sums outstanding under the mortgage. However, the difficulty with this approach is that, in many cases, borrower default will not produce any actual loss to the lender. The 'potential damage' resulting from a negligent overvaluation may have been covered by the 'cushion' or eliminated by a rise in the property market. If the value of the security is greater than the sums outstanding, no loss will be suffered. Actual loss will be suffered on borrower default only if the security is inadequate. As a result, it cannot be said that, in every case, the cause of action will accrue on borrower default: the value of the security must also be considered.

[44] See also *BBL v Eagle Star* [1995] QB 375, 419F.
[45] See Evans, *ibid*, 185.
[46] (1955)166 EG 37; doubted in *London & South Building Society v Stone* [1983] 1 WLR 1242, 1254, but not on this point.

5.4.5   Date on which the rights acquired by the lender are worth less than the lender's loss

The fourth possibility is that the lender suffers actual loss when the value of all the rights which he acquires is less than his capital outlay plus interest. This approach takes into account the fact that the lender's loss is contingent because the borrower might not default. When the lender makes a loan he advances money and receives, in return, the borrower's covenant plus the security. The argument is that actual (as opposed to contingent) loss is only suffered when the value of the bundle of rights acquired by the lender (the borrower's covenant plus the value of the security) is worth less than the amount outstanding.

This possibility is supported by the decision in *UBAF v European American Banking*.[47] In that case, a bank advanced money in reliance upon an alleged misrepresentation by the defendant. The borrowers defaulted. The writ was issued more than six years after the date of the loan, and the plaintiff alleged that had it known the truth it would not have entered into the transaction. On the defendant's application to have leave to issue out of the jurisdiction set aside, it was held that the action was not necessarily statute-barred because it was not inevitable that the plaintiff had suffered damage at the time of entering into the contract of loan. Ackner LJ held[48] that it was:

> ... possible, although it may be improbable, that, at the date when the plaintiff advanced its money, the value of the chose in action it then acquired [ie the borrower's contractual obligation to repay] was, in fact, not less than the sum which the plaintiff lent, or indeed even exceeded it.

This would be a matter of evidence. *Forster* was distinguished on the ground that the plaintiff in that case, on entering into the deed of mortgage, 'suffered actual damage ... encumbering her freehold and reduced the value of her property'.

This approach appears to be consistent with the decision of the Court of Appeal in *Humberts*: in that case, the value of the lender's rights became less than the value of the security at some date after March 1984. It is noteworthy that Saville LJ places that case in the same category as *UBAF* and *Wardley*.[49]

This approach is also supported by Gaudron J in *Hawkins v Clayton Utz*[50] in which it was said:

> If the interest infringed is an interest in recouping moneys advanced it may be appropriate to fix the time of accrual of the cause of action when recoupment becomes impossible rather than at the time when the

47   [1984] 2 All ER 226.
48   At 234j.
49   *Ibid*, at 679d.
50   (1988) 164 CLR 539, 601.

antecedent right to recoup should have come into existence, for the actual loss is sustained only when recoupment becomes impossible.

Brennan J took a similar approach in *Wardley*:[51]

> A transaction in which there are benefits and burdens results in loss or damage only if an adverse balance can be struck. If the balance cannot be struck until certain events occur, no loss is suffered until those events occur.

However, this approach also gives rise to enormous practical difficulties. It is difficult to see how the value of the borrower's covenant can be assessed whilst the loan is performing. In most cases, it only becomes clear that the value of the borrower's covenant was less than the sum advanced when there is substantial borrower default. It is submitted that, as a result, in the absence of specific evidence as to the borrower's financial position, it should be assumed that the value of the borrower's covenant is greater than or equal to the sum outstanding.

This would mean that the cause of action would accrue on the later of two dates:

(a) the date of substantial borrower default; or
(b) the date on which the value of all the security taken by the lender becomes less than the lender's loss.

5.4.6 Date of realisation of the security

The fifth possible date for accrual of the cause of action is the date on which the security was realised. This approach receives support from Sir John Megaw in *Swingcastle v Gibson*[52] when he said:

> No loss is incurred, nor can anyone foretell whether any loss is going to be incurred, as a result of the surveyor's negligent valuation, unless and until the third party, the borrower under the loan contract with the lender, defaults on the payments due under the loan contracts, the lender seeks to exercise his right to enforce the security and the proceeds of the security prove to be less than the total amount which the lender is then entitled to recover from the borrower under the terms of the loan contract. Up to that time, or at any rate up to the time when the lender decides to enforce the security, there may be a potential loss, but there is no actual loss.

This approach has the advantage of certainty. It is, however, inconsistent with both *Forster v Outred* and *UBAF*. It would also have two consequences which the courts would be likely to regard as unacceptable. First, it would mean that there would be no 'time pressure' on a

---

[51] (1992) 109 ALR 247, 262.
[52] [1990] 1 WLR 1223, 1235–6.

dilatory lender to enforce his security. A lender could, in effect, choose when the limitation began to run. Secondly, it would mean that a diligent lender could not bring a claim in tort until he was able to realise the security. It is common for sales to be delayed for considerable periods by matters such as title difficulties. In such a case, the lender would not be entitled to issue negligence proceedings until the sale had finally taken place.

5.4.7   Some conclusions

The issue of limitation in property finance negligence cases is a difficult one. The authorities are not wholly consistent and unless and until the issue is dealt with by the House of Lords, all conclusions must necessarily be tentative. The appeal to the House of Lords in *First National Bank v Humberts* was heard by the House of Lords in July 1996 but was settled before judgment was given. As far as the authors are aware, no other appeal on this point is pending. However, it is submitted that on the present state of the authorities, in lender cases the fourth possibility is the correct one: the cause of action will not accrue until the rights acquired by the lender are worth less than the lender's loss (being the sum of the advance and loss of interest).

In practice, as stated above, it may be difficult to value the bundle of rights acquired. In particular, the value of the borrower's covenant will usually be extremely difficult to assess. However, this approach can be used in practice by making the assumption, in the absence of evidence to the contrary, that prior to substantial borrower default, the value of the borrower's covenant plus the security is sufficiently valuable to cover the full advance plus interest. However, once the borrower well and truly defaults, the court is then entitled to assume that his covenant is worthless. The cause of action will, therefore, accrue at the date of borrower default or the date on which the value of the security is less than the lender's loss, whichever is later.

Although the use of this date will, in some cases, produce a considerable extension of the limitation period, this seems unlikely to place undue burden on solicitors and valuers as they will usually have written records relating to the transaction. If the prospect of actions more than six years after the date of the advance is burdensome, professionals are at liberty to contract on terms which restrict their liability in time as well as amount. At the same time, this approach places the onus on the lender to monitor repayment carefully and to proceed expeditiously after borrower default. If the lender delays in realising his security then time will run against him. The lender is not able to sit back in the knowledge that time will not run against him until the sale of the security takes place. For these reasons, it is suggested that this approach is consistent with principle and authority and should be adopted in property finance cases.[53]

5.5 Latent damage

5.5.1 Introduction

Prior to 1986, the law relating to the limitation of actions was liable to cause potential injustice to litigants who only became aware that damage had been suffered after the lapse of the statutory six year period from the accrual of a cause of action in contract and tort. In 1980, The Law Reform Committee was asked to consider the law relating to 'latent defects' and as a result of its report[54] the Latent Damage Act 1986 was enacted, introducing new ss 14A and 14B into the Limitation Act 1980.

The 'latent damage' provisions of the 1980 Act apply to claims against valuers and solicitors both in negligence and negligent misstatement and in relation to all types of damage sustained, whether physical or economic.[55]

Under s 14A, the plaintiff can, in an 'action for damages for negligence',[56] take advantage of a limitation period that exists independently of that prescribed by s 2 of the 1980 Act. The courts have strictly interpreted the ambit of the section to apply only to actions for negligence: this section does not apply to claims in contract, even where the alleged breach of contract involves, or is founded upon, an allegation of careless or negligent conduct.[57] This 'secondary limitation period' is 'three years from the starting date', if that period expires later than the six year primary period of limitation.[58]

The definition of the 'starting date' is to be found at s 14A(5) of the Act:

> For the purposes of this section, the starting date for reckoning the period of limitation under subsection 14A(b) above is the earliest date on which the plaintiff or any person in whom the cause of action was vested before him first had both the knowledge required for bringing an action for damages in respect of the relevant damage and a right to bring such an action.

It is for the plaintiff to plead (whether in the statement of claim or in

---

[53] See generally, Evans, *ibid*, pp 184–6.
[54] No 24, Cmnd 9390, November 1984.
[55] See *Horbury v Craig Hall & Rutley* [1991] EGCS 81; and *Campbell v Meacocks* [1993] CILL 866. The Law Reform Committee certainly envisaged this: see para 1.2 of its 24th Report.
[56] Section 14A(2).
[57] See above, p 119.
[58] Section 14A (4) (*b*).

reply) and prove a date within three years of the commencement of proceedings when he acquired the relevant knowledge.[59]

5.5.2 'Date of knowledge'

The key concept that emerges from this section is the notion of an ascertainable 'date of knowledge' which sets the three year clock of the extended limitation period running. 'The knowledge required for bringing an action for damages in respect of the relevant damage' is then given an extended definition:

(1) It means knowledge of 'the material facts about the damage in respect of which damages are claimed'.[60] This is then expanded upon by ss 14A(7):

> ... the material facts about the damage are such facts about the damage as would lead a reasonable person who had suffered such damage to consider it sufficiently serious to justify his instituting proceedings for damages against a defendant who did not dispute liability and was able to satisfy judgment.

But mere knowledge that 'damage' has been sustained is not in itself enough to activate the three year period.

(2) The prospective plaintiff must also have knowledge:
   (a) that the damage was attributable in whole or in part to the act or omission which is alleged to constitute negligence; and
   (b) of the identity of the defendant; and
   (c) if it is alleged that the act or omission was that of a person other than the defendant, the identity of that person and the additional facts supporting the bringing of an action against the defendant.[61]

The word 'attributable' at paragraph (a) above means 'capable of being attributable' to the act or omission of the prospective defendant.[62]

It is also important to be clear about the meaning of the word 'damage'. The situation often arises in cases brought by purchasers in which the surveyor on whose report and valuation the plaintiff relied fails to draw attention to a number of defects. The purchaser may discover one defect much earlier than the others. It is now clear that, if a surveyor fails to draw attention to a series of defects, the purchaser's claim is statute-barred when the relevant limitation periods have expired in relation to the defect which was, or ought to have been, discovered first.

---

[59] *Nash v Eli Lilly & Co* [1993] 1 WLR 782, 796.
[60] Section 14A(6)(a).
[61] Section 14A(8).
[62] Per May LJ, *Davis v Ministry of Defence* (1985) *The Times*, 7 August.

The point was considered by the Court of Appeal in *Hamlin v Edwin Evans*.[63] In that case, three years after purchasing the property, the purchasers noticed dry rot infestation which was eradicated, at a total cost of £4,000. They complained to the defendant, who compromised the action. Five years later the plaintiffs became aware of an enlarging crack, which proved to be due to subsidence. The plaintiffs brought a second claim. The Court of Appeal upheld the judge in deciding that the claim was statute-barred: in contrast to building cases, where there may be different causes of action against different contractors for different types of damage,[64] in a case against a valuer or surveyor there was one single, indivisible cause of action arising out of one negligent act—the making of the single report. As a consequence the cause of action arising out of that negligent act accrued when damage (whether small or large) was suffered for the first time.

This decision is difficult to justify in terms of the policy of the section, which was enacted precisely to prevent good claims against defendants becoming statute-barred prior to the plaintiff having knowledge of them. In *Hamlin* there was no suggestion that the plaintiffs should have discovered the material facts relating to the subsidence prior to the date when they did discover them. Moreover it is noteworthy that s 14A(6)(*a*) defines the necessary 'knowledge' as knowledge 'of the material facts about the damage in respect of which damages are claimed'. In *Hamlin*, the plaintiffs were claiming damages in respect of the failure to report on the subsidence, not the dry rot.

The word 'knowledge' has been interpreted in a number of cases in the context of s 14 of the 1980 Act (which governs personal injury actions) and there is no reason to think that it has any different meaning in the context of s 14A. In *Halford v Brookes*,[65] Lord Donaldson of Lymington MR said:

> The word has to be construed in the context of the purpose of the section, which is to determine a period of time within which a plaintiff can be required to start any proceedings. In this context 'knowledge' clearly does not mean 'know for certain and beyond possibility of contradiction'. It does, however, mean 'know with sufficient confidence to justify embarking on the preliminaries to the issue of a writ, such as submitting a claim to the proposed defendant, taking legal and other advice and collecting evidence'. Suspicion, particularly if it is vague and unsupported, will not be enough, but reasonable belief will normally suffice.[66]

---

[63] [1996] EGCS 120; [1996] 1 PNLR 398 following conflicting decisions in *Horbury v Craig Hall & Rutley* [1991] EGCS 81; and *Felton v Gaskill Osborne & Co* [1993] 2 EGLR 176.

[64] See, for example, *Steamship Mutual Underwriting Association v Trollope & Colls (City) Ltd* (1986) 33 BLR 77.

[65] [1991] 1 WLR 428.

[66] At 443.

Lord Donaldson said that May LJ's comment in *Davies v Ministry of Defence*[67] that 'reasonable belief or suspicion are not enough' for time to start running should not be followed, though he did consider that that case had been correctly decided on its facts.[68] However the mere fact that the prospective plaintiff has consulted a solicitor will not in itself be sufficient to set time running.[69]

5.5.3   The nature of the plaintiff

The definition of 'knowledge' needs to be considered in the context of the particular plaintiff who is seeking to rely upon s 14A. Although knowledge is a 'condition of mind which imports a degree of certainty', the degree of certainty necessary to constitute knowledge to set time running is that which, for the particular plaintiff, 'may reasonably be regarded as sufficient to justify embarking upon the preliminaries to the making of a claim for compensation such as the taking of legal or other advice'.[70]

Thus, for instance, a building society would be expected to have greater sophistication in the assessment of information which comes into its hands than the lay plaintiff who had relied upon a negligent survey in purchasing a domestic property. An institutional lender may be fixed with knowledge at an earlier date than the lay plaintiff. However Purchas LJ went on to qualify the above proposition by noting:

> ... a firm belief held by the plaintiff that [the damage he has sustained] was attributable to the act or omission of the defendant, but in respect of which he thought it necessary to obtain reassurance or confirmation from experts, medical or legal, or others, would not be regarded as knowledge until the result of his enquiries was known to him or, if he delayed in obtaining that confirmation, until the time at which it was reasonable for him to have got it.[71]

On the other hand, where the plaintiff does not think it necessary to obtain reassurance or confirmation from experts, time can run from the date that a confident assertion of liability is made. In *Spencer-Ward v Humberts*[72] the plaintiffs purchased a house in reliance upon a valuation and report prepared by the defendants. Some years later they wished

---

[67]   (1985) *The Times*, 7 August.
[68]   See also *Dobbie v Medway Health Authority* [1994] 4 All ER 450, 455 where it was stated that Lord Donaldson's test was not (usually) hard to apply.
[69]   *Nash v Eli Lilly & Co* [1993] 1 WLR 782, 800; *Wilson v Le Fevre Wood and Royle* [1996] PNLR 107, 117.
[70]   *Nash v Eli Lilly & Co* [1993] 1 WLR 782, 792, per Purchas LJ.
[71]   At page 796. Of course the situation might well arise where a plaintiff suspects (or even firmly believes) that he has sustained damage attributable to the defendant, but the expert he has sought confirmation from gives negative advice. It would appear in that situation that time would only start running when a second expert gives positive advice.
[72]   [1995] 1 EGLR 123.

to sell the house and were told by neighbours that the house was probably of a defective 'Woolaway' type construction. They wrote a letter to the building society which had retained the defendant surveyor to survey the house prior to the offer of a mortgage, complaining that the valuation was 'grossly misleading and inaccurate' in failing to mention this fact. The letter claimed that the house was worth £30,000 less as a result. The writ was issued more than three years after this letter was written. It was argued by the plaintiffs that at the time of writing the letter they did not have the benefit of expert advice and did not know what defects the house might have. The argument failed: while expert evidence would no doubt be needed for the purpose of litigating the case, as at the date of the letter the plaintiffs were in possession of the essential factual material to mount a claim for damages. The case might well have been decided differently had the plaintiffs' letter made their allegations contingent on the obtaining of expert evidence to confirm their suspicions.

In *Wilson v Le Fevre Wood & Royle*,[73] the plaintiffs had complained to the defendants, only to receive a flat rejection (and explanation) of their allegations. That explanation was accepted by the plaintiffs, who revived their allegations only at a later date after the damage had persisted. The Court of Appeal left open the question whether time ran from the date when the plaintiffs had initially complained. It was argued by the defendants that once actual knowledge had been acquired then supervening doubts could not stop the clock running. It is submitted that in circumstances where the plaintiff's firm belief that damage has been sustained which is attributable to the default of the defendant is scotched by a negative expert report, the plaintiff only acquires knowledge when a second expert report is affirmative; this analysis should pertain even where the 'expert' is in fact the prospective defendant.

In *Spencer-Ward* the plaintiff suffered the cost of being too confident too early. In general, however, knowledge will depend upon positive expert evidence to substantiate a claim. In *Campbell v Meacocks*,[74] another case brought by house purchasers, the plaintiffs had received a letter from a firm of loss adjusters instructed by their neighbours. The letter told the plaintiffs that their house needed underpinning because of subsidence and invited them to agree to a common raft for both houses. The plaintiffs took no action and some years later received expert advise from a structural engineer informing them that the house suffered from subsidence. It was held that, for the purposes of s 14A, the plaintiffs only had knowledge of the surveyors' negligence in failing to discover subsidence when they obtained the structural engineer's report. The earlier letter did not fix them with such knowledge and it was reasonable

---

[73]   [1996] PNLR 107.
[74]   [1995] EGCS 143.

for them not to follow up the letter, having purchased the house in reliance upon the defendant's report only 20 months earlier. For that reason the plaintiffs were not fixed with knowledge under s 14A(10).[75]

A further argument that is sometimes raised by plaintiffs is that, although they are aware at a particular date that damage has been caused by the defendant, they did not know until some later date that the damage was caused by the defendant's fault. Section 14A(9) makes it clear that knowledge that the act or omission constituted negligence in law is not necessary to fix a plaintiff with knowledge. But s 14A(8)(*a*), by implication, goes further: all that the plaintiff need know is that the damage is 'attributable in part to the act or omission which is alleged to constitute negligence'.

In *Higgins v Hatch & Fielding*[76] the plaintiffs obtained an expert report in 1990 which stated that the house they had purchased in reliance upon the defendants' report was suffering from long-standing subsidence. The writ was issued in 1994. It was argued that the plaintiffs were lay-men and were unable therefore to understand the import of the report as calling into question the original valuation and therefore rendering the defendants vulnerable to an action in negligence. The Court of Appeal held that it was irrelevant to the making out of the elements of knowledge as set out at ss (7) and (8) whether the plaintiffs knew that they had a 'cause of action': knowledge of the facts founding that cause of action was sufficient. It had been emphasised in *Dobbie v Medway Health Authority*[77] that knowledge, for the purposes of s 14A, was not dependent upon the knowledge that damages were attributable to the *fault* or *actionable negligence* of the defendant, but simply the *act* or *omission* of the defendant.

However the act or omission of which the plantiffs must have knowledge must be that which is causally relevant for the purposes of an allegation of negligence.[77a]

5.5.4   Objective test

However, the test to ascertain whether a plaintiff has knowledge or not is not simply a subjective one. Section 14A(10) gives a second, objective definition of the plaintiff's 'knowledge':

> For the purposes of this section a person's knowledge includes knowledge which he might reasonably have been expected to acquire—
> (a)   from facts observable or ascertainable by him; and
> (b)   from facts ascertainable by him with the help of appropriate expert advice which it is reasonable for him to seek.

---

[75]   See section 5.5.6 below.
[76]   [1996] 10 EG 162.   [77]   [1994] 4 All ER 450, 456, 463.
[77a]   *Hallam-Eames v Merrett Syndicates*[1995] 7 Med LR 122; *Dobbie v Medway Health Authority* [1994] 4 All ER 450; *Broadley v Guy Clapham & Co* [1994] 4 All ER 439.

Thus in *Heathcote v David Marks & Co*[78] one of the arguments advanced by the plaintiffs was that although they may have known that there was a serious defect in the house which had not been referred to in the report and valuation, they did not know the identity of the valuer until a later date. This argument was rejected. The judge held that if there *was* any doubt as to the identity of the party that provided the report (which he doubted) the plaintiffs or their solicitor need only have asked.

No doubt for the purpose of fixing a plaintiff with constructive knowledge so as to commence the three year period, the courts will take into account the type of plaintiff in any particular case, in the sense that it will be astute to expect the relevant facts to be more readily observable by an institutional plaintiff than by an individual one.

This is starkly illustrated by the case of *Finance for Mortgages v Farley*.[79] In that case, the writ was issued in April 1994. The lender had lent in reliance on an allegedly negligent overvaluation. The primary limitation period expired in July 1993 and the action had to proceed under s 14A of the Limitation Act 1980. The lender claimed that its earliest date of knowledge was August 1991, after the date when possession was obtained, and relied upon s 14A(5). The defendant valuer alleged that the lender had been guilty of unreasonable delay in taking possession, and accordingly the date of knowledge should be earlier than the date of actual knowledge by reason of s 14A(10).

It was held that the plaintiff's claim was statute-barred. A reasonably prudent lender would have commenced proceedings earlier, after it became clear that the borrower did not intend to continue payments under the mortgage, and pursued them with vigour. The judge held that it should take no longer than twelve months from commencement of the possession action to the obtaining of physical possession. Here proceedings should have been issued by January 1990, so that possession would have been obtained by January 1991. Where a lender obtained vacant possession it was normal to expect it to proceed to an early valuation. Therefore the lender should have obtained a valuation (which would have disclosed the facts necessary to institute proceedings) by mid-March 1991. Accordingly the plaintiff was fixed with constructive knowledge from that date.

The judge appears to have considered that 'facts observable' by the plaintiff included facts that would have come into its knowledge simply by reason of the normal reactions of a lender to a common situation: the reasonableness of the plaintiff's behaviour was not limited to an analysis of when it should have drawn the proper conclusions on the evidence before it. Instead the judge, adopting a robust approach, took into account extrinsic matters to determine the date when the lender

[78]   [1996] 03 EG 128.
[79]   [1996] NPC 19.

would (had it behaved in the normal way) have come into possession of the relevant information to found a claim against the valuer.

5.6   Other claims

5.6.1   Contribution

Section 10 of the 1980 Act provides that, where under s 1 of the Civil Liability (Contribution) Act 1978 a person becomes entitled to a right to recover contribution in respect of any damage from any other person, then 'no action shall be brought after the expiration of two years from the date on which that right accrued.'[80]

The date on which the right to recover contribution will arise is either the date when judgment has been given against the person entitled to recover contribution or the date when that person has compromised the main action.[81]

The effect of these provisions is to extend the period of time for which a person is at risk of being sued in respect of damage for which he is jointly liable with someone else.

5.6.2   Breach of trust

Section 21(3) of the Act provides a six year limitation period in cases of breach of trust. In the case of a solicitor paying away advance monies in breach of trust, the limitation period will run from the date of such payment away.

---

[80]   Section 10(1).
[81]   See s 10(3) and 10(4) of the 1980 Act.

6 Apportioning Responsibility: Contributory Negligence and Contribution

6.1 Introduction

The apportionment of responsibility arises as an issue in property finance negligence cases in two situations. Firstly, when the plaintiff lender is partly to blame for the loss which he suffers. In such a case, defendant professionals can rely on the defence of contributory negligence: the apportionment of blame between plaintiff and defendant can lead to a reduction in the damages recoverable by the plaintiff.

Secondly, where more than one defendant is liable for the same damage, the courts can apportion liability between them under the Civil Liability (Contribution) Act 1978. This is important in property finance negligence claims as, in many cases, the lender plaintiff will have concurrent negligence claims against both solicitors and valuers (and, sometimes, accountants and credit reference agencies).

6.2 Contributory negligence

6.2.1 Introduction

Contributory negligence has become an extremely important issue in property finance negligence cases. After some initial doubt is it is now clearly established that, in an ordinary case, damages can be reduced to reflect imprudent lending by the plaintiff. It is now commonplace for both parties to call evidence from 'lending experts' to consider whether or not the plaintiff lender has acted prudently in lending to the borrower.[1] A successful plea of contributory negligence can have a major impact on the quantum of damages awarded.

The general principle is that where the defendant can show that the plaintiff's damage was in part caused by its own negligence the

---

[1] For the admissibility of such evidence, see Chapter 7 below.

defendant will be entitled to a reduction of the damages which would otherwise have been payable. The precise reduction will depend upon the plaintiff's and the defendant's relative degrees of fault.[2] In assessing the degree of contributory negligence it is necessary to consider the blameworthiness of each party and the 'causative potency of the relevant conduct'.[3] The burden of proving contributory negligence is on the defendant.[4]

6.2.2   The basic principles

The jurisdiction to make a deduction from damages by reason of a plaintiff's contributory negligence is based on s 1 of the Law Reform (Contributory Negligence) Act 1945 ('the 1945 Act') which provides:

> Where any person suffers damage as the result partly of his own fault and partly of the fault of any other person or persons[5] a claim in respect of that damage shall not be defeated by reason of the fault of the person suffering the damage, but the damage recoverable in respect thereof shall be reduced to such extent as the Court thinks just and equitable having regard to the claimant's share in the responsibility for the damage.

In seeking to establish contributory negligence, the defendant must show that there was a *causal link* between the fault of the plaintiff and the damage complained of.[6] The mere fact that the plaintiff has acted carelessly is not, in itself, sufficient to justify a reduction. Fault which does not cause any damage is irrelevant. However:

> It is well-established that in considering questions of causation and contributory negligence the Court should adopt a broad and practical approach in considering the transaction in question.[7]

Furthermore, if the result of the plaintiff's negligence has been simply to exacerbate the extent of the damage he has suffered, rather than to cause the event which led to the damage, then a reduction may still be made.[8]

---

[2]   See *Clerk and Lindsell* 17th edn, 3-09 *ff.*
[3]   See *Davies v Swan Motor Co (Swansea) Ltd* [1949] 2 KB 291.
[4]   See *United Bank of Kuwait v Prudential Property Services Ltd* [1995] EGCS 190. The court may however make a finding of contributory negligence on the basis of the plaintiff's evidence, or simply by way of inference from the facts as found.
[5]   The wording of the section would make a finding of 100 per cent contributory negligence illogical: see *Pitts v Hunt* [1992] 1 QB 24, 50, per Beldam LJ.
[6]   See *Caswell v Powell Duffryn Associated Collieries Ltd* [1940] AC 152, 165, per Lord Atkin.
[7]   Per Evans-Lombe J, *Britannic Securities v Hirani Watson* (1995) unreported, transcript, p 63.
[8]   For example, in 'seat-belt' and 'crash helmet' cases: see *Capps v Miller* [1989] 2 All ER 333 and the cases there referred to.

For the purpose of s 1 'fault' is defined by s 4 of the 1945 Act as 'negligence, breach of statutory duty or other act or omission which gives rise to liability in tort or would, apart from this Act, give rise to the defence of contributory negligence'. So, there is no doubt that this section applies to claims for the tort of negligence. It does not, however, apply when the plaintiff's claim is for damages for deceit[9] or for breach of trust or fiduciary duty. However, it is possible that compensation for breach of fiduciary duty will be assessed on the footing that the plaintiff should accept some share of the responsibility.[10]

The question whether the defence of contributory negligence was available when the plaintiff's claim was for breach of contract was long a matter of debate.[11] The issue was resolved by the decision of the Court of Appeal in *Forsikringsaktieselskapet Vesta v Butcher*[12] which indorsed the division of breaches of contract into three types:

(a) where the defendant's liability arises under a contractual provision the breach of which does not depend on negligence on the part of the defendant;

(b) where the defendant's liability arises from a contractual obligation to take care (or the equivalent) but there is no corresponding tortious duty which would exist on the facts independently on the contract; and

(c) where the defendant's liability in contract is the same as the corresponding liability in the tort of negligence.[13]

It is clear that the defence of 'contributory negligence' applies in cases within category (3)[14] but does not apply in cases within category (1).[15] The availability of the defence in relation to category (2) cases remains uncertain.

Most property finance negligence claims fall into category (3). However, some aspects of some claims may be in category (1). Thus, in *Bristol*

---

[9] See *Alliance & Leicester Building Society v Edgestop* [1993] 1 WLR 1462. In that case the argument that the innocent employer, vicariously liable for the actions of a fraudulent employee, should be entitled to plead contributory negligence was rejected.

[10] See *Day v Mead* [1987] 2 NZLR 443, 451; see also *Doiron v Caisse Populaire D'Inkerman* (1985) 17 DLR (4th) 695; *Canson Enterprises Ltd v Boughton & Co* (1992) 85 DLR (4th) 129; and Spry, *Equitable Remedies* 3rd edn (1984) where, at p 610, it is stated that if part of the injury sustained by a plaintiff is caused or contributed to by his own unacceptable conduct, a court could reduce equitable damages to achieve a just result.

[11] See the historical survey in *Basildon District Council v J E Lesser (Properties) Ltd* [1985] QB 839.

[12] [1988] 2 All ER 43; *affd* [1989] AC 852. The Court of Appeal adopted Pritchard J's compelling reasoning in *Rowe v Turner Hopkins & Partners* [1980] 2 NZLR 550.

[13] See also *Lipkin Gorman v Karpnale Ltd* [1989] 1 WLR 1340, 1360.

[14] It was held in *Gran Gelato v Richcliff (Group) Ltd* [1992] Ch 560 that the same reasoning applies in cases where there are concurrent claims in negligence in tort and under the Misrepresentation Act 1967.

[15] See *Tennant Radiant Heat Ltd v Warrington Development Corp* [1989] 1 EGLR 41; and, most recently, *Barclays Bank v Fairclough* [1995] QB 214.

& West Building Society v A Kramer & Co[16] the solicitor was in breach of a 'sweeping up' clause requiring the lender to be informed of any matter known to him which might prejudice the lender's security. Blackburne J regarded the breach as dependent upon the knowledge which the solicitor had, not as dependent upon the solicitor's negligence, and the fact that it did happen also to be negligent did not make the obligation into one dependent on negligence.

However, since *Kramer*, plaintiffs seem to have accepted that property finance negligence claims generally fall within category (3) and this argument has not been widely raised. Nevertheless, if a plaintiff lender is able to establish that the defendant professional is in breach of a duty which does not correspond to a common law duty of care, then the court has no jurisdiction to take 'contributory negligence' into account in assessing damages.

6.3   Contributory negligence: the standard of care

6.3.1   General approach

To establish contributory negligence the defendant must prove on a balance of probabilities that the plaintiff failed to use reasonable care to protect its own interests. Contributory negligence does not, therefore, necessarily involve a breach of duty owed by the plaintiff to the defendant: the concept of a duty of care is irrelevant to the consideration of the question whether the plaintiff has suffered damage which has been partially caused by his own fault.[17] The defendant must establish that the injured party did not 'in his own interest take reasonable care of himself and contributed, by this want of care, to his own injury'.[18] However:

> ... the standard of care in contributory negligence is what is reasonable in the circumstances, which in most cases corresponds to the standard of care in negligence ... [Therefore] contributory negligence requires foreseeability of harm to oneself.[19]

On the other hand, the court will not lightly hold a plaintiff at fault for relying on advice given by a professional adviser who owes a duty of care to the plaintiff.[20] The general question of contributory negligence was said by Phillips J in *BBL v Eagle Star*[21] to turn on whether there

---

16   (1995) *The Independent*, 26 January; [1995] TLR 57.
17   *UBK v Prudential Property Services* (1995) unreported, 27 November, transcript, p 17.
18   *Nance v British Columbia Electric Railway* [1951] AC 601, 611.
19   *Clerk and Lindsell, ibid*, at 3–22. Glanville Williams, in *Joint Torts and Contributory Negligence* (1951), suggested that the actual standard of care which the law requires of the plaintiff is in practice lower in comparison to that required of the defendant: 'the reasonable defendant is not allowed lapses, but the reasonable plaintiff is' (at 353).
20   *BBL v Eagle Star* [1995] 2 All ER 769, 824.
21   *Ibid*, 819 *ff*.

were features of the transactions which should have led a reasonably prudent bank to decline to grant the facilities or to question the valuations relied upon. In other words: 'Did the plaintiff fall short of the standards of prudence reasonably to be expected of them?'[22]

In recent years, however, the practice has developed in property finance negligence cases of calling 'lending practice experts' to give evidence as to the way in which reasonably prudent lenders would have conducted themselves in the circumstances of the case. The Court of Appeal has accepted that such evidence is relevant and admissible[23] though it is not absolutely essential to a defendant being able to raise a case of contributory negligence.[24]

In assessing such 'prudent lending' evidence, however, the court, will be astute not to view the plaintiff's conduct with 'the omniscient gaze that hindsight brings'.[25] Furthermore, 'lending practice' evidence cannot, of course, be conclusive: the court remains the ultimate arbiter of what constitutes 'fault' and can always take the view that all lenders were acting imprudently in a particular type of situation.

For example, it has been suggested that the practice which developed of centralised lenders making 'non-status' loans in the late 1980s was imprudent, despite the fact that such loans were made by most lenders at the time. This was the view of Sir John Vinelott who, in *Birmingham Midshires v Parry*[26] put it as follows:

> There may be good commercial reasons which lead those engaged in a business enterprise to take risks, pressure of competition or desire to break into a new market … During the period from 1985 to 1989 the market for residential properties seemed set for an almost indefinite rise. Interest rates were high. A new type of lender, the centralised lender with no high street presence and with ready access to finance, was attracted to the field. To establish a position in the market the centralised lender was willing to lend money on a non-status mortgage—that is to rely to an excessive extent on the value of the security and, as regards the personal covenant, to rely on self-certification. That was, in my judgment, a risky course.[27]

---

[22] *UBK v Prudential Property Services* (1995) unreported, 27 November, CA, transcript, p 17 per Evans LJ.

[23] See *United Bank of Kuwait v Prudential Property* [1995] EGCS 190. However, there are no relevant authoritative statements of principle from an appropriate professional body (such as RICS guidelines) which might provide a firm foundation for a finding as to what the reasonably competent financial institution should do, or what steps it should take, to protect its interests, and so the evidence of lending experts should, it has been suggested, be approached with 'considerable circumspection': *Nyckeln Finance Co Ltd v Edward Symmons & Partners* (1996) unreported, transcript, pp 88–9.

[24] *UBK v Prudential Property Services* (1995) unreported, 27 November, transcript, p 22, per Evans LJ.

[25] *Ibid*, p 36, per Peter Gibson LJ.

[26] (1996) unreported, 23 February.

[27] Transcript, p 43. Compare *HIT Finance v Lewis & Tucker Ltd* [1993] 2 EGLR 231, 236,

However, it is clear that evidence of lending practice is an essential starting point for the assessment of contributory negligence. It is submitted that the court should approach the question by having regard to the particular type of lending involved. Lenders should be judged by reference to the prevailing standards of the lending category into which they fit. Thus, for example, secondary lenders form a distinct category with their own standards and so a plaintiff secondary lender should be judged against such standards.[28] This is quite unlike the position in the general law of negligence where, in general, the 'status' of the defendant does not affect the 'standard of care' required.

It must also be borne in mind that the relevant question is not 'Did the lender make mistakes?' but, 'Were the mistakes such that no reasonably competent lender of that category could have made them?' Mere 'errors of judgment' would not give rise to a deduction for contributory negligence.[29]

6.3.2   Contributory negligence by an agent

Contributory negligence must be based on the fault of the lender or of someone for whom he is vicariously liable. Therefore it appears that a claim for contributory negligence cannot be based on the fault of an agent or independent contractor.[30]

Thus, in *AXA Equity & Law Home Loans v Goldsack & Freeman*[31] the lender's solicitors could have deduced that the borrowers had histories of mortgage arrears but it was held that there was no contributory negligence. The solicitors would not have known what information the lender had and it was not their function to act as detectives on the lender's behalf.

6.4   The effect of contributory negligence

6.4.1   Introduction

If the court finds that there was contributory negligence, the burden of

and *Britannic Securities v Hirani Watson* (1995) unreported, transcript, p 64.

[28]   See *HIT Finance v Lewis & Tucker, ibid,* and *Nyckeln Finance Co Ltd v Stumpbrook* [1994] 2 EGLR 143, at 148D. So, in *BBL v Eagle Star* [1995] 2 All ER 769 Phillips J, at 821, said: 'The conduct of BBL has to be judged against the standard of the reasonably competent merchant bank at the time'. See also Jackson and Powell, *ibid,* 4th supp, 3–103A.

[29]   See *SAAMCO v York Montague* [1995] 2 EGLR 219, 229C; *BBL v Eagle Star, ibid,* 821, citing *Saif Ali v Sydney Mitchell & Co* [1980] AC 198, 220.

[30]   See *BFG Bank AG v Brown & Mumford* [1995] EGCS 21. It was said in *Kendall Wilson Securities v Barraclough* [1986] 1 NZLR 576, at 594, per Cooke J, that 'a lender may not normally be identified with his solicitor for the purposes of the contributory negligence legislation'. See also *Blackburn, Low & Co v Vigors* (1887) 12 App Cas 531, 538.

[31]   [1994] 1 EGLR 175.

the loss is apportioned according to the parties' relative degrees of responsibility. The court reduces the amount recoverable by such extent as it considers just and reasonable, having regard to: (1) the degree of blameworthiness; and (2) the causative potency which can be attached to the relevant conduct. In practice contributory negligence reduces to 'palm tree justice': each case is a matter of subjective assessment. It has been said that:

> ... the issue of negligence is a straightforward question of fact. Did the Plaintiffs fall short of the standards of prudence reasonably to be expected of them?[32]

This accords with the approach in other common law jurisdictions:

> The Canadian practice is to look at the 'causative conduct in terms of relative or comparative blameworthiness or culpability'. The court takes a 'common sense approach', free of 'definitions and refinements'. The degree of fault of each party is a question of fact.[33]

The only useful general guidance which can be given is that however badly the lender has looked after his own interests, the cases suggest that judges are reluctant to impose 'contributory negligence reductions' of more than 30 per cent. This appears to be the highest percentage reduction imposed in any English case in which the plaintiff has been successful on liability.[34] However, much higher percentages have been suggested, *obiter,* in cases in which the plaintiff failed on liability. Thus, in *Nyckeln Finance Co Ltd v Edward Symmons & Partners*[35] the judge said that, given the 'staggering recklessness' of the loan, a reduction of 75 per cent would have been made if the plaintiff had succeeded on liability.[36]

6.4.2   Failures directly relating to advice

Such failures have been the basis of findings of contributory negligence in a number of cases. The most well-known examples are the cases in which the lender has failed to inquire whether there is any explanation for the valuation and the sale prices being different. This failure has led

---

[32]   *United Bank of Kuwait v Prudential Property* [1995] EGCS 190; 'Thomist' logic is not appropriate to the application of the 1945 Act; *Kendall Wilson Securities v Barraclough* [1986] 1 NZLR 576, at 595, per Cooke J. See also as a recent example *Chelsea Building Society v Goddard & Smith* [1996] EGCS 157.

[33]   See Allen, *Canadian Tort Law* 5th edn, 445.

[34]   But note that reductions of 50 per cent have been made in Commonwealth cases: *Marble Developments Ltd v Pirani* (1994) 18 CCLT (2d) 229; and *Austrust Pty Ltd v Astley* (1993) 60 SASR 354.

[35]   (1996) unreported.

[36]   See also *First National Bank plc v Andrew S Taylor (Commercial) Ltd* (1995) unreported, where the judge said that he would have made a 75 per cent reduction in the plaintiff's damages had he found the defendants liable; and *P K Finans International v Andrew Downs & Co* [1992] 1 EGLR 172 (80 per cent); see below.

to damages reductions in a number of substantial cases.

Thus in *BBL v Eagle Star*[37] the valuations far exceeded the purchase prices of the various properties being lent on, and it was held that the lender should not have proceeded without an adequate explanation for this relating to the circumstances of sale. A finding of 30 per cent contributory negligence was made. In *Nyckeln Finance Co Ltd v Stumpbrook*[38] there was a finding of 20 per cent contributory negligence as some, albeit inadequate, steps had been taken to explain the discrepancy.

Similarly, where the lender obtains two valuations, one of which is lower than the other, and decides to lend in reliance upon the higher valuation, then a finding of contributory negligence may properly be made, on the basis that the lender may be thereby put on inquiry as to the reliability of the valuation. However the defendant will have to establish how the lender's failure to make inquiries caused the damage.[39]

A failure to follow up on non-negligent advice which was given could form the basis of a substantial finding of contributory negligence. For example, it was said *obiter* in *PK Finans International v Andrew Downs & Co*[40] that a failure to pass a valuation report to a solicitor when a valuer had recommended verification of his planning assumptions would have led to a finding of 80 per cent contributory negligence.[41]

A failure to inform a defendant valuer of facts relevant to the value of the property could also lead to a substantial finding of contributory negligence. An example of this would be where the plaintiff failed to show recent accounts to the valuer which would have been relevant to his valuation of the leasehold. As was said in *Craneheath Securities v York Montague*:[42]

> ... where a valuation has been given to a man and that man has, and knows he has, more information affecting the valuation than the valuer had, he is very likely to find himself at least partly at fault if he seeks to act in reliance on the valuation without first giving the valuer that information for comment.

A similar failure occurred in *SAAMCO v York Montague*[43] where the plaintiff was held to have failed to give proper or sufficiently explicit instructions to the valuer as to the basis and assumptions upon which the valuation should be made. A reduction of 25 per cent was made.

Attempts by professionals to contend that the lender was unreasonable

[37] [1995] 2 All ER 769.
[38] [1994] 2 EGLR 143.
[39] See *Cavendish Funding Ltd v Henry Spencer* (1996) unreported, 21 March, transcript, pp 16–17.
[40] [1992] 1 EGLR 172.
[41] See also *Mirage Entertainment Corp Ltd v Arthur Young* (1992) 6 NZCLC 96–577.
[42] [1994] 1 EGLR 159.
[43] [1995] 2 EGLR 219.

to rely on their advice have in general received short shrift from the courts. In *Nyckeln Finance Co Ltd v Stumpbrook Continuation Ltd*,[44] Judge Fawcus said:

> ... it lies ill in the mouth of a professional valuer, who is given a valuation for mortgage lending purposes, to say that it was unreasonable for the party to whom such valuation was given to rely on it.

This is not in fact an example of contributory negligence in the strict sense of something which the defendant does which might reduce damages but of an all or nothing defence to liability.[45]

It is sometimes argued that the lender was negligent simply for lending at a high loan-to-value ratio. This argument obviously has more force in a commercial lending situation than an ordinary domestic lending one (where up to 95 per cent loan-to-value ratios are common), but will in general fail, for a variant of the reason given by Phillips J in *BBL v Eagle Star*, namely that, while in that case 90 per cent loan-to-value was a greater proportion than was prudent, that could go to reduction of damages only if 'the risk of a fall in the market value of the property was a relevant consideration'.[46] On the other hand in *Platform Home Loans Ltd v Oyston Shipways Ltd*,[47] Jacob J made a finding of contributory negligence on the ground that lending at above 70 per cent loan-to-value ratio was not prudent in the case of non-status loans as large as £1 million.

In *BBL*, the plaintiff argued further that it was necessary, when considering the issue of contributory negligence, to take into account the fact that the lender had taken out a mortgage indemnity guarantee. The existence of such a policy obviously strengthens the overall security which the lender has protecting a loan. Phillips J held that, just as the court must disregard any receipts which a lender might have obtained under a MIG when assessing damages,[48] so the court should, when considering contributory negligence, disregard the fact that the lender had insured an element of the loan.

6.4.3 Failing to investigate the borrower's creditworthiness

The most common allegation of contributory negligence concerns failures by the lender to investigate the creditworthiness of the borrower. It was initially argued by plaintiffs that the defence of contributory negligence could not be relied upon in a case where the specific purpose of the lender in retaining the valuer was to advise on the value of the

---

[44] [1994] 2 EGLR 143.
[45] See *Davies v Idris Parry* [1988] 1 EGLR 147; *SAAMCO v York Montague, ibid*, 228.
[46] [1995] 2 All ER 769, 822.
[47] (1996) unreported, 29 July, transcript, p 7.
[48] On the principle of *res inter alios acta*; see p 97.

proposed security so as to make the strength of the borrower's covenant irrelevant. This argument was rejected in *United Bank of Kuwait v Prudential*[49] and it is now clear that defendant valuers can rely on the 1945 Act in order to reduce any damages awarded against them.[50]

The courts appear to accept that a lender should take some steps to investigate the borrower's income and creditworthiness. Even where the loan is self-certifying, a prudent lender who knows that the borrower's financial position is uncertain (eg income from his own company appears to fluctuate between £40,000 and £100,000 in a single year) should make additional enquiries and ask further questions.[51] The steps required, however, are not extensive. In both *HIT Finance Ltd v Lewis & Tucker Ltd*[52] and *United Bank of Kuwait v Prudential*[53] the trial judge found that the lender had insufficient grounds on which to doubt the borrower's creditworthiness.[54] Furthermore, in appropriate cases, taking into account (1) the purpose and time scale of the loan and (2) the margin of equity relied upon, the lender may be entitled to rely on the borrower's own statements about his finances without further investigation.

In *HIT Finance Ltd v Lewis & Tucker Ltd*,[55] Wright J, in considering *Kendall Wilson Securities v Barraclough Ltd*,[56] said:

> Somers J went on to observe: 'I have no doubt that the prudent lender would enquire into the ability of a possible borrower to meet his obligation without recourse to any proffered security'.
>
> As a statement of general principle, this remark is doubtless entirely unexceptional—but its impact upon any individual case must depend upon all the relevant circumstances. Given that it is incumbent upon the prudent lender to make *some* enquiries into the status of his prospective borrower, the nature and extent of the enquiries may vary widely according to the facts of the case. An important factor will be the margin of safety provided by the security offered.
>
> In the circumstances of the present case, even if I had found the plaintiff guilty of a want of reasonable care in the enquiries that it made into the circumstances of the loan and the substance of its borrower and the persons associated with it, I should have found it far from easy to see how any such want of care was in any way causative of the loss suffered by the Plaintiff in this case. In my judgment the overwhelming operative cause of that loss was the over-valuation of the security by the Defendant.

---

[49]   [1994] 2 EGLR 100, 105.
[50]   See also *Trade Credits Ltd v Ballieu Knight Frank (NSW) Pty Ltd* (1985) Aust Tort Rep 80-757.
[51]   See *Crédit Agricole Personal Finance v Murray* [1995] EGCS 32 (15 per cent deduction, *obiter.*)
[52]   [1993] 2 EGLR 231.
[53]   [1994] 2 EGLR 100.
[54]   See also *Nykredit Mortgage Bank plc v Edward Erdman Group Ltd* (1993) unreported, 1 October.
[55]   [1993] 2 EGLR 231.
[56]   [1986] 1 NZLR 576.

However, if the plaintiff had evidence giving it substantial reason for suspecting the honesty of the borrower, the contributory fault will be substantial.[57]

The courts have drawn a distinction between long-term finance (such as a domestic mortgage), where the lender clearly relies primarily upon the borrower meeting the repayments out of his income, and short-term bridging finance. In both *Britannic Securities & Investments Ltd v Hirani Watson*[58] and *Cavendish Funding Ltd v Henry Spencer*[59] the lenders had made short-term loans (repayable within a matter of months). The defendants argued that the lender should have investigated the ability of the borrower to repay the loan from his own resources apart from the security. In both cases, Evans-Lombe J emphasised the impracticality of the steps proposed having regard to the nature of the particular transactions. In both cases, it was plain to the plaintiff lenders that the loans were only going to be repaid either from the proceeds of a further advance or from the sale of the property. Given the nature of the loan, there was no contributory negligence.

In *United Bank of Kuwait* it was alleged that when the borrower's application for a loan was being considered the bank failed to analyse and inquire into accounts and cashflow projections of the borrower which, if they had done so, ought to have made the bank aware that the borrower was in serious financial peril and was probably unable to service the loan. The bank argued that in circumstances where (a) the bank sought security to obviate any risk in making the loan and (b) the whole purpose of retaining the services of the valuer was to establish whether the proposed security was, adequate there could be no finding of contributory negligence. Gage J preferred the evidence of the lender's expert to that of the valuer's, and, as a result, was not satisfied that the lender fell below the standards required of reasonably competent bankers.

Similarly, in *HIT Finance Ltd v Lewis & Tucker Ltd*,[60] Wright J said:

> I am not suggesting that the prudent lender, merely because he had the comfort of more than adequate security, is entitled to shut his eyes to any obviously unsatisfactory characteristics of the proposed borrower. Plainly a lender would not be acting prudently if he made a loan in circumstances where he had substantial reason for suspecting the honesty of the borrower.

Generally this will be a potent defence only if the margin of equity is narrow.[61] The narrower that margin is, the more the plaintiff will be

[57] *HIT Finance Ltd v Lewis & Tucker Ltd* [1993] 2 EGLR 231, 236.
[58] [1995] EGCS 46.
[59] (1996) unreported, 26 March, Evans-Lombe J.
[60] [1993] 2 EGLR 231, 235.
[61] See *HIT Finance Ltd v Lewis & Tucker Ltd, ibid*, 236; *Britannic Securities v Hirani Watson* (1995) unreported, transcript, p 63; *United Bank of Kuwait v Prudential* [1994] 2 EGLR 100, 109; *Cavendish Funding Ltd v Henry Spencer* (1996) unreported, 26 March, transcript, p 15.

regarded as relying on the creditworthiness of the borrower as well as on the security, so making it all the more important for it to have investigated the borrower's credit and income. It is noteworthy that, whilst in the *BBL* case the margin of equity was 10 per cent, in *HIT*[62] the margin was 25 per cent.[62a]

A lender is not guilty of contributory negligence merely because it has failed to make detailed investigations into the value of additional security. Thus, in one case, the bank had taken out personal guarantees from directors which turned out to be worthless. The judge rejected criticism of the bank for failing to investigate the financial standing of the guarantors.[63]

6.4.4   Breach of lending guidelines

Another common criticism of lenders is that they have failed to follow their own lending guidelines. This approach has not, in general, found favour with the courts.[64] As was said in *HIT Finance Ltd v Lewis & Tucker Ltd*:[65]

> It is in my judgment important to consider the precise purposes for which these rules and guidelines come into existence. Obviously a sensible commercial finance house would wish, in an ideal world, to make loans only to borrowers who would meet their obligations thereunder both as to repayment of capital and interest on time and in all respects exactly in compliance with the contractual terms so that the lender would never have to have recourse to the underlying security. It is entirely clear to me that the rules and guidelines are formulated with that very desirable object in mind. No doubt, if a credit controller in a finance house persistently ignored requirements of the kind enshrined in the guidelines, so that his company regularly had to have recourse to the underlying security in order to recoup its investment, even though the whole of its losses and expenses were covered thereby, he would be regarded with disfavour by his employers. By contrast, the whole purpose of the taking of security, and the valuation of that security, is to ensure that the lender has an adequate safety net in the event that the borrower defaults, whether that default should have been foreseeable by the lender had he taken appropriate precautions or not.

---

[62]   [1993] 2 EGLR 231.

[62a]   See also *Crédit Agricole Personal Finance v Murray* [1995] EGCS 32; referred to above at p 150.

[63]   See *BFG Bank AG v Brown & Mumford* [1995] EGCS 21—the judge said the bank was not expected to carry out a 'DTI inquiry' into their affairs.

[64]   In *Nyckeln Finance Co Ltd v Edward Symmons & Partners* (1996) unreported, the judge rejected the defendant's argument that the plaintiff's lending guidelines themselves amounted to contributory negligence (transcript, p 87).

[65]   *Ibid.*

There is some doubt as to whether breach of guidelines can ever, of itself, be a reason for making a deduction for contributory negligence. Phillips J made it clear in *BBL v Eagle Star* that he could see no relevance in allegations of this kind:

> The important issue in the case of each transaction is whether it was intrinsically prudent and I cannot see that it matters whether or not ... [a particular set of guidelines] were breached.[66]

It has, however, been suggested that breaches of lending guidelines may be relevant as a prudent lender would adopt guidelines and follow them. This issue remains unresolved.

6.4.5 Examples of findings of contributory fault

Three cases illustrate the approach taken by the court when a number of allegations of contributory negligence are found to have been established.

In *BNP Mortgages v Key Surveyors Nationwide*[67] the plaintiff was aware that there was a high risk of default by self-certifying borrowers. As a result, the plaintiff established a system of 'spot checks'. However, the plaintiff failed to carry out the 'spot checks' in that case. The judge held that, if these checks had been carried out, they would have revealed the unsatisfactory nature of the application with the result that no loan would have been made. The judge concluded:

> I am left in no doubt ... that BNP's lack of care for their own interest was causative of the damage they suffered. Clearly however their blameworthiness was markedly less than that of Key Surveyors. BNP were entitled to place much reliance on [the valuation].[68]

In these circumstances, a finding of 25 per cent contributory negligence was made.

In *SAAMCO v York Montague*[69] the lender:

(a) failed to read the report carefully enough to see that it was not really what they wanted (they wanted a valuation of the land but were given a valuation on the viability of a joint venture scheme which could be applied to the land);

(b) wrongly assessed the risk classification of the loan (in breach of their own guidelines); and

---

[66] [1995] 2 All ER 769, 829j.
[67] (1994) unreported, 20 June, HHJ Fox-Andrews.
[68] Judgment, p 38.
[69] [1995] 2 EGLR 219.

  (c) were vague in their instructions to the valuers;
and it was found that these matters contributed causatively to the plaintiff's loss. Had they not occurred no loan might have been made. The
judge made a deduction from damages for contributory negligence of
25 per cent.

In *Platform Home Loans v Oyston Shipways Ltd*[70] the lender was held to
be imprudent because:

  (a) it made a loan of £1.05 million with a loan-to-value ratio of 70
       per cent with virtually no inquiries of the borrower; and
  (b) it failed to require the borrower to complete the section of its
       application form which concerned the date and amount of the
       original purchase.

If the lender had asked about the original purchase price, it would
have discovered that the borrower had bought the house two years
earlier for £375,000 at the top of the market, whereas the defendants
stated that it was worth £1.5 million. Taking these two findings together,
Jacob J assessed the total contributory negligence at 20 per cent.

6.4.6   Contributory negligence and 'scope of duty'

Prior to the decision of the House of Lords in *BBL v Eagle Star*[71] the question of apportionment was a simple exercise: once it had been decided
that a reduction should be made the court determined the total amount
of damages recoverable and then reduced that amount by the appropriate percentage. However, as a result of the *BBL* decision, the court must
first ascertain the total loss which actually flowed from the breach and
then consider whether it falls within the 'scope of the defendant's duty'.
The question arises as to at which point any contributory negligence
reduction should be made. Should the percentage reduction be applied
to the total loss or to the 'capped' figure?

The wording of the 1945 Act suggests that the reduction should take
place after the damages have been 'capped'. Section 1(1) provides that,
if a finding of contributory negligence can be made then 'the *damages
recoverable* ... shall be reduced to such an extent as the court thinks just
and equitable' (emphasis added). Given that the law now provides that
a lender can recover damages only in respect of any damage which
falls within the scope of the duty then the reduction should be applied
to the capped figure. This point was considered in *Platform Home Loans
v Oyston Shipways Ltd*.[72] In that case the judge had found the plaintiff
contributorily negligent in two respects, firstly in relation to its general

[70] (1996) unreported, 29 July, ChD.
[71] [1996] 3 WLR 87.
[72] [1996] EGCS 146.

policy of lending on too high a loan-to-value ratio, and, secondly, in its handling of the particular transaction. The plaintiff argued that contributory fault which had nothing to do with the negligent valuation should not be taken into account and that, as a result, the judge should only take into account the contributory negligence under the second head.

This argument was rejected by Jacob J who held that the 1945 Act did not envisage such a 'subtle distinction',[73] and that all forms of contributory negligence, within the broad word 'fault' which is used at s 1 of the 1945 Act, could be taken into account when reducing a plaintiff's damages.

Secondly, the defendant argued that the reduction for 'contributory fault' should be applied after the court decided how much of the loss fell within the scope of the defendant's duty. Unfortunately, this argument was not dealt with by Jacob J in *Platform Home Loans* because all the loss suffered by the plaintiff was held to be within the scope of the defendant's duty. As a result, the plaintiff recovered its full loss, after deduction of contributory fault.

The question as to when the reduction for contributory negligence is applied is an important one which, potentially, has a substantial impact on the quantum of damages recovered in property finance cases. Take, for example, a case in which the total loss is £750,000, the amount of the overvaluation is £500,000 and there is a 30 per cent reduction for contributory negligence. If the reduction is made before considering the scope of the duty the damages will be £500,000; if it is applied afterwards the damages will be reduced to £330,000.

It is submitted that the defendant's argument in *Platform Home Loans* is correct. The proper approach is to take contributory negligence into account after the court has decided how much of the loss falls within the scope of the duty. If all the loss falls within the scope of the duty then the reduction is applied to that figure. If only part of the loss falls within the scope of the duty then the reduction is applied to that part of the loss.

6.5 Contribution proceedings

6.5.1 Introduction

It is common for a lender to have causes of action against both a solicitor and valuer (and possibly accountants). It is not infrequent that proceedings are brought against both the valuer and solicitor retained in

---

[73] Transcript, p 42.

the original loan transaction.

Two questions arise:

(a) Firstly, if, for any reason, the lender chooses to bring proceedings against only one professional, what steps can the particular party sued take to seek contribution from any third parties?

(b) Secondly, if both valuer and solicitor are jointly sued, and both are found liable to the lender, how should the total quantum of damages awarded to the lender be apportioned as between the two defendants?

6.5.2   The Civil Liability (Contribution) Act 1978

The Civil Liability (Contribution) Act 1978 ('the 1978 Act') considerably extended the existing common law right (as modified, in relation to tortfeasors, by s 6(1)(c) of the Law Reform (Married Women and Tortfeasors) Act 1935) to seek contribution, a right which had been described as 'bottomed and fixed on general principles of justice [which did] not spring from contract, though contract may qualify it'.[74]

Thus, prior to the 1978 Act there was, whether at common law or under the 1935 Act, no right of contribution as between a person liable in contract and a tortfeasor, even though liable for the same damage. Nor could there be contribution between two persons liable to the same plaintiff for the same damage but under separate contracts.[75]

Section 1 of the 1978 Act provides that:

> ... any person liable in respect of any damage suffered by another person may recover contribution from any other person liable in respect of the same damage (whether jointly with himself or otherwise).

The 1978 Act in effect created a statutory cause of action in its own right[76] which allows joint wrongdoers, whether they be joint contractors, joint tortfeasors, joint debtors, joint trustees, or joint sureties, to seek contribution *inter se*. However the Act is drawn in the widest terms, so that the person seeking contribution simply has to show that the person against whom contribution is sought is liable to the plaintiff in respect of the same damage. The basis of the liability is irrelevant: 'A person is liable in respect of any damage for the purposes of this Act if the person who suffered it ... is entitled to recover compensation from him in respect of that damage (whatever the legal basis of his liability whether tort, breach of contract, breach of otherwise)'—s 6(1) of the 1978 Act.

The liability of the 'contributor' and 'contributee' need not arise out of breach of the same duty, or be in relation to the same cause of action.

---

[74] *Dering v Winchelsea* (1787) 1 Cox 318.
[75] *McDonnell v Lynch-Robinson* [1957] NI 70.
[76] See *The Supreme Court Practice* (1997), 16/1/3.

Thus in *UCB Bank v Dundas & Wilson, CS*,[77] where the lender brought proceedings against the solicitors who had allegedly failed to tell the lender that the land was subject to a serious risk of subsidence, the solicitors were held entitled to issue third party contribution proceedings against the valuers who, although instructed by the borrower, owed a duty in negligence to the lender. The fact that the solicitors' duty to the lender was founded on the contractual relationship between them whilst the valuer's duty was founded on a tortious duty did not prevent the issue of the third party notice.

More recently it has been held that a person liable to a plaintiff for breach of contract may seek contribution against a person liable to the plaintiff under a restitutionary claim: under s 6(1) liability to contribute is not dependent on any breach of duty or default.[78]

However, care must be taken in identifying the precise 'damage' in respect of which the various parties are liable. In *Birse Construction Ltd v Haiste Ltd*[79] a company (B) constructed a reservoir in breach of contract. The employer (A) brought proceedings which were settled on the basis of B building a second reservoir. B brought proceedings against the consulting engineers (H) who had been retained for the performance of the original contract, seeking contribution for its losses. H in turn brought contribution proceedings against an engineer (N) employed by A. The question arose whether both H and N were liable in respect of the same damage. The Court of Appeal held that the damage suffered by A was physical, whereas that suffered by B was financial and therefore H could not claim contribution from N in respect of B's losses.

The right to seek contribution may be exercised even where the party sued has compromised the main claim: s 1(2) of the 1978 Act. Thus in *Bristol & West Building Society v Christie*[80] solicitors were sued by the lender. The claim was compromised and the lender assigned its claim against the valuers to the solicitors who then brought contribution proceedings against the valuers. In those circumstances the initial defendant in effect must establish what the plaintiff would have had to show had it brought independent proceedings against the party against whom contribution is sought. The initial defendant should seek contribution in respect of the compromise figure, not the amount of damages which the plaintiff could have obtained had he proceeded to trial (so that the person against whom contribution proceedings are brought can take the benefit of any negotiated reduction). This is explicitly recognised by the wording of s 1(2) of the 1978 Act which envisages separate contribution proceedings being taken relating

---

[77] 1989 SLT 243 (a Scottish case).
[78] *Friends Provident Life Office v Hillier Parker* [1995] 4 All ER 260.
[79] [1996] 1 PNLR 1.
[80] [1996] CILL 1139.

to the 'payment in respect of which the contribution is sought'.[81] However where the person against whom contribution is sought seeks to argue that the plaintiff's claim overall was less than the compromise figure then it can defend on that basis independently of any liability defence: so in *Christie* the valuers argued that insurance monies received by the plaintiff under a MIG would have reduced their damages.

Moreover the party against whom contribution proceedings are brought after compromise of the main action can defend the claim not simply on the basis that it would not have been found liable to the plaintiff, but also, in limited circumstances, on the basis that the party seeking contribution was not liable either. However, if the party seeking contribution has compromised the claim with *bona fides*, then it will be entitled to recover contribution:

> ... without regard to whether or not he himself is or ever was liable in respect of the damage, provided, however, that he would have been liable assuming that the factual basis of the claim against him could be established.[82]

It is not clear how this provision sits with the earlier statutory requirement, contained in s 1(2), that a party who seeks contribution after compromise of the main action must have been 'liable [in respect of the damage in question] immediately before he made or was ordered to make the payment in respect of which the contribution is sought'. However it is clear that the person seeking contribution who has settled the main action need not show that he was liable to the plaintiff.[82a]

6.5.3 Procedure

The means by which the defendant may seek to recover contribution from a non-party is through the third party notice procedure (RSC Ord 16, r 1), or, if the party is a co-defendant, through a contribution notice (RSC Ord 16, r 8). However, where solicitor and valuer are jointly sued as tortfeasors liable in respect of the same damage (the usual case), it will not be necessary for each to issue a contribution notice against the other.[83] The usual practice is for a letter to be written by a defendant to the other defendants expressing his intention to seek an apportionment in the event of judgment being given against both (or all) defendants. If that eventuality arises the judge will be asked after judgment to apportion responsibility between the defendants.[84]

However where one of the defendants seeks discovery or to administer interrogatories against another, then a contribution notice

---

[81] See also *Comyn Ching v Oriental Tube* (1979) 17 BLR 47, applying *Biggin & Co Ltd v Permanite Ltd* [1951] 2 KB 314.

[82] 1978 Act, s 1(4).

[82a] See also *Arab Monetary Fund v Hashim* (No 8) (1993) *The Times*, 22 June.

[83] See *The Supreme Court Practice* (1997), commentary at 16/8/2.

[84] See *Croston v Vaughan* [1938] 1 KB 540.

should be served.[85] Where the party seeking contribution has already settled the main claim then it can take separate contribution proceedings against the party against whom it seeks contribution, relying upon the statutory cause of action contained in s 1(1) of the 1978 Act.

Often the reason why the lender sues one professional but not another is because the limitation period has expired against one, but not the other (indeed, in general this will be because the lender can take advantage of s 14A of the Limitation Act 1980 against the solicitor, but not against the valuer). Where a direct action between the lender and a party who is liable in respect of the same damage is statute-barred, what effect does this have upon the person seeking contribution? The answer lies in s 10 of the Limitation Act 1980, which provides that where under s 1 of the 1978 Act a person becomes entitled to a right to recover contribution in respect of any damage from any other person, then 'no action shall be brought after the expiration of two years from the date on which that right accrued'.[86] The right to recover contribution will arise where either judgment has been given against the person entitled to recover contribution or where that person has compromised the main action. The effect of this section is to extend the period of time for which a person is at risk of being sued in respect of damage for which it is liable.

It may be noted that a frequent step taken by negligent professionals, when action is brought against them by lenders, is to compromise the claim on terms that the benefit of the mortgage interest owned by the lender is assigned to the professional. The professional can then attempt to claw back some part of the compensation paid from the borrower, who of course will remain personally liable under the mortgage contract. Of course, where the lender brings proceedings against the allegedly negligent professional prior to borrower default or sale of the security,[87] the defendant could seek contribution from the borrower as liable in respect of the same damage.

Where the lender has successfully obtained judgment against both valuer and solicitor, then, although the judgment will be in a single sum, each defendant will be jointly and severally liable to the plaintiff for the whole amount. Therefore, if the plaintiff demands payment from the insurer of one of the defendants in the whole amount, that payment cannot properly be withheld. However, as an ancillary issue in any case where professional defendants are jointly sued in respect of the same damage, the court will be asked to apportion liability on a percentage basis as between the defendants. This apportionment will be of no interest to the plaintiff, though the usual result will be, in practice, for the defendants to pay over directly to the plaintiff sums proportionate

---

[85]   *Clayson v Rolls Royce* [1950] 1 KB 746.   [86]   Section 10(1).
[87]   See, for instance, *Eagle Star v Gale and Power* (1955) 166 EG 37.

to the percentage apport of the full judgment sum. However, in the event of one of the defendants being called upon to pay the full amount, the apportionment percentages (which will form part of the judgment), will allow that defendant to obtain an indemnity from a co-defendant for the percentage amount for which he is liable, and, if necessary, to maintain a contribution action.

6.5.4   Apportionment under the 1978 Act

On what principles does the court act in deciding how to determine the amount of the contribution sought from a party or how to apportion liability between joint defendants? Section 2(1) of the 1978 Act simply requires the court to make an apportionment having regard to the justice and equity of the case having regard to *the extent of the responsibility of the person from whom contribution is sought for the damage in question.* Although s 2(1) specifically relates to contribution proceedings, the principle set out applies equally to cases where apportionment is sought after judgment as between co-defendants where the contribution procedure has not been followed, whether by third party notice or by separate contribution proceedings.[88]

The court's jurisdiction to apportion responsibility as between the parties is qualified by s 2(3) of the 1978 Act which limits the amount the person from whom contribution is sought may be required to pay in respect of the damage to the amount he could have been liable for had proceedings been brought against him directly by the person who suffered the original damage, having regard, amongst other considerations, to any reduction which would have been made pursuant to s 1 of the Law Reform (Contributory Negligence) Act 1945. Thus if a judgment in the sum of £100,000 has been awarded against a solicitor in a claim brought by a lender, and the solicitor subsequently takes contribution proceedings against the valuer, the valuer is entitled to show that, had it been sued direct by the lender then any damages awardable against it would have fallen to be reduced by, say, 30 per cent because of the lender's contributory negligence. If this argument is accepted by the court in the contribution proceedings then the maximum amount which the solicitor could recover in the contribution proceedings against the valuer would be £70,000, that being the maximum amount the lender could have obtained by way of direct action. It would require very special circumstances for the valuer to be required to make contribution for the full amount of his maximum liability to the lender to the solicitor in such a case.

There is only one fully reported case relating to apportionment as between professional defendants in a property finance negligence case.

---

[88]   See *Croston v Vaughan* [1938] 1 KB 540.

In *Anglia Hastings & Thanet Building Society v House & Son*[89] the defendant valuers were sued by the plaintiff building society for negligent
valuations. They admitted liability and issued a third party notice
against the solicitors who had acted for the lender, claiming contribution. The valuers' own expert conceded that the valuations which had
been provided were 'wildly wrong'. Bingham J held that although the
plaintiff would not have sustained any loss if either of the professionals had not breached its duty, nonetheless the solicitor should be liable
for 70 per cent of the damage sustained on the ground that its default
involved a failure to disclose a conflict of interest, not, as with the valuer,
simple negligence. The solicitor had acted not merely for both the borrowers and the lender, but also for the vendor:

> ... the default of the [valuer] was an act of pure misjudgment in the course
> of a relatively brief involvement in this transaction. There was in their
> case no question of putting themselves in a position where their interest
> and their duty conflicted.

While the apportionment in the *Anglia Hastings* case was certainly
justified on its facts, note should be taken of the Court of Appeal's decision in *Bristol & West Building Society v Mothew*, where Millett LJ held
that even though a solicitor could be described as a fiduciary, the usual
breach, involving as it did carelessness and negligence, rather than dis-
honesty or the calculated putting of one principal's interest before
another's (where the solicitor was acting for both lender and borrower),
could not sensibly be described as a breach of trust or fiduciary duty,
but simply gave rise to tortious/contractual liability. In future, unless
breaches of fiduciary duties can be shown in the circumstances outlined by Millett LJ, the solicitor's responsibility might be more force-
fully argued to be only equal to the valuer's. In *Bristol & West Building
Society v Christie*[90] the judge split contribution on a 50/50 basis, on the
simple basis that if either party had been non-negligent the lender would
not have lent.[91] Occasionally a complete indemnity will be awarded.[92]

In the light of the House of Lords decision in *BBL v Eagle Star*[93] the
potential extent of the liability of valuers will in certain circumstances
be narrower than that of solicitors in relation to the same transaction.
This disparity, just as the availability of a contributory negligence allegation to one, but not both, professionals will undoubtedly affect the

---

[89] (1981) 260 EG 1128. Another case is *Chelsea Building Society v Goddard & Smith* [1996]
      EGCS 157.
[90] [1996] CILL 1139.
[91] For other examples of apportionment in different spheres see *Computastaff Ltd v
      Ingledew Brown Bennison & Garrett* (1983) 268 EG 906; *Bell v Holmes* [1956] 1 WLR
      1359; *Baker v Willoughby* [1970] AC 467.
[92] *Lister v Romford Ice and Cold Storage Co Ltd* [1957] AC 555, 579.
[93] [1996] 3 WLR 87.

apportionment exercise. On the other hand where the negligence of both the valuer and solicitor relates to the valuation (for example where as in *Mortgage Express Ltd v Bowerman & Partners Ltd* [94] the solicitor fails to report a disparity between the purchase price and the price paid by an intermediate purchaser), then, applying *BBL*, the scope of both professionals' duty is the same. The approach to apportionment suggested by Professor Dugdale is convincing:

> As [the valuer] had the primary responsibility for the valuation, he should bear the heavier portion of the liability, perhaps 70 per cent as against 30 per cent for [the solicitor]. [95]

---

[94]   [1996] 3 All ER 836.
[95]   [1995] JBL 533, 539.

7 Experts

7.1 Introduction

In any professional negligence action the court has to decide whether the conduct of the professional fell below the standard of care of the reasonably careful and skilful professional practising in the same discipline. In general a court will not be prepared to criticise the conduct of a person practising in a highly specialised area unless it has the benefit of an expert who can give the court an opinion as to the proper conduct of a professional in the particular circumstances.[1]

The more specialised the professional field in which the case arises the more dependent the judge will be upon the expert evidence which is adduced. However it is clear that the court is not bound to accept the evidence given. In most cases there will be a conflict of evidence. Even where no conflict arises, the court remains the final arbiter of whether an act or omission is, in law, negligent.

In this chapter we begin by considering the nature of expertise and the duties of the expert to the court. We then consider the difficult question of the issues on which expert evidence is admissible. In particular, we consider the contentious problems of how far experts can go in expressing opinions as to whether or not the defendant was negligent. We then consider expert evidence in valuers' and solicitors' cases respectively. The final section deals with procedural issues relating to expert evidence.

7.2 The nature and ambit of expert evidence

7.2.1 Expertise

There is no statutory definition of what criteria need to be fulfilled before a person may be termed an expert. Section 4(1) of the Civil Evidence Act 1972 ('the 1972 Act') appears to suggest that expertise might be derived from 'knowledge or experience'.[2] For the purpose of

---

[1] See, generally, Hodgkinson, *Expert Evidence: Law and Practice* 1st edn (1990).
[2] See also *Longley (James) and Co v South-West Thames Regional Health Authority* (1983) 25 BLR 56, 62.

admissibility, there can be no precise test as to who is an 'expert' and who is not. In practice the question is not one of admissibility but of weight. Nevertheless, when the court is satisfied that a person purporting to give expert evidence has no credentials, it will exclude his evidence entirely.[3] Section 3(1) of the 1972 Act makes expert evidence admissible only on any relevant matter 'on which [the person] is qualified to give expert evidence'.

In a professional negligence case, the expert must be qualified in the same field as the defendant. In a negligent valuation case, where a civil engineer and an architect gave 'expert' evidence as to the surveyor's conduct, Auld J disregarded such evidence:

> However competent they may be in their respective professions, [they] cannot speak with authority on what is to be expected of the ordinarily competent surveyor.[4]

In *Investors in Industry Commercial Property v South Bedfordshire District Council*[5] an architect's evidence was preferred to that of three engineers, because while they were expressing opinions in a 'profession other than their own', the architect's was the only directly relevant evidence.

7.2.2   The relationship of the expert to the court

The expert must be careful not to lose his objectivity or become partisan in the adversarial process. Similarly the lawyers who instruct the expert must ensure that they do not pressure or persuade him to take a position on paper which does not reflect his actual view. The over-zealous expert will not, in the end, promote his client's interests. As Lord Wilberforce said in *Whitehouse v Jordan*:[6]

> It is necessary that expert evidence presented to the Court should be, and be seen to be, the independent product of the expert, uninfluenced as to form or content by the exigencies of litigation. To the extent that it is not, the evidence is likely to be not only incorrect but self-defeating.

In *National Justice Compania Naviera SA v Prudential Assurance Co*,[7] Cresswell J gave a summary of the duties and responsibilities of an expert witness which can be summarised as follows:

(a)   the expert evidence should be, and be seen to be, the independent product of the expert, and should not be influenced by the exigencies of the litigation in which it is given;[8]

---

3   See *R v Silverlock* [1894] 2 QB 766, 769.
4   *Whalley v Roberts* [1990] 1 EGLR 164.
5   [1986] 1 All ER 787, 808–9.   6   [1981] 1 WLR 246.
7   [1993] 2 Lloyd's Rep 68.
8   See *Kerridge v James Abbott & Partners* [1992] 2 EGLR 162. See also *Alliance & Leicester Building Society v Edgestop Ltd (No 3)* [1994] 2 EGLR 229.

(b) the expert should act as an independent assistant to the court whose duty is to provide an objective unbiased opinion on matters which are within the expertise of the witness;

(c) the expert should never assume the role of advocate in the cause of his client;

(d) the facts or assumptions upon which the opinion of the expert is based should be stated, along with the material facts or matters which could detract from the concluded opinion;

(e) the expert should make it clear when a question or issue falls outside the ambit of his expertise;

(f) if insufficient data is available in order to research properly a particular part of the opinion, then that deficiency should be clearly stated and also it should be indicated that any opinion reached is provisional;

(g) if, after exchange of reports, the expert changes his mind on a material matter, then the change of mind should be communicated to the other side through the legal representatives without delay and, if appropriate, to the court; and

(h) all documents and exhibits referred to in the expert evidence should be exchanged at the same time as the reports themselves.[9]

7.3 The issues on which expert evidence is admissible

7.3.1 The limits of expert evidence

Section 3(1) of the 1972 Act allows expert evidence to be adduced on 'any relevant matter'. By s 3(3) 'relevant matter' includes 'an issue in the proceedings in question'. The boom in the 'expert industry', with the emergence of people purporting to be expertly qualified to give evidence on all manner of subjects has been met with recent reaffirmations by the courts of the extent of that principle. As was said in *Liddell v Middleton*:[10]

> An expert is only qualified to give expert evidence on a relevant matter, if his knowledge and expertise relate to a matter *which is outside the knowledge and experience of a layman*.

This case concerned a road accident. The plaintiff adduced evidence from an 'expert' who gave his views, on the basis of the eyewitness evidence, that the defendant had been negligent. The objection to the

---

9   See further *Cala Homes (South) Ltd v Alfred McAlpine Homes East Ltd* [1995] FSR 818; and *Mount Banking Corporation v Brian Cooper & Co* [1992] EGLR 142, where the judge described the evidence of one expert as being 'unbending to the point of unreasonableness and somewhat dogmatic'; and see Edenborough, "Experts in Court" (1995) 139 SJ Supp 18.

10 [1996] PIQR 36, 41, per Stuart-Smith LJ.

expert evidence was that it was evidence which was about matters within the province of the judge on which he did not require the assistance of an expert. Although the judge held that the evidence related to a 'relevant matter' it was of little or no probative value and so was inadmissible. Moreover it was irrelevant what the 'expert' thought, when the judge could perfectly easily come to his own conclusions.[11] As a result, the Court of Appeal held that the expert's evidence was wholly irrelevant and therefore inadmissible. The question of whether the defendant was negligent or not was a matter for the judge based on the evidence and on such inferences as he drew from the primary facts found. Such 'expert evidence' involved a usurpation of the judge's role: 'We do not have trial by expert in this country: we have trial by judge'.[12]

The same point has been made in *Smoothysigns v Metro Products (Accessories & Leisure) Ltd*[13] where the judge held that there was no need for expert evidence in relation to a simple patent. As Lawton LJ said in a criminal case:

> An expert's opinion is admissible to furnish the court with scientific information which is likely to be outside the experience and knowledge of a judge or jury. If on the proven facts a judge and jury can form their own conclusions without help, then the opinion of an expert is unnecessary. In such a case if it is given dressed up in scientific jargon it may make judgment more difficult.[14]

The question was also considered in the recent property finance negligence case of *United Bank of Kuwait v Prudential Property Services*.[15] Evans LJ said:

> The nature and permissible scope of expert evidence varies widely. In all cases it is admissible to inform the court of relevant practices in an area where the conduct on the particular occasion is said to have been negligent. In other words, such as no reasonably competent practitioner would undertake. Sometimes, however, it may be unnecessary so to inform the court. An obvious example is in the case of a motor accident where private cars and pedestrians are involved. It might be otherwise, however, if a specialist vehicle was involved in the particular case. Another example might be the straightforward need to translate a document from a foreign language. Evidence might be unnecessary in the case of even elementary French, whereas it would almost certainly be necessary in the case of even elementary Mandarin Chinese. The object throughout and always is that the Court should reach a fully informed decision and by way of comparison one might refer to the kind of expert evidence in a personal injury road accident case which, for example, might explain what can be deduced

---

[11]   See Hodgkinson, *ibid*, pp 121 *ff*, and *Cross and Tapper on Evidence* 8th edn, pp 545 *ff*.
[12]   *Ibid*, at 43.
[13]   [1995] 10 EIPR D-289.
[14]   *R v Turner* [1975] QB 834, 841.
[15]   [1995] EGCS 190 .

from certain tyre marks or other real evidence after the road accident.[16]

Jacob J made the same point in *Routestone v Minories Finance Ltd*:[17]

> You do not need an expert to tell you whether or not someone should have sounded their horn or driven slower.

But where the expert evidence relates to the experience of practitioners in a specialised field, the court will not be able to rely on its own experience and the evidence will be admissible.

Parties who adduce irrelevant or unnecessary expert witness evidence should expect to be penalised in costs. The taxing master has power under RSC Ord 62, r 12 to disallow costs unreasonably incurred.[18]

7.3.2 Expert evidence of 'negligence'

In a number of cases, defendants have sought to challenge the admissibility of expert evidence on wider grounds. In the *United Bank of Kuwait* case one of the issues which arose was whether the plaintiff lender had been guilty of contributory negligence by failing to properly investigate the borrower's ability to service the loan. The defendant argued that the opinions of experts on the question of whether or not the plaintiff was negligent or not were strictly inadmissible: the expert's role was limited to informing the court of current practice in the relevant areas of expertise.[19] This argument was rejected by the Court of Appeal in the following terms:

> The decision whether or not there was negligence is always one for the Court. So the question raised by [counsel's] submission is this: can there never be cases where the expert can say what he would have done or not done or would have expected to have been done if he had been placed in the relevant situation? Clearly there are cases where such evidence is admitted. One might say that it happens every day, especially in medical cases where, for example, an allegation of negligence is made against a surgeon. It may be that in practice this kind of evidence would be indistinguishable, although not always necessarily so, from the expert witnesses' evidence of what current good practice required. Section 3 of the Civil Evidence Act 1972 establishes that opinion evidence of this kind is properly admissible.[20]

The defendant's argument in *United Bank of Kuwait* involved a resurrection of the debate as to whether an expert is entitled to give evidence on the 'ultimate issue' in a case.[20a] It has often been suggested that an expert cannot give evidence 'on the very question which the

---

[16] Transcript, p 6.
[17] (1996) unreported, 16 May.
[18] In *Liddell v Middleton*, Stuart-Smith LJ actively encouraged the use of this power.
[19] Citing *Boyce v Rendells* [1983] 2 EGLR 146, 149, per Lawton LJ; *Midland Bank Trust Co Ltd v Hett, Stubbs & Kemp* [1979] Ch 384, 402, per Oliver J. See below at p 172.
[20] Transcript, pp 6–7, per Evans LJ.
[20a] See generally Cross and Tapper, *ibid*, p 552.

court has to decide'.[21] In other words, applying this argument in professional negligence cases, an expert cannot say that, in his opinion, the defendant has been negligent.

It is now established that this argument cannot be sustained. The evidence of experts *is* admissible on the very issue which the court has to decide. In *Glaverbel SA v British Coal Corporation*[22] it was held that the 'supposed rule' to the contrary had been abrogated by s 3 of the Civil Evidence Act 1972.[23] The 1972 Act was passed following the 17th Report of the Law Reform Committee[24] which specifically recommended that expert opinion on the ultimate question should be admissible.

This decision was followed by Jacob J in *Routestone v Minories Finance Ltd*.[25] In that case the plaintiff's expert refused to state in evidence that he considered that the defendant estate agents had fallen below the proper standard of a competent estate agent. As a result, the plaintiff sought to exclude this aspect of his own expert's evidence on the basis that, since it went to the 'ultimate question', it was inadmissible. Rejecting the argument, the judge drew a distinction between evidence as to what was the legal test of negligence in any given field of professional activity (which is solely a matter for the court), and evidence of the type which the plaintiff's expert had given:

> It by no means follows that the court must follow it [that is, the evidence as to whether there has been a breach of duty]. On its own (unless uncontested) it would be a 'mere bit of empty rhetoric'. What really matters in most cases is the reasons given for the opinion. As a practical matter a well constructed expert's report containing opinion evidence sets out the opinion and the reasons for it. If the reasons stand up the opinion does, if not, not. What happens if the evidence is regarded as inadmissible is that expert's reports simply try to creep up to the opinion without openly giving it. They insinuate rather than explicate.[26]

Jacob J pointed out that it was useful, in practice, for everybody to know whether the expert took the view that the defendant had been negligent.

It has also been suggested that there is something objectionable in principle to an expert stating what he would have done in the relevant situation. In *United Bank of Kuwait v Prudential Property* the question was posed:

> ... can there never be cases where the expert can say what he would have done if had been placed in the relevant situation?[27]

21 See, for example, *Midland Bank Trust Co Ltd v Hett, Stubbs & Kemp* [1979] Ch 384, 402.
22 [1995] RPC 254.
23 Per Staughton LJ, at 277, lines 9–29.
24 Cmnd 4489 (1970).
25 (1996) unreported, 16 May, ChD; see also *Molnlycke v Proctor & Gamble (No 5)* [1994] RPC 49, 113.
26 Transcript, p 11.   27   Transcript, p 6D.

It was held that there were clearly cases in which such evidence was admissible[28] but that it was a question of fact and degree.

Those opposing the admission of such evidence have often relied on a *dictum* of Oliver J in *Midland Bank Trust Co Ltd v Hett, Stubbs & Kemp*[29] to the effect that:

> ... evidence which really amounts to no more that an expression of opinion by a particular practitioner of what he thinks that he would have done had he been placed, hypothetically and without the benefit of hindsight, in the position of the defendants is of little assistance to the court.

However, this does not appear to be an objection of principle to the reception of such evidence. In *Routestone*, Jacob J suggested that such evidence was 'of little assistance' because it was not directed to the relevant question, namely: 'was the conduct such that no reasonably well-informed and competent practitioner in this type of practice could have made?' If the expert focuses not on what *he* would have done but on what a *reasonably competent practitioner* would have done, the evidence is potentially highly relevant.

7.4   Evidence in valuers' cases

7.4.1   Introduction

In a valuer's negligence case the plaintiff must adduce expert evidence that a valuation is (1) wrong and (2) negligently prepared. Such evidence is a precondition for a finding of negligence:

> A valuer will only be liable if other qualified valuers, who cannot be expected to be harsh on their fellow professionals, consider that taking into consideration the nature of the work for which the valuer is paid and the object of that work, nevertheless he has been guilty of an error which an average valuer, in the same circumstances, would not have made ...[30]

Similarly in a case involving allegations of negligence against an architect it was said that:

> Expert evidence from suitably qualified professional persons is, in our judgment, admissible to show what competent architects in the position of [the third party architects] could reasonably have been expected to know and do in their position at the relevant time. Indeed, in our judgment, there could be no question of the court condemning them for professional negligence ... unless there were appropriate expert evidence to support the allegation that their conduct fell below the standard which might reasonably be expected of an ordinarily competent architect.[31]

---

28   *Ibid*, p 6D–E.
29   [1979] Ch 384, 402.
30   Per Lord Templeman in *Smith v Eric S Bush* [1990] 1 AC 831, 851.
31   *Investors in Industry Commercial Properties v South Bedfordshire District Council* [1986] 1 All ER 787, 808. See also *Worboys v Acme Investments Ltd* (1969) 4 BLR 13, 139.

Both passages show that courts are not prepared to conclude that a person was negligent in cases concerning the conduct of professionals in specialised disciplines without the guidance of expert evidence.

A good example of this attitude is *Strover v Harrington*[32] where a purchaser's surveyor was told, wrongly, by the vendor that the property had mains drainage, whereas in fact it was served by a septic tank. Relying on this statement and without verifying its truth, the surveyor reported to his client that the property had mains drainage. The purchaser did not adduce any expert evidence relating to the surveyor's omission to qualify his report or his reliance on the vendor's statement, but simply asserted that the surveyor's conduct was self-evidently wrong. His action against the surveyor failed. The judge held that, in the absence of expert evidence, it was not even necessary for him to decide the question of whether the surveyor had been negligent:

> As a professional man [the surveyor] can only be held liable for negligence in the conduct of his profession if he acted in a way which no surveyor of ordinary skill would be guilty of, if acting with ordinary care. No expert evidence was led as to the practice of careful surveyors, and the burden is on the purchasers to prove negligence. Therefore, in my judgment, there is no evidence on which I could hold [the surveyor] to have been negligent, even if, contrary to my inclinations, I thought he had been.[33]

This position is an acknowledgment that judges, being lawyers (and not doctors, surveyors, accountants, etc), cannot in general presume to know whether certain acts or omissions fall below the standard of the ordinarily competent professional. Nonetheless to the extent that the 'ultimate question' (that is, whether the act or omission constitutes negligence sounding in damages) is a legal, not a factual, question, and remains solely within the province of the judge, it is submitted that this approach is wrong. However, the thrust of these passages is clear, and is borne out in practice: many professional negligence cases (and this is especially true of valuers' negligence cases) are won or lost by the cogency and strength (or otherwise) of the expert witness(es) called by the parties.

7.4.2   Areas of expert valuation evidence

The expert in a valuer's negligence case will be commonly asked to give evidence relating to various matters:

(a) what the actual value of the property was at the time of the valuation;

(b) the highest value which a reasonably competent valuer could

---

[32]   [1988] Ch 390.
[33]   At 405.

have attributed to the property at the time of the valuation, and
the 'margin of error' that is appropriate for the particular
property;

(c) any particular facts and considerations which the valuer took
into account in valuing the property which a reasonably competent valuer should have disregarded or to which he should have
given less weight;

(d) any particular facts and considerations which a competent valuer
should have taken into account in valuing the property which
were not taken into account or were given insufficient weight;

(e) the nature and extent of any defects which were present in the
property at the time of the valuation; and

(f) whether a reasonably competent valuer producing the type of
report which was in fact produced should have detected those
defects at the time when the valuation was carried out.

7.4.3   Proving comparables

One issue which has given rise to difficulty is that of the admissibility
of the evidence which will be relied upon by any expert who is called
in a valuer's negligence case. Expert valuers called by the parties to
litigation will generally rely upon comparables in giving their opinion
of the true value of the property at a given date. In *English Exporters
(London) Ltd v Eldonwall Ltd*[34] the judge distinguished between the *opinion* evidence given by a valuer (which would inevitably involve the
expert drawing from his general experience, which would be derived
from textbooks, journals and other hearsay sources) and *factual* evidence,
where the normal rules relating to hearsay evidence applied. The effect
of this distinction was that the expert could not specifically adduce evidence of comparable transactions of which he did not have direct,
firsthand knowledge.

The strict enforcement of this rule would create considerable difficulties in having specifically to prove separate comparables. However
in *BBL v Eagle Star*, the defendants insisted that the lender plaintiff
should be put to strict proof of any comparables upon which they relied.
Phillips J[35] distinguished *Eldonwall* and held that, given that the valuer,
when conducting his primary task of valuing property, must have regard
to 'market intelligence which is hearsay', the court, when considering
whether the valuation was negligent:

> … not only may but must have regard to the hearsay material that a com-
> petent valuer could and should have had regard to when performing the
> valuation.

[34] [1973] 1 Ch 415.
[35] In an unreported interlocutory decision, 26 February 1993.

In a valuer's negligence case comparables are not adduced for the purpose of proving that a particular property sold for a particular amount at a particular time, but that such a comparable was available to the valuer and should have both been considered by him and influenced him.

On that basis alone *Eldonwall* may be distinguished in valuers' negligence cases. But the Court of Appeal in *Abbey National Mortgages v Key Surveyors Nationwide*[36] went further and refused to accept that *any* valuation expert is confined to giving evidence based only on comparables of which he has direct firsthand knowledge.

7.5   Expert evidence in solicitor cases

The admissibility of expert evidence in solicitors' negligence cases is a matter of some controversy. The difficulties probably spring from the fact that, unlike in other categories of professional negligence, the conduct being impugned is that of a lawyer. As a result, courts have shown themselves to be far less willing to admit evidence of proper practice in relation to particular transactions involving solicitors, precisely because judges have taken the view that they, as lawyers, are able to consider the question of whether another lawyer has breached the standard of care owed, without the assistance of expert evidence which will, necessarily, come from lawyers.

This view received its first modern exposition in *Midland Bank Trust Co Ltd v Hett, Stubbs & Kemp*[37] where Oliver J said, of evidence from practising solicitors:

> I doubt the value, or even the admissibility of this sort of evidence ... The extent of the legal duty in a given situation must, I think, be a question of law for the court. Clearly if there is some practice in a particular profession, some accepted standard of conduct which is laid down by a professional institute or sanctioned by common usage, evidence of that can and ought to be received. But evidence which really amounts to no more than an expression of opinion by a practitioner of what he thinks that he would have done had he been placed, hypothetically and without the benefit of hindsight, in the position of defendants, is of little assistance to the court, whilst evidence of the witnesses' view of what, as a matter of law, the solicitor's duty was in the particular circumstances of the case is, I should have thought, inadmissible, for that is the very question which it is the court's function to decide.

This approach was followed by the Court of Appeal in *Bown v Gould & Swayne*[38] in which the judge's decision to refuse the plaintiff leave to call the evidence of a conveyancing expert was upheld. The submission

36   [1996] 3 All ER 184.
37   [1979] Ch 384.
38   [1996] PNLR 130.

that the evidence was a 'matter of practice' was rejected. Simon Brown LJ commented:

> I entirely share the view of the judge below that ... the evidence here sought to be adduced falls foul of Oliver J's dictum. It would amount to no more than an expression of opinion by the expert, either as to what he himself would have done, which could not assist, or as to what he thinks should have been done, which would have been the very issue for the Judge to determine.[39]

Millett LJ stated that good practice in investigating title is a matter of law, saying that:

> ... the practice of investigating title has settled down sufficiently to be well established and recorded in the textbooks. If it is necessary to assist the Judge to understand the proper machinery for the deduction and investigation of title, the proper way to do it is to cite the textbooks such as Emmett, Farrand, Williams and Dart, if necessary supplemented by Law Society opinions. In fact, this is a straightforward case in which I doubt that even such references would be necessary. I deplore the suggestion that it is either helpful or necessary to call evidence from high street solicitors whose individual practices may be eccentric and differ and whose practice certainly does not make the law of the land.[40]

The decision in *Bown* appears to rest on three points. First, the contention that expert evidence is not admissible on the 'very issue that the court has to decide'. In fact, a number of relevant and binding authorities were not cited. Most importantly, no reference was made to *United Bank of Kuwait v Prudential Properties*[41] where, of course, Evans LJ had stated expressly that evidence of what the expert thinks the competent practitioner should have done was admissible.[42] In so far as the *Bown* decision was based on this first point it was *per incuriam* and should not be followed.

Secondly, the court of Appeal in *Bown* appears to have accepted without analysis the submission that the question of the 'extent of the legal duty' is a matter of law on which expert evidence is not admissible. This is true but only if the phrase 'extent of the legal duty' is understood in a narrow sense. The question as to what general 'standard of care' is applicable (for example that of the generalist or the specialist) is a question of law for the court. However, the precise content of the legal duty is a mixed question of law and fact. The court cannot determine, without evidence (whether from 'judicial notice', textbooks or experts), what reasonably competent solicitors do in particular factual situations.

[39] At p 135.
[40] At p 137.
[41] [1995] EGCS 190.
[42] See above at p 166.

The third factor which influenced the court in *Bown* is the fact that the issues raised were matters of ordinary conveyancing practice and did not require specialist knowledge. Expert evidence will not be admitted in areas on which a judge can properly rely on his own experience. This would mean that where the case relates to the experience of practitioners in a specialised field, the court will not be able to rely on its own experience. The court cannot reach a view on the precise contents of the duty owed by the specialist solicitor without receiving evidence of the features particular to the specialism. This is implicitly acknowledged in *Bown* by the reference to 'textbooks' and Law Society opinions. Such guidance is not available in, for example, complex commercial cases. In the absence of 'textbooks' and Law Society opinions, it is submitted that the court will need the assistance of a 'live' solicitor expert.

In summary, therefore, it is submitted that no special principles apply in relation to the reception of solicitor expert evidence. Such evidence is admissible on the 'very issue' which the court has to decide, provided that the issue relates to a 'specialist' area on which the court requires guidance. In property finance cases this would mean that a solicitor of expert evidence will be admissible on:

(a) issues concerning the practice of solicitors, particularly in relation to past practice;

(b) issues relating to complex commercial conveyancing practice;

(c) issues concerning the practice of solicitors in acting for commercial lenders.

7.6   Procedure

7.6.1   General procedural considerations

The 1972 Report of the Law Reform Committee considered the procedure relating to expert evidence. Their recommendations led to the Civil Evidence Act 1972 and to RSC Ord 38, rr 35–44. The general policy behind these provisions was to promote full disclosure of evidence and early resolution of the matters in issue between the parties. The court may order, at or before trial, that the number of expert witnesses who may be called at the trial shall be limited to a particular number.[43] This question will usually be dealt with at the summons for directions.

It had been considered that this power did not extend to excluding expert evidence altogether.[44] In *Bown v Gould & Swayne*[45] the first instance judge made an interlocutory order disallowing the plaintiff from

---

[43] RSC Ord 38, r 4; and see Ord 38, r 6.

[44] *Sullivan v West Yorkshire Passenger Transport Executive* [1985] 2 All ER 134.

[45] (1996) unreported, 24 January.

adducing expert evidence at trial. It was argued on appeal that he had no jurisdiction to do this. The Court of Appeal held that, where the judge was specifically invited prior to trial to rule on admissibility, there was jurisdiction to make such an order.

In property finance cases, expert reports will invariably be ordered to be exchanged prior to trial.[46] The practice, first initiated in Official Referee's cases, of ordering a 'without prejudice' meeting of experts prior to trial, has now become widespread. The purpose is to identify those parts of the evidence which are in issue and those parts which are not. The experts are often directed to prepare a joint report stating what is agreed and what is not. Experts at such meetings have no implied authority to agree facts in any form other than the joint statement.[47]

7.6.2   The court expert

The court has power under RSC Ord 40, r 1 to appoint an independent 'court expert'. This power had, until recently, been relatively little used.[48] However, the large volume of valuers' actions over the last few years has prompted courts to make more frequent use of this power in conjunction with the power to limit the number of experts called contained in RSC Ord 38, r 4 in an attempt to reduce the time and expense of litigation. In *Abbey National Mortgages plc v Key Surveyors Nationwide Ltd*, a consolidated action involving discrete allegations of negligence relating to 51 separate properties, the Official Referee limited the number of experts who could be called by each party to one and appointed a court expert to advise on the value of all the properties.[49] The Court of Appeal[50] recognised that the orders were 'bold and innovatory', but refused to interfere with the order. It was held that Ord 38 r 4 was not confined to questions of a scientific or technical kind and was not limited to questions subsidiary to the main issue.[51]

One of the issues the Official Referee's order in *Abbey National Mortgages* raised was the question of the admissibility of the evidence which will be relied upon by any expert who is called in a valuer's negligence case. One of the objections raised by the defendant against the appointment of a single court expert was that he would not (given that the properties were located all over the country) have local experience, and therefore would not have firsthand knowledge of comparables. In fact

---

[46]   Ord 38, r 37.
[47]   *Carnell Computer Technology v Unipart Group* (1988) 45 BLR 100; see also *Richard Roberts Holdings v Douglas Smith Stimson* (1989) 47 BLR 113; *Murray Pipework v UIE Scotland* (1990) 6 Const LJ 56.
[48]   See *The Supreme Court Practice* (1997), 40/1–6/2.
[49]   [1995] 2 EGLR 134.
[50]   [1996] 3 All ER 184.
[51]   At 189.

the judge's interpretation of Ord 40 was that the court expert was not 'a witness' in the normal sense of the word, and did not give 'evidence' but rather 'furnished information to the court'.[52] Therefore the strict rule of hearsay did not apply:

> [I]n giving [the court expert] instructions under r 1(3) the court can empower him to conduct his inquiry by any fair means authorised by those instructions, even if for example that results in the incorporation in his report of material which in the evidence of a witness would be inadmissible hearsay.[53]

52   RSC Ord 40, r 2(3).
53   The Court of Appeal to some extent agreed at [1996] 3 All ER 184, 189.

8 Practice and Procedure

8.1 Introduction

The purpose of this chapter is to highlight issues of practice and procedure which tend to arise when bringing or defending a property finance negligence claim. Although some of these points will be familiar from other areas of litigation, property finance negligence litigation can give rise to a number of particular procedural issues.

8.2 Beginning an action

8.2.1 Initial investigations

It is not unusual for a lender to ask for a large number of loan files to be 'trawled' in order to see whether potential claims lie against the professionals who were involved in the transaction. To detect a claim against a valuer a rigid formula can be used to see if a claim is worth referring for a retrospective valuation.

An example of the working of such a formula (there are many variations) which builds in an allowance (represented by the figures 0.8 and 10) for the decline in values between 1988 and 1994 is as follows:

Repossession value (A)	£60,000
Value given by potential defendant (B)	£100,000
B-A = C	£40,000
C/B = D1, the percentage difference	40%
Difference in months between A and B = E	24 months
E × 0.8 + 10 = D2	29.2%

The rule is then that if D1 is greater than D2, the matter should be referred for a retrospective valuation.

Such a mechanistic approach is not possible in relation to claims against solicitors. The person carrying out the trawl should simply try to work out whether the underlying cause of the loss which the lender has suffered is something which relates to an inaccuracy or omission in the advice given by the solicitor at the time of completion of the loan.

In each case, in addition, the person carrying out the investigation will have to have regard to the limitation period for bringing any claim.[1]

8.2.2   Which court?

A property finance negligence claim can be brought in a number of different courts. In the High Court, a case relating to property in or around London can be brought in the Queen's Bench Division, the Commercial Court, the Official Referee's Court or the Chancery Division. A District Registry case could be brought in the Queen's Bench Division and, in some centres, the Chancery Division, the Official Referee's Court or the Mercantile Court.

The advantage of the Commercial Court, the local mercantile courts and the Official Referee's Courts is that the timetable for the whole action will be determined at the outset and a trial date fixed at an early stage. The Commercial Court and the Mercantile Lists are, in general, only suitable for substantial commercial lending cases. However, domestic valuer cases are now commonly brought in the Official Referee's Courts. Cases against solicitors are usually brought in the Chancery Division or, sometimes, the Queen's Bench Division.

Although the High Court and the county court have concurrent jurisdiction for contract and tort cases without any financial limit, under para 9 of the Practice Direction of 1 July 1991[2] a professional negligence action is treated as suitable for trial in the High Court. In practice, only a small proportion of property finance negligence claims are dealt with by the county court.

It should be borne in mind that it is not possible to transfer between Mercantile Lists or Official Referee's Courts for the purpose of trial. As a result, the case must be started in (or immediately transferred to) the court in which the trial will take place. This will usually be the court which is closest to the property itself. However, when an action is commenced in the ordinary Queen's Bench or Chancery Lists or in the county court, the general principle is that, for interlocutory matters, the plaintiff's solicitors have the choice of forum.[3] The place of trial is then determined at the summons for directions stage and the action is not usually transferred to the court in which trial is to take place until setting down.

Section 2(1) of the Courts and Legal Services Act 1990, amending s 40 of the County Courts Act 1984, provides that a case can be struck out for being commenced in the wrong court. In practice, however, it will usually be simply transferred.[4]

---

[1]   See Chapter 5.
[2]   [1991] 1 WLR 643.
[3]   See *The Supreme Court Practice* (1997), 4/5/1.
[4]   *Restick v Crickmore* [1994] 1 WLR 420, CA.

8.3   Pleadings

8.3.1   Introduction

Pleadings are the written statements of the parties to a case of all the material facts on which each relies for his claim or defence. The purpose of a pleading is to tell the other party to the case what is being said against him and so prevent him being taken by surprise. The importance of pleadings cannot be over-emphasised:

> ... pleadings continue to play an essential part in civil actions, and although there has been since the Civil Procedure Act 1833, a wide power to permit amendment, circumstances may arise where the grant of permission would work injustice or, at least, necessitate an adjournment which may prove particularly unfortunate in trials with a jury. To shrug off a criticism as 'a mere pleading point' is therefore bad law and bad practice. For the primary purpose of pleadings remains and it can still prove of vital importance. The purpose is to define the issues and thereby to inform the parties in advance of the case they have to meet and so enable them to take steps to deal with it.[5]

8.3.2   The statement of claim

The statement of claim sets out the basic facts which the plaintiff will seek to prove to establish its claim. If there are omissions in the statement of claim or if it is drafted incorrectly, the action can go wrong in ways which can be costly, if not impossible, to put right. The general rule is that a party is not entitled to give evidence at trial of facts which have not been pleaded and, in a surprisingly large number of cases, claims are dismissed because of defective pleadings.

In property finance negligence claims it is particularly important to ensure that the statement of claim is accurate because many claims are brought towards the end of the limitation period and any amendment the effect of which is to add a new cause of action after the limitation period has expired can only be made in narrow circumstances.[6]

A plaintiff must be careful to ensure that he is suing the right party. A firm of solicitors can be sued either in the name of the firm or, because their liability is joint and several,[7] in the names of the individual partners at the time of the negligence complained of. The latter is advisable if the firm concerned has been reconstituted or dissolved since the time of the transaction. The business of many valuers is conducted through limited companies and it is important to make sure that the defendant has the same registered number as the company which carried out the

---

5   *Farrell v Secretary of State for the Defence* [1980] 1 WLR 172, 180A–B.
6   See p 199 above, and RSC Ord 20, r 5.
7   Partnership Act 1890, ss 9 and 12.

valuation even if the name of the company has changed or the trading style has altered. In domestic valuation cases, establishing the correct defendant can prove difficult where, often, only the name of the individual valuer who conducted the valuation is written on the valuation report.

The following pleading points should be noted in relation to statements of claim in property finance negligence cases:

(a) the duties owed by the solicitors (whether express or implied) should be fully set out—it is rarely sufficient to rely on a simple 'duty to use reasonable skill and care';[8]

(b) the plaintiff should specifically plead the basis on which loss is claimed, for example 'no loan' or 'lesser loan'. In a 'no loan' case, the plaintiff should plead that 'had the defendant properly reported' etc, no loan would have been made, setting out the factual reasons for this. In a case in which the plaintiff is alleging a misrepresentation he can simply plead 'reliance'.[9] However, it is suggested that in these circumstances the 'no loan' case should be pleaded in the alternative in any event;

(c) it is now advisable to plead that the loss suffered fell within the scope of the defendant's duty—it is obligatory if a contention to this effect involves specific factual allegations; and

(d) all claims for special damages should be specifically pleaded.[10] As a result, a lender should specifically plead all the expenses incurred in realising the security and the 'interest as damages' claim (cost of funds or losses in not having the money available to lend). It is common to place these in schedules.

8.3.3   Defence

The traditional defence to a negligence claim was a short document consisting largely of non-admissions and bare denials. Although this is a permissible form of pleading, it is important to note that if the defendant wishes to raise any affirmative case at trial such a case must be pleaded. If, on a particular issue, the defendant simply denies the plaintiff's case and puts it to proof:

> ... it is not even permissible [for them] to proceed to put forward some affirmative case which they had not pleaded or alleged; and it is not, therefore, right that they should, by cross-examination of the plaintiffs or otherwise, suggest such an affirmative case.[11]

---

[8]   If specific duties are relied on, the plaintiff may be able to resist a contributory negligence defence: see Chapter 6.

[9]   See Chapter 3.

[10]   See *Ilkiw v Samuels* [1963] 1 WLR 991, 1006.

[11]   *Regina Fur Co Ltd v Bossom* [1958] 2 Lloyd's Rep 425, 428, per Lord Evershed MR.

In many cases, defendants do not seek to set out their positive case on matters such as the particulars of negligence pleaded by the plaintiffs. In these circumstances, strictly speaking, the defendant is not entitled to advance any affirmative case at trial.

The following points should be noted in relation to the pleading of defences in property finance negligence cases:

(a) a defendant valuer should make clear his case as to the true value of the property, either by asserting that the figure contained in the valuation was within the range of figures at which a competent valuer could have arrived, or by stating his alternative figure;

(b) the burden is on the defendant to show that the plaintiff failed to mitigate his loss. Any positive case on failure to mitigate should be pleaded. In many cases this cannot be done until after discovery. There is nothing to be gained by the bare plea that 'the plaintiff is put to proof that he took reasonable steps to mitigate';

(c) the burden is also on the defendant to establish that the plaintiff was guilty of contributory negligence. Each alleged failure to measure up to the standard of a reasonably prudent lender should be specifically pleaded. Once again, it is often impossible for this case to be properly pleaded until after discovery. It is usually unwise for a defendant to commit himself to a contributory negligence case until he has obtained a preliminary view from a lending expert; and

(d) the defendant must specifically plead any limitation defence it relies upon. Otherwise the plaintiff has 'no opportunity to raise the point that the [Limitation Act] does no apply'.[11a] When a limitation defence is raised the burden of pleading and proving that the action was brought within the limitation period shifts to the plaintiff.[11b]

8.3.4   The reply

If a plaintiff does not serve a reply there is an 'implied joinder of issue'[12] with the defence. In other words, unless a reply is served the plaintiff is taken to have denied the factual allegations in the defence. As result, a plaintiff needs to serve a reply in only one of two situations:

(a) where he wishes to admit some of the factual allegations in the defence to narrow the issues; or

(b) where he wishes to raise additional factual matters to rebut pleaded defences.

[11a] *Dismore v Milton* [1938] 3 All ER 762, 764.
[11b] *Cartledge v Jopling & Sons Ltd* [1963] AC 758, 784 and see generally *Atkin's Court Forms* 2nd edn (1994), vol 25, p 243 *ff.*
[12]   RSC Ord 18, r 14(1).

The second of these situations commonly arises if the defence pleads failure to mitigate, contributory negligence, or that the action is statute barred. The plaintiff will usually need to deal with the particular factual contentions raised. For example, if it is said that the plaintiff failed to make adequate investigations of the financial position of the borrower, the plaintiff will usually need to plead the investigations which he, in fact, carried out.

8.3.5   Requests for particulars

The function of particulars is described in *The Supreme Court Practice*[13] as follows:

> (1) to inform the other side of the nature of the case they have to meet as distinguished from the mode in which that case is to be proved ...
> (2) to prevent the other side being taken by surprise at the trial ...
> (3) to enable the other side to know what evidence they ought to be prepared with and to prepare for trial ...
> (4) to limit the generality of the pleadings ... or of the claim or the evidence ...
> (5) to limit and define the issues to be tried, and as to which discovery is required ...
> (6) to tie the hands of the party so that he cannot without leave go into any matters not included ... But if the opponent omits to ask for particulars, evidence may be given which supports any material allegation in the pleadings.

Requests for particulars, however, have frequently been used not just for these purposes but in the course of tactical manoeuvring in order to involve the other side in time and trouble. This phenomenon was one of the main reasons for Lord Woolf concluding in his interim report of June 1995 that the basic function of pleadings has been lost sight of.[14]

Until Lord Woolf's recommendations are implemented (which replace pleadings with Statements of Case and Requests for Further and Better Particulars and interrogatories with Requests for information) the courts have made a start in limiting the scope for lengthy requests. In the Practice Direction of 24 January 1995[15] it is said that RSC Ord 18, r 7 (which provides that facts, not evidence, must be pleaded) will be strictly enforced and that failure by practitioners to conduct cases economically will be visited by appropriate orders for costs, including wasted costs orders.

In *Pension Trustees Ltd v Sir Robert McAlpine and Sons Ltd*,[16] Saville LJ

---

[13] (1997), para 18/12/1—we have omitted the authorities cited in support of these propositions.
[14] Chapter 20, para 4.
[15] [1995] 1 WLR 262.
[16] (1994) 72 BLR 26.

stated that there has been, in recent times, a tendency to forget the basic purpose of pleadings and to seek particularisation solely to cause delay and lead to expensive and unnecessary interlocutory battles. He emphasised that pleadings were not a game to be played at the expense of litigants.[17]

It is particularly important that a party who has been served with a request for further and better particulars does not agree, on pain of an application for an order for their answer, to submit to a consent order which provides that the requests be answered within a certain time period. If he does, he cannot change his mind later and say that the party who served the requests is not entitled to the answers after all.[18]

8.4 Third party proceedings

A professional who is sued by a lender will often claim contribution or indemnity from another party or parties. Three situations in which this occurs in property finance negligence cases are:

(a) when a solicitor (or valuer) seeks to allege that a valuer (or solicitor) also retained in the transaction by the lender is liable in respect of the same damage as is claimed against him by the lender;

(b) where an employee of a valuer or solicitor who is sued in his own name by a lender wants to allege that his employer is liable, the act complained of having been carried out whilst acting on behalf of that employer, or, more usually, vice versa; for example where a partnership or company wants to allege that the responsibility for the act complained of is that of the employee, not the firm or partnership; or

(c) where a professional seeks to bring his insurer into the action if that insurer is disputing the indemnity of the professional under his insurance policy.

A defendant brings a new party into existing litigation by means of a third party notice.[19] A claim for contribution against an existing defendant is brought by contribution notice.[20] The subject is dealt with in greater detail in Chapter 6.

8.5 Discovery

8.5.1 General principles

Within 14 days of the close of pleadings in a High Court action each

---

[17] See article by Doug Masson 'Setting a Fairer Agenda for Trial' (1995) 139 SJ 92.

[18] This follows from the general principle that an order by consent cannot be altered by the court without the consent of the parties: *Hill v Deakin* (1974) 118 SJ 389, CA; *Tigner-Roche v Spiro* (1982) 126 SJ 525, CA; *Fearis v Davies* (1986) *The Times*, 5 June.

[19] RSC Ord 16, r 1(1) and CCR Ord 12, r 1(1).

[20] RSC Ord 16, r 8 and CCR Ord 12, r 5.

party must make and serve: 'a list of the documents which are or have been in his possession, custody or power relating to any matter in question between them in the action'.[21] When litigation is contemplated or, in the case of a defendant, when the writ is served, the solicitor must take prompt steps to ensure that his client is aware of the duty of discovery and the importance of not destroying relevant documents.[22] The obligation to give discovery is a continuing one and covers documents which come into a party's possession at any time in the course of litigation.[23]

A broad definition is given to documents for the purposes of discovery. A tape recording which records relevant information or evidence is a 'document' and must be disclosed on discovery.[24] A computer database is also discoverable.[25] All copies of a particular document must be disclosed.[26]

It is important to note that all documents must be included on the list—even if they are no longer in the possession, custody or power of the party or if privilege is claimed for them. The list should give a complete picture of all the relevant documents which a party has ever had, whatever their nature.

The category of 'relevant' documents is extremely wide. The classic definition is that it includes any document which it is reasonable to suppose 'contains information which may enable the party to advance his own case or to damage that of his adversary or which might fairly lead him to a train of inquiry which may have either of these consequences'.[27] Furthermore, a document is discoverable whether or not it is admissible in evidence.[28] However, discovery which goes simply to credit will not be ordered.[29]

A party who has served a list of documents must allow the party on whom it has been served to inspect the documents referred to in the list.[30] However, if an objection is taken to the production of a particular document or class of documents, then the party entitled to inspection must make an application to the court for an order for production for inspection.[31] An order for production for inspection will not be made:

> ... unless the Court is of the opinion that the order is necessary either for disposing fairly of the cause or matter or for saving costs.[32]

21   RSC Ord 24, r 2(1).
22   See *Rockwell Machine Tool v E P Barrus* [1968] 2 All ER 98.
23   *Mitchell v Darley Main Colliery Co* (1884) Cab & E 215.
24   *Grant v Southwestern and County Properties* [1975] Ch 185.
25   *Derby v Weldon (No 9)* [1991] 1 WLR 652.
26   *Dubai Bank v Galadari (No 2)* [1990] 1 WLR 73.
27   *Compagnie Financiere v Peruvian Guano Co* (1882) 11 QBD 55.
28   *O'Rourke v Darbishire* [1920] AC 581.
29   *Ballantine v FER Dixon* [1974] 1 WLR 1125; *Thorpe v Chief Constable of Greater Manchester Police* [1989] 1 WLR 665, CA.
30   RSC Ord 24, r 9; CCR Ord 14, r 3.   31   RSC Ord 24, r 11(1).
32   *Ibid*, r 13.

In relation to discovery, the burden of proof is on the party who objects to disclosing a document to show that disclosure is *not* necessary. In contrast, in relation to inspection, the burden is reversed: it is on the party who seeks inspection to show that it *is* necessary for those purposes.[33] The position was recently summarised in *Wallace Smith Trust v Deloitte Haskins & Sells*[34] as follows:

Disclosure will be necessary if:

a.   It will give 'litigious advantage' to the party seeking inspection—see Sir Thomas Bingham, MR in *Taylor v Anderton*[35] and

b.   The information sought is not otherwise available to that party by, for example, admissions, or some other form of proceeding (eg interrogatories) or from some other source—see, for example, *Dolling-Baker v Merrett*[36] and

c.   Such order for disclosure would not be oppressive, perhaps because of their sheer volume ...

The result is that the fact that a document is disclosed on discovery does not mean that the other party is automatically entitled to inspect it. It is always open to the party who has disclosed the document to resist an order for inspection on the ground that disclosure of the particular document or class of documents is not necessary.

If a claim to privilege is to be made the existence of the documents in question is made known to the other side, but it is indicated that privilege is being claimed. If the claim to privilege is successful then, unless the privilege is waived, the other party is not entitled to see the documents in question.

The most important category of privilege in property finance negligence cases is 'legal professional privilege', which covers communications with both in-house and external lawyers. It comprises two sub-categories: 'advice privilege' and 'litigation privilege' .

Advice privilege: All confidential communications between a client and his legal advisers are privileged from disclosure if they are made in relation to the giving of legal advice.[37] However, this privilege does not extend, without limit, to all communications between solicitor and client upon matters within the ordinary business of the solicitor, such as advice which would also be given by an estate agent. Nevertheless, the privilege can cover commercial as well as strictly 'legal' advice.[38]

Litigation privilege: In addition to the documents covered by 'advice privilege', this category also covers communications with third parties

---

[33]   *Dolling-Baker v Merrett* [1990] 1 WLR 1205.
[34]   (1996) *The Times*, 12 July.
[35]   [1995] 1 WLR 447, 462.
[36]   [1990] 1 WLR 1205, 1214.
[37]   *Balabel v Air India* [1988] Ch 317, CA.
[38]   *Nederlandse Reassurantie Groep Holding NV v Bacon & Woodrow* [1995] 1 All ER 976.

provided these are 'for the purposes' of actual or contemplated litigation. There must, however, be a 'definite prospect' of such litigation but it is not essential that a cause of action has arisen.[39] The 'dominant purpose' of the communication must be the seeking of advice for the contemplated litigation.[40] Any statements or reports made before litigation was contemplated will not be privileged under this head. Nor will documents which come into existence for reasons unconnected with the litigation in hand but which come into one party's hands for the purposes of such litigation be privileged.[41]

As legal professional privilege is that of the client (though the solicitor has a professional duty to protect it until waived by the client) it can be waived by the client. When a client sues his former solicitor for negligence there will an implied waiver of privilege on all relevant documents.[42] This includes documents which were created in the course of previous retainers of the same solicitor by the client and, if the fair conduct of proceedings requires, documents prepared by a former solicitor in the context of previous proceedings (though relating to the same subject matter as present proceedings) which are in the hands of the solicitor being sued.[43]

Documents received as a result of discovery will be subject to an implied undertaking given by the party receiving them not to use them for any purpose other than for the action in which they were disclosed, such as the commencement of a second action on the basis of documents disclosed in the first.[44] Until the privilege is lost or waived by, for instance, the document being read out in court[45] the documents, being the property of the party who disclosed them, remain subject to such an undertaking.

The undertaking has particular application in property finance negligence cases because there are often a number of cases relating to different properties between a lender and a professional. Documents disclosed in one action between a particular lender and a particular professional cannot be used in another case between the same lender and the same professional. The court does, however, have jurisdiction to relax or modify the undertaking in appropriate circumstances, for example if it can be done without prejudicing the position of the party who gave the discovery because, for instance, the documents could eventually be obtained elsewhere in any event.

---

[39]   *Bristol Corp v Cox* (1884) 26 ChD 678.
[40]   *Waugh v British Railways Board* [1980] AC 521.
[41]   *Ventouris v Mountain* [1991] 1 WLR 607, CA.
[42]   *Lillicrap v Nalder & Son* [1993] 1 WLR 94.
[43]   *Kershaw v Whelan* [1996] 1 WLR 358.
[44]   *Crest Homes v Marks* [1987] AC 829; *Riddick v Thames Board Mills* [1977] QB 881; *Miller v Scorey* (1996) *The Times*, 2 April.
[45]   RSC Ord 24, r 14A and CCR Ord 14, r 8A, reversing *Home Office v Harman* [1983] 1 AC 280, HL.

8.5.2 Discovery in property finance negligence cases

The plaintiff in a property finance negligence case will be obliged to give discovery of all documents relating to the underwriting and making of the loan (including its lending criteria), instruction of the professional, default of the borrower and efforts to sell the property. Agreements with any syndicated lenders are also likely to be discoverable as relevant to the issue of whether the cause of action vests in the named plaintiff. Documents relating to any agency on behalf of the plaintiff will also be discoverable.

The valuer's file of papers relating to his valuation and the solicitor's conveyancing file will be discoverable against them in any action brought against such a professional. In the latter case, however, there is guidance from the Law Society as to the documents which ought to be shown to a lender upon the lender's request (ie even before an action is commenced on the basis that the documents belong to the lender or belong to both the lender and the borrower on the basis that they had a common interest in their creation) where the solicitor had been acting for both the lender and the borrower.

Documents which the lender is entitled to see both at this stage and, *a fortiori*, once an action is commenced (under an order for discovery) include its instructions to the solicitor, the mortgage deed, the report on title, correspondence between the solicitor and the lender or between the solicitor and a third party (written or received on the lender's behalf) the contract for sale, enquiries before contract, the abstract or epitome of title/office copy entries and plan, requisitions on title, the draft purchase deed, any draft licence to assign and Land Registry application forms.

In one case an order was made against a lender for discovery of documents relating to earlier loan transactions entered into by the same lender with other companies controlled by the individual who was the moving spirit behind the borrower in the particular loan which gave rise to the action. It was held that such documents were relevant to the questions of contributory negligence and the extent to which the plaintiff relied upon the defendant's valuaton.[45a]

In another recent case, where the lender alleged that the solicitors negligently failed to tell it of their knowledge that the borrowers were in financial difficulties, the judge held that the legal advice privilege that could be maintained by the defendant's solicitors could be no greater than that which could be maintained by the borrowers. In circumstances where the lender has shown a strong case that the borrowers' application was fraudulent such privilege could not be maintained

---

[45a] *Nyckeln Finance Co Ltd v Edward Symmons* [1996] PNLR 245, applying the test in *Compagnie Financière du Pacifique v Peruvian Guano Co* (1882) 11 QBD 55.

and the lender's application for specific discovery was granted.[46]

8.5.3 Interrogatories

Interrogatories are often regarded as being a form of pleading. This is not correct as they are not pleadings but a form of discovery—discovery of facts and not documents. The distinction has been put as follows:

> The object of the pleadings is to ascertain what the issues are. The object of interrogatories is not to learn what the issues are but to see whether the party who interrogates cannot obtain an admission from his opponent which will make the burden of proof easier than it otherwise would have been.[47]

The primary function of interrogatories is therefore to obtain discovery of facts which will assist the party's case or damage the opposite party's case.[48] They are used to obtain more information from the other side, to reveal weaknesses in their case, to narrow the issues and to try to force admissions on matters which otherwise would have to be proved. Often a fact is not ascertainable in disclosed documents nor (because the defence consists of denials or non-admissions) can a request for further particulars be made.

Interrogatories may now be served without leave not more than twice.[49] Although they must relate to 'matters in question between the parties', they can extend to any facts the existence or non-existence of which is relevant to the existence or non-existence of facts directly in issue.[50] They must be necessary either for disposing fairly of the cause or matter or for the saving of costs. In general, neither 'fishing interrogatories' nor interrogatories relating solely to credit are allowed.

The party interrogated must answer to the best of his knowledge, information and belief after making all necessary inquiries of his servants or agents.[51] He may object to answering on the ground of privilege in his answer to the interrogatories.[52] If his answers are insufficient the court may order further answers by either affidavit or oral examination.[53] However, a request for further and better particulars of the answer

---

[46] *Bristol & West Building Society v Nelsons*, (1996) unreported, October.

[47] Tomlin J in *Duke of Sutherland v British Dominions Land Settlement Corporation Ltd* [1926] 1 Ch 746.

[48] *Plymouth Mutual Co-Op and Industrial Society Ltd v Traders Publishing Association Ltd* [1906] 1 KB 403; *Rockwell International Corp v Serck Industries Ltd* [1988] FRS 187.

[49] RSC Ord 26; CCR Ord 14, r 11; Ord 1, r 6. Interrogatories with leave can be served an unlimited amount of times though they are now quite rare. The following notes 50–61 relate to the position in relation to interrogatories without leave.

[50] *Marriott v Chamberlain* (1886) 17 QBD 154, CA.

[51] *Anderson v Bank of Columbia* (1876) 2 ChD 644.

[52] RSC Ord 26, r 5(1).

[53] *Ibid*, r 5(2).

does not count as serving a second set of interrogatories.[54]

Where a party fails to answer interrogatories or to comply with orders, the court may make any order it thinks just including a debarring order[55] or even committal in the case of refusing to answer ordered interrogatories.[56]

If the party upon whom the interrogatories are served believes that the serving party has no right to the answers sought, he must apply to the court within 14 days of service for the interrogatories to be varied or withdrawn. If the objection is that of privilege (only), objection may be taken in the answer.

If interrogatories are not answered within the minimum 28-day period for their answer, the court retains a jurisdiction under RSC Ord 26, r 6(1) to refuse interrogatories which have not been answered, notwithstanding that the party on whom they were served has not applied to the court for their variation or withdrawal.[57] This jurisdiction, however, probably relates only to the question of whether the answering of the interrogatory would effect a fair disposition of the action, *not* whether the interrogatory is admissible.[58]

In the case of *Det Danske Hedeselskabet v KDM International plc*,[59] Colman J expressed concern about the excessive use of interrogatories and laid down a number of guidelines, in the following terms:

> There are … some very specific yardsticks which it is worth bearing in mind …
>
> First, unless the answers are essential for the preparation of the requesting party's case for trial and cannot reasonably be expected to emerge from requests for further and better particulars and further discovery or witness statements, interrogatories will not normally be ordered. For this reason, the service of interrogatories before witness statements have been exchanged will almost always be premature.
>
> Secondly, information which is relevant to matters in issue only in the sense that it may lead to further inquiry or that questions about it could be asked in cross-examination at the trial will not be essential information for the purposes of the first consideration.
>
> Thirdly, requests for information which, although it may be relevant to matters in issue, can be provided only by means of detailed research or investigation which the party interrogated would not otherwise carry out for the purpose of preparing for trial will hardly ever qualify as being necessary either for disposing fairly of the cause or matter or for saving costs.
>
> Fourthly, hypothetical questions should not normally be asked.

---

[54]   *Ibid*, r 5(3).   [55]   *Ibid*, r 6(1).
[56]   *Ibid*, r 6(2).
[57]   *Maxiplus v Lunn* (1992) *The Times*, 27 February, CA.
[58]   *Tate v Durham County Council* [1992] CLY 3523, Darlington Cty Ct.
[59]   [1994] 2 Lloyd's Rep 534.

Fifthly, requests for information ascertainable by cross-examination at the trial are inappropriate unless the party questioning can establish that it is essential for the proper preparation of his case that such information is made available to him before trial, in the sense that if the matter is left until cross-examination at the trial that party will, or probably will, be irremediably prejudiced in his conduct of the trial or the trial may be unduly interrupted or otherwise disorganised by the late emergence of the information.

In *Hall v Selvaco*[60] the Court of Appeal said that the guidance given by Colman J should be regarded as applicable generally. The result is that interrogatories served before witness statements have been exchanged are likely to be regarded as not 'necessary' and therefore are liable to be ordered to be withdrawn.

The only exception to the principle that interrogatories should not usually be served before exchange of witness statements appears to be where they can be justified on the basis that a clear litigious purpose would be served. In *Hall v Selvaco* the Master of the Rolls put the principle in these terms:

... it would not be necessary to interrogate to obtain information likely to be contained in discoverable documents or witness statements unless, exceptionally, a clear litigious purpose would be served.

This means that a party will still be entitled to obtain an order for interrogatories if he can show that they are necessary to obtain some information which is not likely to be available from documents or witness statements. Thus, in *UCB Bank plc v Halifax (SW) Ltd*,[61] a property finance negligence case, Mr Goldblatt QC held that such a purpose was served when the interrogatories related to the issue of the valuer's methodology and the material he relied on in reaching his valuation. He found that it was not possible to say that this information would necessarily emerge from another source (such as witness statements) and that there was a clear litigious purpose in knowing the information at a relatively early stage of the proceedings.

It is submitted that questions about the comparables used by a valuer and the basis of figures appearing in his rough notes should be legitimate subjects for interrogatories even before exchange of witness statements. In a case against a solicitor, interrogatories concerning the state of knowledge of the solicitor at the material time may be permissible. For a defendant, interrogatories about the application of the plaintiff's lending criteria or its compliance with prudent lending practice generally would also be permissible.

[60]   (1996) *The Times*, 27 March.
[61]   [1996] 36 EG 148.

8.6 Summary judgment and interim payment

8.6.1 Summary judgment

In principle an application for summary judgment can be made at any time. Even though such applications are normally made before a defence is filed, there is nothing to preclude an application at a later stage in the proceedings. The mere fact of delay is irrelevant.[62] Such an application will rarely be appropriate in a valuer's negligence case where liability is disputed and where a finding of negligence will require expert evidence. In *European Partners in Capital (EPIC) Holdings BV v Goddard & Smith*[63] the Court of Appeal held that cases in which the plaintiff was seeking to attack the defendant's professional opinion were not, as a general rule, suitable to be resolved on a summary judgment application. Scott LJ said:

> ... this is a case ... in which leave to defend should have been given upon the footing that it is based upon the incompetence of an expression of professional opinion which the defendants responsible for that opinion desire to stand by at trial and support. I accept that there may be some cases in which summary judgment could be given notwithstanding the desire of a professional to stand by and justify his professional opinion. Such a case would, in my judgment, be a rare one and I can see nothing in the present case to take the case out of what I would regard as the general rule that would permit a professional who desired to support his professional opinion to do so at trial.

The position in relation to solicitors' negligence cases is less straightforward. After the decision of the Court of Appeal in *Target Holdings v Redferns*[64] a large number of summary judgment applications against solicitors were pursued on the basis of 'breach of trust'. This continued after the decision of the House of Lords on the basis of 'constructive trust' claims.[65] The decision of the Court of Appeal in *Bristol & West Building Society v Mothew*[66] meant that 'breach of trust' claims could not be pursued in ordinary negligence cases. As a result, applications for summary judgment on this basis are inappropriate.

However, the decision in *Mothew* suggests that summary judgment is still available in one category of solicitors' cases. After allowing the appeal, the Court of Appeal proceeded to enter interlocutory judgment for the lender for damages to be assessed. This was on the basis that, where 'incorrect advice' has been given, the lender does not have to

---

[62] *Brinks Ltd v Abu Saleh* [1995] 4 All ER 65.
[63] [1992] 2 EGLR 155.
[64] [1994] 1 WLR 1089.
[65] See *Bristol & West Building Society v May, May & Merrimans* [1996] 2 All ER 801 and generally Chapter 1.6 above.
[66] (1996) unreported, 24 July.

show that he would have acted differently if the correct advice had been given: proof of reliance is sufficient.[67] Whereas the question of 'what the lender would have done' almost always gives rise to a triable issue,[68] the proof of reliance will often be straightforward: it will usually be clear and incontestable that a lender has relied on the solicitor's confirmation that all the conditions of the advance had been fulfilled. As a result, it will often be appropriate for lenders to seek summary judgment for damages to be assessed in 'incorrect advice' cases.

In the rare case that the point in issue is a pure point of law, either party may use RSC Ord, r 14A for a determination of such issue without a full trial. All relevant factual issues must, however, be agreed.

8.6.2   Interim payment

Similar principles would probably apply in relation to any application under RSC Ord 29, r 9 for an 'interim payment' on account of any damages which a defendant may be held liable to pay at trial. Unless the plaintiff can show that he *will* succeed at trial (which, where there are conflicting professional opinions, will be unlikely) the interim payment provisions of RSC Ord 29 will be inapplicable.[68a]

8.7   Other interlocutory matters

8.7.1   Directions

Once the pleadings are closed directions must be given for the further progress of the action. In most cases in the High Court this is done at the hearing of a 'summons for directions'.[69]

Parties are expected to deal with all interlocutory matters which can be dealt with at the summons for directions stage, at that stage. Matters which could have been dealt with but are not, and require a subsequent application, may involve the court penalising in costs the party who did not raise such matters on the summons for directions.

In the Chancery Division, it is now necessary to lodge a pleadings bundle and statement of value not less than two clear days before the hearing of the summons. This has to be accompanied by an information sheet (in the form of completed answers to a questionnaire).[70] In the Commercial Court a similar information sheet is required to be completed.

---

[67]   For analysis and criticism of this point see 3.2.4 above.
[68]   See *Bristol & West Building Society v May, May & Merrimans* [1996] 2 All ER 801.
[68a]   *British & Commonwealth Holdings plc v Quadrex Holdings Inc* [1989] QB 842.
[69]   RSC Ord 25.
[70]   See *Chancery Guide*, 3.10.

In the county court automatic directions apply from 14 days after delivery of the defence or 28 days after any defence and counterclaim. The particular directions are set out in CCR Ord 17, r 11.

In addition to pleadings (including amendments) and discovery, the following matters are likely to be dealt with on the summons for directions:

(a) the exchange of witness statements, Civil Evidence Act notices and other directions in relation to evidence;
(b) notices to admit facts;
(c) leave to call expert evidence and exchange of experts' reports;
(d) the listing of a 'false trial date' for the purposes of obtaining documents from third parties; and
(e) directions as to the future conduct of the action and for trial.

8.7.2 Witness statements and other factual evidence

In all property finance negligence cases witness statements will have to be exchanged in accordance with RSC Ord 38, r 2A. Exchange will be 14 weeks after the summons for directions or within such other time as the court may order. The court also has power to order exchange to be on different dates for different issues.

There is no general right to call evidence at trial which has not been disclosed nor to add to the evidence of those whose statements have been disclosed. Leave of the court is required. In *Beachley Property Ltd v Edgar*[71] it was held that evidence could not be called at trial where it was contained in witness statements exchanged late without good excuse even if the other side were not prejudiced by the delay. One had to consider as well the inconvenience and disruption to the administration of justice caused by late service.

If a witness refuses to give a statement than it is advisable to apply to the court for a direction that this witness be allowed to give oral evidence without a statement having been exchanged. It will usually be granted (on sight of an affidavit from the solicitor explaining the difficulties in respect of this witness) on terms that the other side are told of the witness's name and address and the gist of the evidence which it is expected will be given.

The statements should be dated and signed and contain a statement by the maker that the contents are true to the best of his knowledge and belief. Any documents referred to should be clearly identified. In most cases witness statements are now ordered to stand as witnesses' evidence in chief.[72]

---

[71] (1996) *The Times*, 18 July.
[72] In the Practice Direction [1995] 1 WLR 262 it is stated that witness statements should stand as witnesses' evidence in chief unless the court specifically orders to the contrary.

Objections to the admissibility of evidence contained in a witness statement can be taken before trial or at trial after the witness has produced his statement and sworn to its truth. It will rarely be appropriate to amend a witness statement. Rather, the witness should be asked to alter or withdraw part of the statement when he comes to be asked about it in the witness box.

If a party who has served a witness statement does not call the witness to whom it relates, no other party may put the statement of that witness in evidence. This suggests that if there is no trial, or if there were and the witness was not called, the statement remains privileged and cannot be used for any purpose other than the litigation in which it was produced. Accordingly, until and unless the maker of the statement confirms the content of it in oral evidence the contents of that statement, although usable in that litigation for, say, an application for specific discovery, cannot be used in related litigation, even between the same parties.[73]

At present, a party who wishes to rely on hearsay evidence at trial must serve notices under the Civil Evidence Act 1968.[74] The timetable for the giving of such notices is usually laid down at the directions stage. Under these provisions, the court may receive firsthand hearsay evidence which is oral or written[75] or hearsay evidence contained in documents which form part of a 'record'[76] compiled by a person acting under a duty.

However, the procedure relating to the calling of hearsay evidence is fundamentally changed by the Civil Evidence Act 1995 which is yet to come into force. The effect of the Act is to allow the calling of hearsay evidence subject to:

(a) reasonable notice to the party against whose case it is called; and

(b) the court attaching such weight to the evidence as reflects its reliability.

New rules of court (which the coming into force of the Act presumably awaits) will provide more detail as to the way in which the new regime will work in practice.

The court may make an order that evidence can be produced in affidavit form rather than having to call oral evidence.[77] It may be useful to seek admission of evidence on uncontroversial matters such as interest rates over a particular period under this provision.

---

[73]   *Black & Decker v Flymo* [1991] 1 WLR 753; *Youell v Bland Welch* [1991] 1 WLR 122; *Prudential Assurance Co v Fountain Page* [1991] 1 WLR 756; *Comfort Hotels v Wembley Stadium* [1988] 1 WLR 872.
[74]   See RSC Ord 38, rr 20–34.
[75]   See *Ventouris v Mountain (No 2)* [1992] 1 WLR 887.
[76]   See *H v Schering Chemicals* [1983] 1 WLR 143.
[77]   See para 14.2 of the *Guide to Commercial Court Practice*.

In property finance negligence cases, there are three areas in particular on which the lender will usually have to lead evidence:

(1) *Underwriting*: Ideally, the lender should have a witness statement from the person who actually made the lending decision in question. If this person is not available then it will usually be necessary to have evidence from someone who worked for the lender at the time and was involved in the decision-making process in relation to the particular advance or advances of that type.

(2) *Possession and sale*: As part of the proof of loss, the lender will require evidence from someone with direct knowledge of the possession and sale process. This will often require evidence from several different people and it may be necessary to give notice of hearsay evidence if all those involved are unavailable.

(3) *'Interest'*: The lender will have to lead evidence as to the 'interest' losses he has suffered. In the case of a lender with excess funds this will be someone from the treasury department who can explain how surplus funds were invested. In the case of a lender who has to go into the market to obtain funds, evidence should be given by someone actually involved in the process. In both cases, it may be necessary to give notice of hearsay evidence as specific individuals are unlikely to be able to recall a specific transaction.

The factual evidence of the defendants is likely to be limited to the solicitor or valuer involved in giving the advice to the lender at the time of the initial transaction. In valuers' cases the factual question as to what was done at the time will often be irrelevant and it may well be that expert retrospective valuation evidence will suffice.

8.7.3   Notices to admit facts

The purpose of a notice to admit facts is to save the time and cost of calling evidence at trial that is not in dispute. One party serves on the other a list of the facts which it seeks to have admitted and the other side must either admit them (thus saving the serving party from having to prove those matters by the calling of evidence) or, if they do not admit them and those facts are then proved at trial, they risk having to pay costs thrown away by the unjustified failure to admit those facts whatever else the result of the trial.[78]

In relation to such matters as the making of the loan, the terms of the loan, the borrower's default and the price on resale—matters which may well involve considerable expense in proof by direct oral evidence, a notice to admit facts is a useful but under-used weapon.

In the High Court a notice to admit facts must be served within 21 days of setting down, unless there is an order to the contrary.

[78]   RSC Ord 27, RSC Ord 62, r 6(7).

8.7.4   Expert evidence

Unless the court gives leave, or all the parties agree, expert evidence cannot be adduced at trial.[79] An application for leave to adduce expert evidence will usually be made at the summons for directions or pre-trial review stage. The procedure in relation to experts is dealt with in Chapter 7 above.[80]

8.7.5   False trial date

In property finance negligence cases, the rules of court make no provision for obtaining discovery from witnesses or third parties. However, third parties can be compelled to bring documents to the trial by means of a *subpoena duces tecum*.[81] This must specify the documents which the party is being required to produce.

It is obviously inconvenient for the documents to be produced, for the first time, in the course of the actual trial. As a result, the practice has developed of fixing a 'false trial date', earlier than the actual one, for the purposes of obtaining documents on subpoena. This practice was approved in the case of *Khanna v Lovell White Durrant*.[82] Once the documents have been produced, the 'false trial' is adjourned, giving the parties time to examine them.

In property finance negligence cases it will often be useful to obtain documents from the borrower and any other professional advisers involved (for example accountants or architects). If these documents are not produced voluntarily then a 'false trial date' should be fixed and subpoenas issued.

8.7.6   Directions as to the future conduct of the action and trial

Such directions could include a direction for consolidation with another action. The conditions for consolidation are set out in RSC Ord 4, r 9(1) and CCR Ord 13, r 9. They involve there being either:

(a)   some common question of law or fact in the two actions; or

(b)   the relief claimed in the two actions being in respect of or arising out of the same transaction or series of transaction; or

(c)   some other reason making it desirable to consolidate the actions.

These conditions will be fulfilled if a number of actions arise out of the same property finance transaction. Thus, the courts often direct the consolidation of an action against a solicitor with one in respect of the same loan transaction against the valuer.

---

[79]   RSC Ord 38, r 36.
[80]   See 7.6.1.
[81]   See RSC Ord 38, r 14.
[82]   [1995] 1 WLR 121.

The court may also consider a direction as to whether particular issues should be heard as preliminary issues, whether there should be a split trial and the venue for trial. The hearing of a preliminary issue is appropriate when (a) a single issue can be isolated, (b) that single issue can be argued on the law alone, the facts being able to be agreed and (c) the determination of such an issue might be determinative of the entire litigation.[83] In property finance negligence cases issues which would be candidates for hearing as a preliminary issue would be whether a duty of care was owed to a particular lender or whether an action was statute-barred. An order for a split trial is rare in property finance negligence cases.

8.7.7   Payments into court and settlement

A payment into court is designed to force a plaintiff to accept an offer of settlement. A defendant can pay a sum of money into court in settlement of some or all of the plaintiff's causes of action, at any time up to judgment. If the plaintiff refuses to accept the payment in and, at trial, recovers damages which are less than or equal to the sums paid into court then he is liable to pay the defendant's costs after the date of payment in. As these costs will usually include the costs of the trial itself, a plaintiff who does not beat a payment in is likely to lose a substantial proportion of his damages in costs.

In a High Court case, the plaintiff has 21 days to decide whether or not to accept a payment in. After the appropriate period has expired the plaintiff can accept only with the leave of the court.[84] The plaintiff cannot apply for leave to accept a payment in once the trial of the action has begun.[85] If a payment in is made during the trial, then the plaintiff has two days to accept and can do so without leave.

The law in relation to the acceptance of payments in by one of several defendants is complex.[86] The implications of acceptance are different depending on whether the claims are 'joint', 'joint and several' or 'several'. The claims by a lender against a solicitor and a valuer in respect of a particular property finance transaction are not 'joint' but 'several'. As a result, if one of the two defendants makes a payment into court, acceptance will not affect the action against the other defendant. The only costs for which the paying in defendant is liable are those in respect of the plaintiff's action against him.[87]

The defendant usually pays into court a lump sum to cover all the plaintiff's causes of action.[88] A plaintiff who wishes to accept a payment

---

[83]   *Allen v Gulf Oil Refining Ltd* [1981] AC 101, HL.   [84]   RSC Ord 22, r 3(1).
[85]   *Gaskins v British Aluminium* [1976] QB 564.
[86]   See, generally, O'Hare and Hill, *Civil Litigation* 7th edn, table 5, pp 334–5.
[87]   See *QBE Insurance v Mediterranean Insurance* [1992] 1 WLR 573.
[88]   RSC Ord 22, r 1.

in can request an amendment of the notice of payment in so as to apportion the lump sum between the different causes of action.[89] A payment in should include an amount for interest.[90]

A defendant who wishes to withdraw a payment in must obtain the leave of the court.[91] The defendant must show some good reason for the withdrawal, such as a change in the relevant law[92] or the discovery of new evidence which supports his case.[93] In view of the rapidly changing state of the law in property finance cases, such applications are not uncommon.

8.8   The trial

8.8.1   Pre-trial reviews

It is now common, in substantial cases, for the courts to conduct 'pre-trial reviews' a short time before the hearing of the action. The purpose of these hearings is to decide on the order of events at trial and to deal with any outstanding interlocutory matters. The trend towards 'active case management' has led judges to take an increasingly interventionist role at these hearings.

In the Chancery Division in cases estimated to last for more than ten days, a pre-trial review should be sought by the plaintiff and, in default, by the defendant. The court can also list a pre-trial review of its own motion. Application by one of the parties is made by summons to a judge. In the Queen's Bench Division and Official Referee's Court the decision whether to hold a pre-trial review is made at the summons for directions or after lodgment of a pre-trial checklist.[94]

Not less than seven days before the pre-trial review the party who applied for it must circulate to the others a list of matters to be considered. The recipients must respond at least two days before the hearing.[95] The advocates who are expected to conduct the trial should appear at the pre-trial review.

8.8.2   Late amendments

Although in principle an amendment to pleadings can be made at any time, amendments just before or at the trial are very carefully scrutinised.

---

[89]   *Townsend v Stone Toms & Partners* (1984) 128 SJ 659.
[90]   RSC Ord 22, r 1(8).
[91]   *Ibid*, r 1(3); CCR Ord 11, r 1(4).
[92]   *Cumper v Pothecary* [1941] 2 KB 58.
[93]   *Metroinvest v Commercial Union* [1985] 1 WLR 513.
[94]   See Practice Direction (Civil Litigation: Case Management) [1995] 1 WLR 262.
[95]   The types of matters to be considered are set out in Appendix 6 of *The Chancery Guide*.

Such amendments may be disallowed on the basis that the other party will be prejudiced in a way which cannot be compensated for in costs. In the case of individual defendants, the courts will take into account the additional personal distress arising out of an adjournment. Furthermore, the court may also take into account the impact of an adjournment on the court lists.[96] If the amendment makes a fundamental alteration to that party's case without which the action will fail, the other party may be entitled to all the costs of the action to the date of the amendment.[97]

Fraud should always be pleaded at the outset of any action, and an amendment to plead deceit will only be allowed if it will not prejudice the defendant and where, on assessment, the plaintiff's claim in deceit appears to have some strength.[97a]

The position is more complex in relation to amendments made after expiry of the limitation period. Any amendment the effect of which is to add a new cause of action cannot be made after the limitation period has expired[98] unless the cause of action arises out of the same or substantially the same facts as are already in issue.[99] The question of whether an amendment introduces a new cause of action is a matter of 'fact and degree'. It is necessary to look at the nature and extent of the breach and the damage.[100] The addition of further particulars of negligence or breach of contract does not amount to a new cause of action.[101] If a new cause of action does arise, then the question of whether it arises out of 'the same or substantially the same facts' is 'essentially a matter of impression' for the judge.[102]

A party can be added to an action after expiry of the limitation period only where 'necessary' for disposal of the action.[103] The most common basis for such amendment is where the amendment is required to correct a mistake as to the identity of the correct party suing or being sued.[104] Such an amendment may be allowed notwithstanding that its effect will be to substitute a new party if the court is satisfied that the mistake was a genuine one and was not misleading or such as to cause any

---

[96] *Ketteman v Hansel Properties Ltd* [1987] AC 189 HL; *Tramp Leasing Ltd v Sanders* (1991) *The Times*, 1 February. See also the post-Woolf concern for such matters in *Beachley Property Ltd v Edgar, ibid.*

[97] *Beoco Ltd v Alfa Laval Co Ltd* [1995] QB 137.

[97a] See *BNP Mortgages Ltd v Black Horse Residential Ltd*, (1995) unreported, 17 February; and see Ord 20, r 8 RSC and the notes thereto in *The Supreme Court Practice* (1997).

[98] *Hancock Shipping Co v Kawasaki Heavy Industries* [1992] 3 All ER 132.

[99] Limitation Act 1980, s 35(5); RSC Ord 20, r 5; CCR Order 15, r 1.

[100] See *Steamship Mutual Underwriting v Trollope & Colls* (1986) 33 BLR 81.

[101] See *Collins v Hertfordshire County Council* [1947] 1 KB 599.

[102] *The Casper Trader* [1991] 2 Lloyd's Rep 237; *Welsh Development Agency v Redpath Dorman Long* [1994] 1 WLR 1409; the decision in *Fannon v Backhouse* (1987) unreported, 30 July, takes too narrow a view of the applicable test.

[103] Limitation Act 1980, s 35(5)(*b*).

[104] RSC Ord 20, r 5(3).

reasonable doubt as to the identity of the relevant party. Mistakes as to the correct defendant are common in actions against valuers because the valuation will often not state precisely the name or title of the firm or company of valuers which provided the valuation. The lender in such cases will often have to research the RICS records and undertake company searches to ascertain the precise legal entity with which it contracted.[105] It is rare for the other categories which define when such amendment is 'necessary'[106] to be applicable.

8.8.3   Documents for trial

It is the plaintiff's duty (unless ordered to the contrary) to prepare trial bundles. It is important that they be delivered to the court in good time and be in good order.[107] Failure to comply can result in a special costs order being made against the party in default.

The advocates should prepare skeleton arguments. In the case of a trial, it should be delivered to the court not less than three days before the date fixed for hearing. The plaintiff should accompany the skeleton argument with a *dramatis personae*, list of issues (agreed if possible) and chronology. A list of the key documents which need to be read to understand the case is also advisable.

8.8.4   Trial

Under the modern procedure, the precise order of events at trial will often depend on what the judge finds most helpful and convenient. It is common, for example, to have the experts of like discipline to give evidence consecutively, after the factual evidence has been completed. The Court of Appeal has encouraged judges to take an interventionist approach with a view to narrowing the issues and saving court time.[108]

In civil trials there is no general rule that witnesses should be kept out of court until they have given their evidence. But an application can be made by either party, at any time:

> ... for an order that all witnesses on both sides other than the one under examination, to withdraw and not to leave the Court again after giving evidence so as to communicate with other witnesses before they give evidence.[109]

---

[105] See, generally, *Evans Construction Co Ltd v Charrington & Co Ltd* [1983] QB 810; *The Sardinia Sulcis and Al Tawwab* [1991] 1 Lloyd's Rep 201; and *IBSSL Ltd v Minerals and Metals Trading Corp* [1996] 1 All ER 1017.

[106] Limitation Act 1980, s 35(6)(b); RSC Ord 15, r 6(6) and RSC Ord 20, r 5(4).

[107] Appendix 2 of *The Chancery Guide* sets out useful guidelines for the preparation of bundles.

[108] See, for example, *Thermawear v Linton* (1995) *The Times*, 20 October.

[109] *Tomlinson v Tomlinson* [1980] 1 WLR 322.

Where there are elements of fraud in a property finance negligence case, such an order may well be appropriate.

Either party may wish to lead 'similar fact evidence', for example previous negligence of a similiar nature by the valuer involved or previous incompetent lending by the plaintiff. When deciding whether to admit such evidence the trial judge must decide whether its probative force is sufficient to make it just to admit it; there is no single manner of determining if the evidence is sufficiently probative so that it need not be strikingly similar.[110] It is unclear whether the rules as to the reception of such evidence which apply in criminal cases are also applicable in civil cases.[111] According to Lord Denning MR:

> In civil cases the courts will admit evidence of similar facts if it is logically probative, that is if it is logically relevant in determining the matter which is in issue; provided that it is not oppressive or unfair to the other side; and also that the other side has fair notice of it and is able to deal with it.[112]

Evidence of 'dissimilar facts' can be admitted to prove the main fact. There are no special procedures by way of notice or pleading in relation to similar fact evidence. In general, a party who wishes to invoke other transactions will have aired the matter on discovery.[113] Questions as to the admissibility of evidence concerning other transactions will generally be a matter for the trial judge.

---

[110] See *R v P* [1991] 3 All ER 337.
[111] See *Phipson on Evidence*, paras 17–65 *ff*.
[112] *Mood Music Publishing Co Ltd v de Wolfe* [1976] Ch 119 at 127; *Sattin v National Union Bank* (1978) 122 SJ 367.
[113] See *Steel v Commissioner of Police* (1993) unreported, 18 February, in which the Court of Appeal ordered discovery of documents relating to 'similar facts'.

Appendix 1   Methods of Property Valuation

A.1   Introduction

This Appendix is intended as a brief introduction to the most common methods of valuation used by property valuers. For a detailed analysis of what can be a very technical and complex subject reference should be made to practitioners' books.[1] At least a working knowledge of such methods is important for a lawyer to be able to identify if, and how, a valuer fell into error.

It is generally acknowledged that valuation is no more than an inexact estimate of what a property is likely to fetch in the market. The more homogeneous the property, the narrower the range of inexactitude. Nevertheless, several different ways of valuing property and several different concepts of value have evolved.[2] Each method and each concept of value is appropriate to particular circumstances. Each method of valuing property uses evidence from comparable property sales. A comparable may be simply a capital sale price which can provide direct evidence of the subject property's capital value. Comparables may also be used to ascertain the likely rental value of a property, which will in turn provide the basis for determining the capital value of the property.

A.2   Direct value comparison

This is the simplest method of valuation, involving a direct comparison of the property to be valued with other comparable properties which have been recently sold or let. It is also known as 'the comparable method'. The more proximate and similar in size, location and amenities

---

[1]   See, for example, Britton, Davies and Johnson, *Modern Methods of Valuation* 8th edn (1989); Darlow, *Valuation and Development Appraisal* 2nd edn (1988); Rees, *Valuation: Principles into Practice* 4th edn (1992); Enever and Isaac, *The Valuation of Property Investments* 5th edn (1995), for detailed analysis of the relevant bases and principles of valuation.

[2]   For example, 'open market value.' See *RICS Appraisal and Valuation Manual*, PS 4.

the comparable properties, the more accurate such a method of valuation will be. As a result such a method can be reasonably accurate when the property to be valued is, for example, a terraced domestic property. The method can be used to value more complex commercial or residential property, but the more unique the property, the less likely it is that another directly comparable transaction will be found. In these circumstances the valuer's skill is in making adjustments to the known value so as to relate it sufficiently to the subject property such that an estimate of its value can be made.

Even where properties appear to be similar, the valuer must nonetheless be aware of, and take into account, such matters as the property's proximity to a main road, state of repair, and internal improvements (eg central heating, double glazing) which may add to, or subtract from, the value as compared to 'comparable' properties. The following characteristics of the Direct Value Comparison (DVC) method should be noted:

(a) the DVC method reflects the fundamental principle of 'value' that, ultimately, it is a factor of price. Open market value is what the market is prepared to pay for the property;

(b) the proper application of DVC requires the valuer to have a well-maintained database of recent comparable transactions in the same locality. The greater the valuer's information base, the more accurate will be the valuation;

(c) the DVC method can be applied to all properties and it will be used to establish rental, as well as capital, values. With complex or heterogeneous properties it may be difficult to compare directly one with another so value can be reduced to a unit rate (e.g. £x per square metre of rental or capital value). This unit rate can then be applied to the subject property by multiplying it by the area of the whole property or different rates may be used for the different parts of the property.[3] When valuing retail property a weighting can also be applied to the front section, ie nearest the street, and to 'zone' the area back from there. The zone A area, at the front, is ascribed the highest rate and each successive zone back is valued as a proportion of the 'zone A' rate. This allows shops of different shape, as well as of different size, to be compared more carefully because a long, narrow shop will be valued less than one having a wide frontage but which is shallower although the floor areas are the same.

A.3 The residual method of valuation

Where, for instance, a developer purchases a site with a view to building

---

[3] The RICS and ISVA have produced a *Code of Measuring Practice* to standardise floor area measurement for different classes of property.

new houses upon it, or a country mansion with a view to converting it into flats, he will be primarily interested in expending such sums on the acquisition of the property itself which will allow, after the payment of his building costs, a profit element. The need to secure this profit will determine the price he is prepared to pay for the property. Therefore the residual method of valuation is often used for the valuation of property which it is intended to develop or redevelop. The advantages of this method are that it takes into account factors specific to the site and the proposed development as primary assumptions in the process of valuation, and is tailored round the need to ascertain what the developer *can afford* to pay for the land. Although most property developers use this method to ascertain what they might pay for a site, having regard to their particular subjective circumstances, when used properly by valuers, the residual method tries to estimate what the *general* market will pay for the property. It is a difficult tool to use and results are likely to be very variable. For this reason the Lands Tribunal has accepted its application with caution unless other comparable evidence is available to test the residual calculation. Nevertheless, it was accepted in *Nykredit Mortgage Bank plc v Edward Erdman Group Ltd*[4] that the residual method of valuation could be an appropriate method of valuation for mortgage purposes. Moreover it was accepted in *Private Bank & Trust Co Ltd v Sallmans (UK) Ltd*[5] that the residual site value should be determined by the gross development value.

On the residual basis, the value is derived by first calculating the estimated post-development value of the property (also known as the gross development value or the gross realisation) on completion of the development. It may be that the developer will wish to sell the developed property immediately on completion (this will generally be the case after the development of residential houses), or, as may be the case when the development is of office buildings, will wish then to let the developed property, retaining the freehold. If the latter is the case then the gross development value will be calculated by the investment method of valuation. From this figure will be deducted the various labour, materials and professional costs involved in the construction and marketing of the development. The residual figure will constitute:

    (a) the amount which is available for the cost of the property, its acquisition and the interest payments required to borrow funds to buy the property; and

    (b) a margin for profit and risk.

The residual method is critically affected by the gross development value and the estimated input costs used. There are many inputs, and if

---

[4]   [1996] 1 EGLR 119, where Staughton LJ remarked, at 120: 'to the uninitiated what is remarkable about this method of calculation is its sensitivity to variables'.

[5]   [1993] 1 EGLR 144.

each is varied by even quite a small amount, the cumulative effect on the end result can be enormous. It is thus a very difficult valuation exercise.

The residual method may be set out as follows:

	Gross development value	
Less	(1)	Cost of building
	(2)	Professional costs associated with the construction of the property
	(3)	Cost of financing borrowing for building.
	(4)	Cost of legal, estate agents' fees, advertising.
	(5)	Profit element
Gives		Residual sum

(1) The cost of building will include the cost of preparing the site for development (demolition, decontamination, ground testing, etc), construction costs, which in the absence of actual tender figures are estimated by using tables, such as those published by the RICS Building Cost Information Service (these indicate the cost per square metre for different types of structure), landscaping, etc.

(2) An architect, engineer and quantity surveyor (and, in the case of large developments, perhaps more than one of each) will generally be retained to oversee the building works. Their professional fees will have to be paid, and it is usual to calculate these at about 10–15 per cent of the building costs.

(3) All development is capital intensive. Substantial funds are required over the period of the scheme, but not all is needed at the start. For instance, if the contractor is to be paid monthly, funds will be spread over the course of the work and called upon as necessary. The valuer will estimate the average time the total funds will be outstanding and from this can be calculated the cost of borrowing. Even where developers are liquid and do not need to borrow, this calculation is necessary to ascertain the opportunity cost of tying capital up until the scheme is complete.

(4) The letting or sale of the developed property will involve the developer incurring costs in the marketing of the property, which will include agency fees and advertising expenses, and the drawing up of leases and conveyances. As a general rule the level of fees for the sale of property is around 3 per cent of the sale price. The legal and agency costs of letting property may be estimated at 15–20 per cent of the rent.

(5) The developer's profit is taken at between 15 and 20 per cent, but this ultimately depends upon the state of the market. The *raison d'être*

of development risk-taking is to make a profit and the margin adopted must also allow for unforeseen circumstances which might increase costs or cause delay. The more risky the project, the greater will be the required margin for profit. Conversely where risk is less, as was seen during the property boom where prices were rising so fast that developers were confident that the value of the completed scheme would increase during the period of the development, margins will be cut so as to increase the residual sum, ie the amount available to spend on the site purchase. Where a builder acts also as the developer, he knows that he can make a 'profit' on the building costs as well as on the finished scheme and, in times of competition for sites, the margin for profit will be pared further.

By the above calculation, the residual sum is the amount of money which the prospective developer can afford to spend on the purchase of the property, the professional fees arising out of the purchase of the land, and the cost of using the amount of money to buy the property for whatever amount of time for which that sum will be tied up (ie until the completion of the development).

Having completed the residual calculation, it is necessary to test the result with known site sales. It is not possible to provide actual comparables because all a valuer can do is to satisfy himself that the result of his residual equation falls within a broad band of site values within the particular geographical location.

A.4   The investment method of valuation

A.4.1   Introduction

It has been seen that the residual method of valuation is appropriate where a buyer of property intends to develop it and then sell it on. However much of the largest proportion of the commercial property stock is owned by and passes hands between investment houses (banks, pension funds, life assurance companies) for the purpose of leasing the property, either as a whole or segmented, the purchaser in those cases will have no other purpose in buying the property, and then continuing to own it, than to generate an income flow from the property, and therefore when assessing the appropriate price to pay for the property, he will have to have regard to its rent potential.

The investment method of valuation involves calculating the yearly monetary return or yield which is likely to be generated by a property and using that figure as a route to arrive at a capital valuation of the property. This method starts from the premise that real property, like shares, bonds or gilts, is a unit of investment which generates an income, the capital value of which is determined by its income generation capacity. Whereas the income generated by the ownership of shares is reflected in the dividend, the income generated by investment property will be generated by the likely passing rent. The investment method of valuation therefore involves the *conversion of an income flow from property into an appropriate capital sum*. The basic principle behind the investment method is that 'an investor wishes to invest capital to obtain an annual return thereon in the form of a net income which represents an acceptable rate of yield'.[6]

The 'net rental value' must be ascertained. This figure is the likely (or the actual, depending on whether the property being valued is already tenanted) yearly income from a property less any yearly outgoings (on, for example, repairs) by the owner. In ascertaining the rental value of a property, the valuer will necessarily have to resort to comparables, looking at current rental income from similar properties. In looking at comparable passing rents, a valuer will give more or less weight to a comparable rent, depending on a variety of factors, including the similarity of the premises, the terms of the lease (what obligations are placed on the tenant, any restriction on user, etc), the date on which the rent was determined and the location of the premises.

Once the full rental value has been ascertained, this figure must be reduced to take into account the freehold owner's likely recurring expenditure. Thus, although the estimated rent value may be, say, £100,000 per year, the lease may not be a repairing lease, so that the freeholder has to spend an estimated, say, £5,000 per year on repairs. Other expenditure which a freeholder may have to make are the costs of insurance, general rates and management. However if in the above example £5,000 is the freeholder's only expenditure in relation to the property, then his *net income* will be £95,000, which will be the figure which will be relevant in ascertaining the value of the property. In ascertaining net income, the valuer will have to have regard to the terms of any existing lease.

A.4.2   The year's purchase or yield

Once the net rental value of the property has been calculated, the capital value of the property can be ascertained by the use of a *multiplier* which will capitalise yearly income. The question of what multiplier is appropriate (also known as *'year's purchase'* or *'YP'*[7]) is obviously of critical importance: the decision to use a multiplier of 5 or 10 will make a

---

[6]   Stated by one of the experts in *Nyckeln Finance v Stumpbrook Continuation Ltd* [1994] 2 EGLR 43, at 148.
[7]   In mathematical terms this is known as the present value of the right to receive £1 for *n* years at *y* per cent.

difference of 100 per cent in calculating the capital value of a property. It is also common to express the YP as a percentage yield. For *freehold* interests, this yield is the reciprocal of the YP. The yield's significance is that it can be readily compared with other forms of investment, or with the cost of borrowing money. The valuation tables are arranged by percentage yields. It will be seen that the YP merely expresses the interest accruing to capital in a year: it is analogous to the price/earnings ratio used in share rating. Thus if a net rental income is valued at £10,000 then, if it is required that this should represent a return on a capital outlay of 8 per cent, then the year's purchase, and so the capital value of the property, will be calculated performing the following calculation:

Required yield = 8%
Year's Purchase = 100/8 = 12.5
Required capital outlay = 12.5 ×10,000 = 125,000

It will be seen that £10,000 is 8 per cent of £125,000.

Ultimately any commercial property, where the freehold and the leasehold are in divided ownership, constitutes a form of investment, from which the investor expects and requires a return. A yearly income from property can be analysed in exactly the same way as a yield from stock, a dividend from shares or an interest payment from a bank deposit and can be calculated as a percentage of capital outlay. Thus if a property is purchased for £100,000 and the net yearly income is £10,000, then the owner obtains a 10 per cent return from his investment. At any given time the prevailing interest rates will provide a benchmark of what return can be achieved by merely depositing money. Prevailing interest rates will obviously have a profound impact on what the investor is prepared to spend on the purchase of property, and thus on property prices at any time. If prevailing interest rates are 12 per cent then the investor, if all else is equal, would be ill-advised to spend £100,000 on property achieving a 10 per cent return when he can, for instance, lend £100,000 with a return of £12,000. As a general rule, the yield required by the investor, in any investment situation, will depend upon the following considerations:

(a) how secure and regular the income flow will be;
(b) the security of the capital, ie the prospect of future growth;
(c) the liquidity of the capital (how quickly it can be released from the investment); and
(d) the transaction costs of investing the capital initially and subsequently freeing it.

A.4.3   Assessing the appropriate yield

The estimation of the appropriate yield will be a critical factor in arriving at the capital value of a particular property. The correct yield will be ascertained by the valuer through an analysis of recent market transactions and so the valuer will have to be abreast of recent sales of similar types of property of comparable condition and location in order to know the comparable yields. The yield ascribed to the particular property in arriving at the capital value will be directly influenced by the yields used in other comparable sales, but will also reflect any differences in condition and location, etc, between the property in question and the comparables.

Similar types of property generally attract similar year's purchase. Thus factories will often have YPs of around 9, and offices around 14: such a disparity reflects the differing degrees of security which the market perceives each property type to offer. Although a lower multiplier means that the property has been bought more cheaply, and gives a return which, expressed as a percentage, is higher, this will reflect the confidence purchasers have in that type of property as long-term investments. This difference in acceptable rates of return is obviously similar to the stock and share market. Investors choose a rate of interest which they consider gives them a yield which adequately reflects the risks involved. The valuer has to decide what yield would be acceptable in the market when preparing his calculation.

In ascertaining value using the investment or capitalisation method the valuer is in effect valuing the right to receive a certain income in perpetuity (if the property being valued is a freehold), or what is referred to as 'the present value of £1 per annum in perpetuity'. Valuing this right depends upon the rate of return which is considered appropriate. Thus the capital value of an annual income of £18,000 receivable in perpetuity discounted at 8 per cent is ascertained by multiplying income by the year's purchase at 8 per cent:

YP in perpetuity at 8% = 100/8 = 12.5
12.5 × £18,000 = £225,000

It will be seen that an 8 per cent yield on £225,000 is £18,000 for a freehold property.

So far it has been assumed that the net future income on any property will remain a constant. However, in practice this will rarely be the case. For instance, where a property is let on a lease which is lower than market rents at the time of valuation, but that lease will fall in, or become subject to a rent review, at a date in the future, it is said that at that future date the property will 'revert' to full rental capacity. In calculating the capital value of a property subject to a low rent, the capitalisation of the net rent received for the period until the reversion to an open market rent will be a separate calculation to the capitalisation of the open market rent for the remainder of the investment (which may be in perpetuity). This method is called the 'term and reversion method'.

Most leases will be subject to upwards-only rent review clauses which mean that, at the date of the rent review, the rent will probably increase to take into account general rental increases since the rent was initially fixed. In those circumstances, a modification of the investment method of valuation known as the 'hardcore, or layer method' will be used. This method assumes a relatively secure continuing rent—the hardcore rent—which will continue throughout the life of the investment (which may be in perpetuity), and a potential future increased rent which, as a further yearly slice of income, incremental on the continuing rent, can be capitalised separately from the continuing hardcore of rent. The more precarious the prospect of the increased income, the higher will be the appropriate yield requirement. The valuer will have to make use of the various valuation investment tables to calculate what the year's purchase is for assessing the present capital value of an income that will only commence at some point in the future.

During periods of recession, the effect of upwards-only rent reviews is that current rents could well be more than the market level so that upon renewal of the lease, the anticipated income in reversion would fall, rather than rise. The 'term and reversion method' can be adapted to this situation whereby the *current* income may be considered to be less secure than the (lower) reversionary income.

Alternatively, instead of performing two calculations to reflect different income periods, the valuer may use the 'equivalent yield method', which involves assessing a single yield which takes into account two or more incomes over future years.

A.4.4   Terminable incomes

Where the property which is proposed to be purchased is a leasehold, rather than a freehold, the income potential on such a property will obviously terminate with the falling-in of the lease. In those circumstances the valuer is not considering an income in perpetuity and therefore the investment method of valuation, while still in general appropriate, will have to be modified to take this into account. Leasehold valuation tables cater for this.

A.5   The mortgage/equity approach

A.5.1   The discounted cash flow method

Where the valuation involves a property which will produce a variable stream of income from some future date, perhaps with an initial outlay in development costs before the income flows, a more sophisticated technique is required to balance outgoings against income. The discounted cash flow method of valuation is used. The method is founded on the theory that an investor values more highly income anticipated in the early days than that receivable at a more distant time. This is of course the theory of all 'present value' tables. A schedule of anticipated outflows and income each year is compiled and each amount is then discounted back to the present day, using 'present value of £1' tables. A balance sheet comprising the total discounted outgoings and income is thus obtained from which the value of the property is estimated.

Of course, the rate of discount is central to the accuracy of this method. It might be that the costs of borrowing money, or the opportunity costs of tying up capital, are the rates used. This will depend on the circumstances of the scheme. The great advantage of the method is that it is very sensitive to small variations in the proposed venture. Its disadvantage is that it may not relate to general market conditions. It is therefore most appropriate for unusual or specialised projects where the value is not readily tested by comparables.

A.5.2 Depreciated replacement cost

This method is not related to market conditions at all and is used only in cases where there is no general market for property, such as public enterprises, buildings used for religious purposes, schools, etc. It is essentially an 'opportunity cost' basis of estimating the worth of a property to the particular type of organisation wishing to use a premises. The method assumes that if the particular property was not available, the owner would need to acquire land and develop his own building for his particular use. Thus the cost of land for the particular use is ascertained to reflect the fact that the property to be valued will probably be less than perfect, as compared with the theoretical cost of building from scratch. It has been seen that the investment method of valuation involves the capitalisation of future income, that income discounted at an appropriate rate of interest depending upon the prevailing economic circumstances and the wider interest expectations from the diversity of investments available. The same basic principle is used in a more sophisticated method of valuation, which is widely used to evaluate a variety of business investments, known as the 'discounted cash flow method'. The value of this method is that it can be modified to take into account fluctuations of future income and future expenditure.

Appendix 2 Extracts from RICS and Law Society Professional Guidelines

1 RICS Appraisal and Valuation Manual (1995)

Practice Statement 4.2: Open Market Value (OMV)

[Revised 3/96 and effective from 1/5/96]

Definition

PS 4.2.1 An opinion of the best price at which the sale of an interest in property would have been completed unconditionally for cash consideration on the date of valuation, assuming:

(a) a willing seller;

(b) that, prior to the date of valuation, there had been a reasonable period (having regard to the nature of the property and the state of the market) for the proper marketing of the interest, for the agreement of the price and terms and for the completion of the sale;

(c) that the state of the market, level of values and other circumstances were, on any earlier assumed date of exchange of contracts, the same as on the date of valuation;

(d) that no account is taken of any additional bid by a prospective purchaser with a special interest; and

(e) that both parties to the transaction had acted knowledgeably, prudently and without compulsion.

Commentary

PS 4.2.2 The use of the expression 'Open Market Value', not qualified by any reference to Existing Use or Alternative Use, implies the value for any use to the extent to which that value is reflected in the price obtainable in the open market.

PS 4.2.3 The definition first requires the Valuer to assume that completion of a sale of the interest in the property took place on the valuation date and then to list further assumptions to be made in relation to that hypothetical sale.

'... the best price ...'

PS 4.2.4   Open Market Value is the Valuer's opinion of the best price which would have been obtained in the market on the date of valuation (subject to the exclusion of any additional bid by a prospective purchaser with a special interest); not a 'fair' price, or an average price or the price which the vendor thinks ought to be achieved.

Hope value

PS 4.2.5   Open Market Value includes such an element of 'hope value' (if any) as the property may have for uses other than the existing use (i.e. Alternative Uses) or for the realisation of any 'marriage value', which the property may have for merger with another property, or which an interest in the property may have for merger with another interest in the same property, but limited to the extent that the expectation of realising such 'hope value' would, in practice, be reflected in offers made in the open market by prospective purchasers (other than the additional bid of 'a prospective purchaser with a special interest').

PS 4.2.6   Therefore, Alternative Use Value should be related to definite information as to statutory and/or other consents, or the prospects thereof (eg superior landlord's approval) regarding change of use or other matters. The Valuer must not make unrealistic assumptions.

PS 4.2.7

(a) It is frequently necessary to value a property capable of development or redevelopment for a purpose for which no planning permission exists. In an open market valuation, planning permission should not be assumed unless the market would make such an assumption, and even then an allowance for risk would be appropriate where the market would do so.

(b) For example, prospective purchasers in the market might make an assumption that planning permission would be granted but nevertheless would make an allowance or deduction from the amount of their offers to reflect the risks involved and the likelihood of delay in obtaining an acceptable permission. In such circumstances, an open market valuation on the assumption that planning permission would be granted should only be made with the corresponding allowance for risk and delay, thus reflecting the view that would be taken in the market in practice.

(c) As a further example, in the case of an outline planning permission already granted, it might be reasonable to consider that prospective purchasers would assume a particular density or plot ratio and value accordingly. In such a case it would be proper to make assumptions about planning which would be made by prospective purchasers in the market without any deduction for risk.

'... sale ... completed ... cash consideration ... on the date of valuation ...'

PS 4.2.8   The Valuer must state the date of valuation in the Report. It may be the same as the date of the Report, or an earlier date, but it must not be a future date. The definition contemplates that the date of valuation is contemporaneous with the completion of the hypothetical sale. 'Cash consideration' means that the price to be paid on completion is to be in money, rather than other valuable consideration such as shares or other securities, goods, materials or services. It is not to be assumed that the purchaser can only be one able to fund the purchase from his own resources, i.e. without recourse to borrowing.

'A willing seller'

PS 4.2.9   The assumption of a 'willing seller' is vital to the definition of Open Market Value because the real circumstances of the actual owner of the property must be ignored and must not be confused with the notional circumstances of the hypothetical 'willing seller'. For the purposes of the definition, the vendor of the property is a hypothetical owner with the right to dispose of the premises. The hypothetical owner is neither an eager nor a reluctant seller, or a forced seller prepared to sell at any price. Thus, the willing seller is not afflicted by personal difficulties such as a cashflow crisis or importunate mortgagees, nor is that seller in the happy position of someone who wishes to sell only if the price he regards as satisfactory is obtained.

PS 4.2.10   Whether the real owner of the property being valued actually considers himself to be a 'willing seller' is irrelevant to the definition of Open Market Value or to the amount of the valuation. One way of explaining the point is to say that a willing seller has to be assumed in the sense that the seller has a genuine intention to sell at the best price (subject to PS 4.2.18 below) which can be obtained in the real market after proper marketing, whatever that price might be.

'... a reasonable period ...'

PS 4.2.11   The length of a 'reasonable period' will have varied according to the circumstances, not just of the particular property itself, but of the economy, of the state of the market and of supply and demand. The Valuer must form a judgement of what constituted a 'reasonable period' in each case, just as the Valuer must form an opinion of value, and the 'reasonable period' may have been longer in a poor market than in a good one but its length is related only to the time necessary to market the property properly, to agree price and terms and to complete the sale.

'… proper marketing …'

PS 4.2.12   Proper marketing means that the interest must be marketed in the most appropriate manner to effect a disposal at the best price having regard to the type of property, its characteristics, locality and the state of the market at the time. The essentials of proper marketing are that the availability of the property for sale and the terms on which it is offered should be brought, by appropriate means, to the attention of an adequate number of potential purchasers and that those potential purchasers should have adequate time in which to obtain such information as they may need in order to make their offers to purchase and, if successful, to complete the transaction.

'… state of the market … on the date of valuation …'

PS 4.2.13   Open Market Value equals the best price which would have been obtained in the market on the date of valuation and, thus, the amount of the valuation must reflect the state of the market and other circumstances on the date of valuation; not on any past or future date. The value is not a price which might be expected some months or years hence when the market may have changed—it is the best price which could have been obtained in the circumstances current on the date of valuation after proper marketing. In a poor or falling market, the Valuer is not entitled to assume that marketing will be delayed until the market has recovered, and, in a rising market, values must not be projected forward.

PS 4.2.14   In practice, it is usually the case that the bargain is struck and the price finally fixed, not on the date of completion of the sale, but on an earlier date when unconditional contracts were exchanged. The Valuer must assume that circumstances, values and market conditions at the date of contract were the same as those prevailing at the date of completion (i.e. the date of valuation).

Evidence of open market transactions

PS 4.2.15   Generally, open market valuations are based on evidence of open market transactions in similar property. A valuation, however, is an exercise in judgement and should represent the Valuer's opinion of the price which would have been obtained if the property had been sold at the valuation date on the terms of the definition of Open Market Value. The Valuer is not bound to follow evidence of market transactions unquestioningly, but should take account of trends in value and the market evidence available to him, whether or not of directly comparable transactions, adjusting such evidence to reflect the OMV definition and attaching more weight to some pieces of evidence than others, according to the Valuer's judgement. It is seldom that a Valuer has evidence of contemporaneous transactions in precisely similar property to that being valued. The art of valuation often involves subjective adjustments to evidence of transactions which are not wholly comparable together with interpretation of trends in value. A Valuer must exercise skill, experience and judgement in valuing and in making such adjustments and comparisons, even to the extent of making an open market valuation (of a property for which it is thought there would have been a market) in the absence of any direct transaction evidence.

PS 4.2.16   In a poor or falling market it is sometimes said that there are few 'willing sellers', that most transactions in the market are the result of 'forced sales' and that prices paid in such a market are not truly representative of Open Market Value and should be ignored by Valuers in favour of some higher level of value. There is little merit in such an argument and there are far fewer truly forced sales (within the meaning of the definition of Estimated Restricted Realisation Price in PS 4.6 below) than is sometimes supposed. Valuers must not ignore the evidence of the market; they should take account of all market evidence, attaching such weight to individual transactions as they believe appropriate. In a depressed market, a significant proportion of sales may be by vendors who are obliged to sell, such as Liquidators and Receivers, but the Valuer should establish whether or not those sales took place after proper marketing for a reasonable period. Liquidators and Receivers are normally under a duty to obtain the best price and their sales should be regarded generally as open market transactions if there has been proper marketing for a reasonable period and the transactions otherwise comply with the definition of Open Market Value.

PS 4.2.17   In a rapidly rising or falling market, undue weight should not be attributed to historic evidence, which may have become outdated, even within a brief period.

'... a prospective purchaser with a special interest ...'

PS 4.2.18
- (a) The definition of Open Market Value requires the assumption 'that no account is taken of any additional bid by a prospective purchaser with a special interest'.
- (b) A purchaser with a 'special interest' (sometimes referred to as a

'special purchaser') may be defined as one to whom the property, or the interest in the property, being valued has a particular attraction which it does not have for the market in general. The special purchaser is, in almost every case, the owner of either:

(i)   an interest in land which has or could have a particular relationship with the property concerned, eg the owner of an interest in a nearby or adjacent property; or

(ii) another interest in the property being valued, eg a superior landlord or an under-tenant.

(c) There is no certainty that the special purchaser will be prepared to make an offer to purchase the property or interest in the property at the date of the valuation, and it is therefore correct to exclude his additional bid from the Open Market Value. However, if the special purchaser is in the market he can usually afford, or be willing, to pay more than any other purchaser, and if he enters the bidding, he may reasonably be expected to succeed in purchasing the property—certainly in theory—by paying 'one bid more' than any other purchaser. In practice, it is often difficult to quantify the special purchaser's additional bid, since he may not need to go to the level he could afford to bid in order to secure the property. On the other hand, in his determination to secure the property, he may overbid by a margin greater than necessary.

(d) A purchaser who is simply prepared to pay a high price is not necessarily a special purchaser. Neither is someone who is a known purchaser of the particular class of property being valued, nor someone who is an active purchaser of property in the locality. A purchaser who is only one of a class of purchasers to whom the property has particular interest, would not be regarded as a special purchaser, eg tax immune funds which purchase short leasehold investment property. Generally, for a prospective purchaser to be a special purchaser there will be an element of additional potential value which is unique to him.

(e) A superior landlord or a sitting tenant, may be a special purchaser because the merging of the two interests might liberate 'marriage value' which would justify a higher price than any other purchaser could afford to pay. It must be remembered however, that the price which a non-special purchaser would pay might include some part of that marriage value because of the hope that the non-special purchaser might eventually be able to re-sell to the special purchaser at an inflated price. Thus 'hope value' and 'marriage value' may legitimately be included in Open Market Value to the extent that offers from non-special purchasers in the open market themselves reflect those elements of value, as in practice they often do. It is only the additional bid of the special purchaser which has to be excluded from the Open Market Value.

(f)   The definition of Open Market Value does not require the Valuer to ignore the existence of the special purchaser, but to take no account of that special purchaser's additional bid, i.e. the amount by which his offer might exceed offers made by non-special purchasers. In practice, the existence of a special purchaser may affect (usually to a limited degree) the level of offers made by non-special purchasers and, to that extent, may be taken into account in arriving at Open Market Value.

'... the parties had each acted knowledgeably, prudently ...'

PS 4.2.19   This presumes that both the buyer and the willing seller are reasonably informed about the nature and characteristics of the asset, its actual and potential uses and the state of the market at the date of valuation. Each is further presumed to act for self-interest with that knowledge and prudently to seek the best price for their respective positions in the transaction. Prudence is assessed by referring to the state of the market at the date of valuation, not with benefit of hindsight at some later date. It is not necessarily imprudent for a seller to sell property in a market with falling prices at a price which is lower than previous market levels. In such cases, as is true for other purchase and sale situations in markets with changing prices, the prudent buyer or seller will act in accordance with the best market information available at the time.

'... and without compulsion ...'

PS 4.2.20   This establishes that each party is motivated to undertake the transaction, but neither is forced or unduly coerced to complete it.

☆ ☆ ☆ ☆ ☆

Practice Statement 8:   Valuation and appraisal of commercial land and buildings for secured lending and disposal purposes

[Revised 6/96 and effective from 1/8/96]

PS 8.1   Introduction

This Statement is for use where the Valuer is to provide services for a Client who is considering whether to lend or extend loan facilities on the security of commercial land and buildings and (although this is not recommended) where a valuation for this purpose is sought by the prospective borrower. It covers also the provision of advice where the Lender is considering whether to take recovery proceedings and the framing of instructions for disposal of such property which has been repossessed.

PS 8.2   Settling the instructions

PS 8.2.1   The Valuer must agree in writing formal Conditions of Engagement before providing the service. The Institution and the British Bankers' Association have drafted model instruction letters which are set out in PSA 8 and PSA 15. Each requires some completion and probably amendment according to the circumstances of the particular case. The Models are drafted for use by banks, but with minor amendment are suitable also for use by Receivers.

PS 8.2.2   There are four principal situations in which the appraisals are most likely to be required and the basis of valuation will need to be agreed in each case. Reference to these bases is made in the PSA 8 and PSA 15. The four situations are:

(a) property which is or is to be held as an investment;
(b) property which is, is to be or has been owner-occupied;
(c) property which is fully equipped as an operational entity (which generally will be valued having regard to trading potential); and
(d) property which is or is intended to be the subject of development/refurbishment.

PS 8.2.3   Before the Valuer's instructions are settled and confirmed, the Client and the Valuer need to identify which of the situations in PS 8.2.2 applies and in the light thereof to agree the valuation basis/bases to be adopted; also which of the other options in the model instruction letters are to apply and the information with which the Valuer is to be supplied. Should the subject property be characterised by more than one of the above situations, or one not within these four, special conditions of engagement need to be agreed.

PS 8.2.4   Usually, however, it will be possible for Valuers to confirm the agreed instructions by written reference to the instruction letters sent to them and such of the matters listed in PS 2.2.2 as are not dealt with therein.

PSA 8 and PSA 15 have been produced on the basis that the Client is the Lender. Parts of the service specified in PSA 8 cannot be provided where this is not the case. PSA 15 may be capable of use with minor adaptation where any client is contemplating framing instructions for disposal of commercial land and buildings.

PS 8.2.5   Where lending on development land and land and buildings in the course of development is contemplated, the valuation or appraisal required is likely to depend on whether the Lender will lend only when planning permission has been obtained and/or upon whether the Lender intends to finance the development. In the latter case, the current estimated value of the development, as proposed to be completed, will be required, in relation to which the Lender may need or obtain from elsewhere an estimate of the development costs. The Lender may have instructed a building or quantity surveyor to advise on the likely cost of proposed development. The service required in such cases must be clearly established between the Lender and the Valuer on each occasion.

PS 8.2.6   In all cases (except where the property to be valued is equipped as a fully operational entity) any additional value attributable to goodwill, or to fixtures and fittings which are only of value *in situ* to the present occupier, is to be excluded.

PS 8.3   Reporting

PS 8.3.1   In view of the purpose of the valuation or appraisal, the Valuer's Report must be addressed and submitted directly to the Lender, notwithstanding that the Lender may choose to supply copies of the Report to its customer.

PS 8.3.2   It is good practice to refer to, and attach the conditions of engagement and letter of confirmation of instructions, to the Report.

PS 8.3.3   The British Bankers' Association and the Institution regard it as important that Client Lenders and Valuers develop close working relationships in respect of valuations and appraisals, especially in the more complex cases, to ensure that the service provided by the Valuer reflects the Client Lender's needs, and the latter fully understands the advice which is being given.

PS 8.4   Investment property (PS 8.2.2(a))

Revenue producing properties are usually valued individually, but lending institutions may wish to be advised as to the value of a property as part of a portfolio of properties. In such cases, a clear distinction as to the assumptions being made must be provided by the Valuer in the Report.

PS 8.5   Owner-occupied property (PS 8.2.2(b))

PS 8.5.1   The valuation is of the property vacant and to let or for sale.
PS 8.5.2   If the Valuer considers that there is a prospect of or potential for change of use or other development of the subject property or those

in the vicinity, which would materially affect the value, this must be reflected in the valuation and declared in the Report.

PS 8.6 Property which is fully equipped as an operational entity (PS 8.2.2(c))

PS 8.6.1 This category includes hotels, public houses, other licensed premises, private healthcare facilities and most types of leisure property. The most appropriate bases of valuation are usually the Estimated Realisation Price or (Open) Market Value, but of the operational entity, unless there is a realistic more valuable alternative use. In providing the valuation or appraisal, regard should be paid to the possible impact of the circumstances envisaged in PS 4.7.1(e)(i) to (vi) and to GN 7, especially GN 7.8.3.

PS 8.6.2 If the Valuer considers that a valuation for an alternative use with vacant possession would assist the Lender, the Valuer should discuss and agree with the Lender whether a valuation of the Estimated Realisation Price should be supplied. This may be appropriate where the demand for the existing use is considered to be particularly limited or where there is a prospective alternative use suggesting significant enhancement of value.

PS 8.7 Development land and buildings (PS 8.2.2(d))

PS 8.7.1 (Also see PS 8.2.5 above.) Lenders may well be as interested, even when only a development site is to be valued, in whether the valuation is founded upon a residual valuation involving an assessment of the estimated costs of development and the resulting value, or upon comparable land transactions.

PS 8.7.2 In those cases where a site is being valued for development into an operational entity, the Valuer should bear in mind the long timescale between the commencement of work and the completion of the project, as compared with most commercial developments. Large operational entities can take long periods to complete and equip and further time may elapse while goodwill develops and trade is built up. Ordinary commercial developments may be pre-let, or the site developed in phases, or sold off as units are completed enabling loans to be repaid at an early date, but operational entity developments, on the other hand, provide reduced security for lending until the development is complete and operational and trading figures become available. A Valuer employing the residual method of valuation must point out to the Lender that there will be risk exposure which may not be covered adequately by value in the intervening period.

☆ ☆ ☆ ☆ ☆

Practice Statement 9:   Valuation of residential properties for mortgage purposes

[Revised 3/96 and effective from 1/5/96]

PS 9.1   Residential mortgage valuations (except in relation to further advances)

PS 9.1.1   Except to any extent notified by or agreed in writing in advance with the Client, the Valuer is to comply with the Specification reproduced in Annex A to this Practice Statement in valuing residential properties for owner-occupation on behalf of building societies, banks and other lenders, for mortgage purposes.

PS 9.1.2

(a) If not previously agreed, terms of engagement should be settled in writing with the Lender before instructions are accepted. Model Conditions of Engagement are provided in Annex B to this Practice Statement and should be used if the Valuer wishes to rely upon the terms of the Specification in that Annex A as defining the task which is to be undertaken. If the Valuer has no written or previously established instructions from the Lender/Client, it is suggested that the Valuer should write confirming the intention to provide a service in accordance with the RICS/ISVA specification for the valuation and inspection of residential property for mortgage purposes on behalf of building societies, banks and other lenders. A copy should be enclosed and confirmation of its acceptability sought in this, and any future cases in respect of which the Valuer may be instructed by the Client.

(b) Where the terms of engagement, documents referred to therein and the Client Lender's instructions in the particular case together cover the matters listed at (a) to (n) of PS 2.2.2, there is no requirement upon the Valuer to confirm in writing receipt of instructions in respect of that case.

PS 9.1.3   It is unlikely that any Lender will seek to limit the normal investigatory procedures of the Valuer. If this should happen, such limiting instructions should be confirmed in writing beforehand and also incorporated in the Report.

PS 9.1.4   It is commonplace for Lenders to disclose the contents of the Valuer's Report to the Borrowers. If the Report is disclosed, it is important that the limits of the form of inspection and Report are conveyed to the prospective purchaser together with a warning that the purchaser should not enter into any legal commitment to the vendor before further investigations are complete. Such warning must, therefore, be included in the Report.

PS 9.1.5   A model report form is provided at PSA 9 for use at the Valuer's discretion.

PS 9.1.6   The Building Societies Act 1986 differentiates between those who are authorised to assess the advance from those who make the valuation for the advance. The duty of the assessor is to decide on the amount of the loan, the duration and other conditions. The Valuer's job is limited to assessing the adequacy of the security. Valuers, therefore, must neither accept instructions to make, nor volunteer recommendations as to the length of the term or the amount to be advanced. These decisions are solely the responsibility of the Lender.

PS 9.2   Reinspection of residential property for mortgage purposes

PS 9.2.1   This paragraph covers 'reinspections' carried out for building societies, banks and other Lenders to which this Practice Statement applies.

PS 9.2.2   A 'reinspection' is a further visit to a property which has already been accepted in principle by the Lender as suitable security for an advance of a specified amount, so that the Valuer can advise:

(a) in connection with consideration of the release of money by way of stage payments applicable to the stage of construction reached; or

(b) as to whether the (new, or newly converted or improved) property has been completed to the state assumed in the initial mortgage valuation report (a mortgage offer having been made in consequence thereof but no advance actually made); or

(c) in circumstances where, part of the advance having been retained until specified works have been undertaken, whether those works have apparently been completed as assumed in the initial Valuation Report, or as otherwise specified by the Lender, to a standard satisfactory to justify lending on them and without significantly affecting the value of the property adversely.

In all of the above cases, whether the previous Valuation Report (which must always be available to the Valuer) remains sufficient to enable the Lender to assess the adequacy of the security when deciding whether or not to release the retention or stage payment.

A Model Report form is provided in PSA 10 for use at the Valuer's discretion.

PS 9.2.3   If, in the course of inspecting the parts of the property with which the service to be provided by the Valuer is concerned, the Valuer:

(a) becomes aware of any material changes or factors, additional to those in the previous Report which would affect the valuation of the proposed, completed security; or

(b) is aware of any other factor which might materially affect the valuation; or

(c) is of the opinion that the valuation of the proposed completed security would be materially different from that previously reported,

the Valuer must report accordingly. Subject to the Lender's specific policy, the Valuer may then be instructed to carry out a revaluation.

PS 9.2.4 In these cases the Valuer's duty is to inspect, to the extent described in Annex A to this Practice Statement, those parts of the property with which the service to be provided by the Valuer is concerned. It is not the task of the Valuer to inspect the whole property.

The Valuer must, however, advise the Lender if in the course of the inspection:

(a) it is considered that the property may have been affected adversely by the works carried out; or

(b) new defects and/or repairing requirements and/or unsatisfactory workmanship are observed; or

(c) it is apparent that the problem which gave rise to the need to carry out the remedial works is now affecting another part of the structure or that part of the structure which is the subject of the required inspection is suffering from a further defect.

Unless asked to do so, the Valuer has no duty to provide a new figure for reinstatement insurance purposes.

PS 9.2.5 If no form is provided by the Lender, the Model Report Forms shown at PSA 10 may be used to form the basis of the Report. Attention is drawn to the caveats and warnings therein which Valuers are encouraged to include in their Reports, whether or not the Lender makes provision therefor and to recommend that copies of their Reports are provided to the Borrowers.

PS 9.3 Valuation of residential property in relation to further advances

PS 9.3.1 This paragraph covers a valuation provided on a property already in mortgage to the lending institution instructing the Valuer, where the lending institution proposes to consider whether a further advance, usually of a specified sum, can be made on the security of the property, or the repayment of a loan rescheduled. The valuation may be of the property as it stands and/or with works proposed to it. Wherever possible the Lender provides to the Valuer the original Report or a copy.

PS 9.3.2 The Valuer's remit is to provide a report on:

(a) the current Open Market Value of the property;

(b) the current Open Market Value, where defined works are contemplated, on the assumption that they have been satisfactorily completed, and a revised estimate for insurance purposes;

(c) any factors likely to affect its value materially; and

(d) changes in the accommodation or its amenities since the previous inspection report.

PS 9.3.3 The matters which a Valuer should consider in preparing the valuation and the extent of inspection are the same as those described in the Annex to this Practice Statement, to which reference should be made.

PS 9.3.4 It occasionally happens that a Valuer is asked for an opinion on a revaluation without inspection. If such an opinion becomes available to a member of the public, including the Borrower, there is a danger of its being misunderstood or misquoted. When a Valuer does provide such an opinion (which should be expressed as approximate) it must be written or confirmed in writing and the manner of valuation and the restrictions under which it is given clearly stated. The Lender must be informed that the value stated in such a fashion must not be quoted to the Borrower or any other party.

PS 9.3.5 The presentation of the revaluation report will normally be dictated by the prescribed form provided by the Lender. In the absence of any such form the Valuer may wish to use the sample form shown in PSA 11.

PS 9.4 Valuation of residential property in connection with possible possession proceedings

PS 9.4.1 This paragraph covers valuations carried out for building societies, banks and other mortgagees to which this Practice Statement applies, where the lending institution is considering whether to take possession of the property. If the Valuer is instructed to produce the valuation without inspection of the inside of the property or with limited information, PS 2.3.1 applies.

PS 9.4.2 Here the Lender's requirement is for an estimate of the price which could be achieved if the property was put on the market at the date of valuation. Accordingly an Estimated Realisation Price (ERP) is required. Notwithstanding PS 3.1.2, there is no obligation to provide also an Open Market Value unless so instructed by the Client. In view of the purpose of the valuation the ERP must be made with the additional assumption that at the date of the valuation the property is vacant. The Client Lender should be recommended to consider the extent to which fixtures and fittings present in the property at the valuation date and included in the valuation may not be present if and when the property is offered for sale by the Client Lender.

PS 9.4.3   If the lending institution requests a 'forced sale value' the Lender must be advised that this is an inappropriate basis and that Estimated Restricted Realisation Price (ERRP) is the more appropriate. An ERP must be provided also. The additional assumption referred to in PS 9.4.2 is to be applied in both cases.

PS 9.5   Valuation of repossessed residential property

PS 9.5.1   This paragraph covers valuations carried out where the lending institution is contemplating the sale of repossessed residential property. Detailed guidance, *The Effective and Efficient Sale of Repossessed Residential Property*, published by the National Association of Estate Agents, of which the Institution was a joint author, was provided in November 1994. Part 1 of that guidance lists the nature of professional advice which lenders are recommended to obtain before deciding on the appropriate mode of sale. Since in normal circumstances the property will already be in possession when the valuation is requested, the appropriate valuation bases are the Estimated Realisation Price (ERP) and the Estimated Restricted Realisation Price (ERRP). In the case of a recommendation that private treaty is the appropriate mode of sale, the recommended asking price may be required also.

PS 9.5.2   The provisions of PS 9.4.2 and PS 9.4.3 above apply also to this paragraph.

PS 9.5.3   On occasion lenders may wish to seek confirmation from an Independent Valuer that the property has been marketed properly in accordance with the agency instructions and that it is that Valuer's opinion that the provisionally agreed sale price is the best reasonably obtainable in the light of prevailing market conditions and the extent of marketing undertaken.

PS 9.5.4   It is never appropriate to provide valuations or opinions on the lines described in this paragraph without an adequate inspection of the property and the relevant information and investigations.

☆ ☆ ☆ ☆ ☆

Annex A to Practice Statement 9: RICS/ISVA specification for the valuation and inspection of residential property for mortgage purposes on behalf of building societies, banks and other lenders

[Revised 12/95 and effective from 1/1/96]

This Specification applies to inspections carried out on or after 1 January 1996 and, in respect of such inspections, supersedes previous published Guidance. The Council of Mortgage Lenders was consulted during the production of this specification.

1 The Valuer's roles

1.1 The roles of the Valuer, who must have knowledge of and experience in the valuation of the residential property in the particular locality, are:

> **1.1.1** to advise the Lender as to the Open Market Value but usually excluding development value (see Sections 4.3 and 4.4 hereof) at the date of inspection;
>
> **1.1.2** to advise the Lender as to the nature of the property (see Section 4 below) and any factors likely materially to affect its value; and
>
> **1.1.3** if required by the Lender, to provide an assessment of the property's estimated current reinstatement cost in its present form (unless otherwise stated) for insurance purposes including garage, outbuildings, site clearance and professional fees, excluding VAT (except on fees).

1.2 The Valuer is not to make a recommendation as to the amount or percentage of mortgage advance or the length of the mortgage term. Nor is it the valuer's responsibility to give advice as to the suitability of the property 'for second mortgage purposes'.

2 The Valuer's inspection

Subject to the Valuer's judgement, a visual inspection is to be undertaken of so much of the exterior and interior of the property as is accessible to the Valuer without undue difficulty. Accordingly, it is to include all that part of the property which is visible whilst standing at ground level within the boundaries of the site and adjacent public/communal areas and whilst standing at the various floor levels, as follows:

2.1 Main building—external

Roof coverings, chimneys, parapets, gutters, walls, windows, doors, pipes, wood or metalwork, paintwork, damp proof courses, air bricks and ground levels.

2.2 Main building—internal

> **2.2.1** Parts not readily accessible or visible are not inspected and furniture and effects are not moved or floor coverings lifted.
>
> **2.2.2** Subject to reasonable accessibility, the roof space is inspected only to the extent visible from the access hatch, without entering it.
>
> **2.2.3** Ceilings, walls, load bearers and floor surfaces are inspected except where covered or obscured. Readings are to be taken with

a moisture meter for rising dampness.

    2.2.4   Cellars are inspected to the extent that they are reasonably accessible, but under floor voids are *not* inspected.

2.3   Services

The Valuer is to identify whether or not there are gas, electricity, central heating, plumbing and drainage services. Testing of services is *not* undertaken.

2.4   Outbuildings

Garages and other buildings of substantial permanent construction, and any structure(s) attached to the dwelling, are to be inspected.

2.5   Site

The inspection is to include the general state of boundaries, structures, drives, paths, retaining walls and the proximity of trees only to the extent that they are likely materially to affect the property's value.

2.6   Neighbouring properties

The nature, use and apparent state of repair of neighbouring properties in the immediate vicinity is to be considered only to the extent that they may materially affect the value of the subject property.

2.7   Flats, maisonettes or similar units forming part of a larger building or group of related buildings

The above provisions apply, but here 'Main Building' means the building containing the proposed security but not including other main buildings physically attached to it.

    2.7.1   *Main building—external*

        The exterior of the proposed security and sufficient of the remainder of the Main Building to ascertain its general state of repair.

    2.7.2   *Main building—internal*

        The interior of the proposed security, the communal entrance areas within the Main Building from which the proposed security takes access and the communal area on the floor(s) of the proposed security. The roof space will only be inspected (as defined in paragraph 2.2.2 above) where access is directly available from within the proposed security.

    2.7.3   *Outbuildings*

        Garaging, car parking, other buildings (excluding sports complexes) of permanent construction and any other structures attached to the Main Building or which serve the Main Building or which serve the proposed security.

3   The Valuer's report

3.1   Subject to covering the matters referred to in Section 1 above, reporting is to be confined strictly to answering questions raised by the Lender.

3.2 If it is suspected that hidden defects exist which could have a material effect on the value of the property, the Valuer is to so advise and recommend more extensive investigation by the intending Borrower prior to entering into a legal commitment to purchase or, in the case of a re-mortgage, as a pre-condition of the mortgage advance. It may be appropriate in exceptional circumstances to defer making a valuation until the results of the further investigations are known.

3.3 If it is not reasonably possible to carry out any substantial part of the inspection (see Section 2 above) this is to be stated.

3.4 Any obvious evidence of serious disrepair to the property or obvious potential hazard to it is to be reported, as should any other matters likely materially to affect the value.

3.5 Where the Valuer relies on information provided, this is to be indicated in the Report, together with the source of that information.

3.6 The Lender is to be informed of the existence of any apparently recent significant alterations and extensions, so as to alert the Lender's legal adviser to any enquiries to be made.

3.7 Where the proposed security is part of a building comprising flats or maisonettes, the Valuer's Report is to identify any apparent deficiencies in the management and/or maintenance arrangements observed during the inspection which materially affect the value, and will provide the amount or estimated current level of the service charges payable on an annual basis.

3.8 Where the apparent sharing of drives, paths, or other areas might affect the value of the subject property, the Valuer is to inform the Lender.

3.9 The form of construction is to be reported and, where non-traditional, the Valuer is to advise accordingly, stating the type of construction and the source of this information if it is not apparent from the inspection.

3.10 Where the Valuer decides to report a necessity for works to be carried out to a property as a condition of any advance and the Valuer identifies the property as being:

3.10.1 of architectural or historic interest, or listed as such; or

3.10.2 in a conservation area; or

3.10.3 of unusual construction,

the Valuer is to advise that a person with appropriate specialist knowledge be asked to give advice as to the appropriate works unless, exceptionally, the Valuer believes he/she is competent to give advice which if adopted would not be detrimental to the property's architectural or historic integrity, its future structural condition or conservation of the building fabric.

3.11 In the case of new properties or conversions where the Valuer is obliged to base the valuation upon drawings and a specification, this fact is to be stated in the Report.

4   The Valuation

4.1   Unless it is made apparent by an express statement in the Report, the Valuer is to make the following assumptions and will have been under no duty to have verified these assumptions:

4.1.1   that vacant possession is provided;

4.1.2   that all required, valid planning permissions and statutory approvals for the buildings and for their use, including any extensions or alterations, have been obtained and complied with;

4.1.3   that no deleterious or hazardous materials or techniques have been used, that there is no contamination in or from the ground, and it is not landfilled ground;

4.1.4   that the property is not subject to any unusual or especially onerous restrictions, encumbrances or outgoings and that good title can be shown;

4.1.5   that the property and its value are unaffected by any matters which would be revealed by a Local Search (or their equivalent in Scotland and Northern Ireland) and replies to the usual enquiries, or by a Statutory Notice and that neither the property, nor its condition, its use, or its intended use, is or will be unlawful;

4.1.6   that an inspection of those parts which have not been inspected, or a survey inspection, would not reveal material defects or cause the Valuer to alter the valuation materially;

4.1.7   that the property is connected to and there is the right to use the reported main services on normal terms;

4.1.8   that sewers, main services and the roads giving access to the property have been adopted, and that any lease provides rights of access and egress over all communal estate roadways, pathways, corridors, stairways and to use communal grounds, parking areas and other facilities;

4.1.9   that in the case of a new property, the construction of which has not been completed, the construction will be satisfactorily completed;

4.1.10   that in the case of a newly constructed property, the builder is a registered member of the NHBC, the Zurich Municipal Mutual, or equivalent and will construct the property to obtain its cover; and

4.1.11   that where the proposed security is part of a building comprising flats or maisonettes, unless instructed or otherwise aware to the contrary, the costs of repairs and maintenance to the building and grounds are shared (except in Scotland) equitably between the flats and maisonettes forming part of the block, that those liable will pay their shares, that there are suitable mutually enforceable covenants between all leaseholders or through the landlord and upon the freeholder/any feuholder, that there are no onerous liabilities outstanding and that there are no substantial defects or other matters requiring expenditure (in excess of the usual level of service charge) expected to result in charges to the leaseholder of the subject property during the next five years equivalent to 10% or more of the Open Market Value being reported; and

4.1.12 that, where the dwelling is leasehold and because the Valuer has no further and better knowledge or information:

(a) the unexpired term of the lease is 70 years, and no action is being taken by an eligible party with a view to acquiring the freehold or to extending the lease term;

(b) there are no covenants exceptionally onerous upon the leaseholder;

(c) the lease cannot be determined except on the grounds of a serious breach of covenant in the existing lease agreement;

(d) if there are separate freeholders, head and/or other sub-head leaseholders, the terms and conditions of all the leases are in the same form and contain the same terms and conditions;

(e) the lease terms are mutually enforceable against all parties concerned;

(f) there are no breaches of covenant or disputes between the various interests concerned;

(g) the leases of all the properties in the building/development are materially the same;

(h) the ground rent stated or assumed is not subject to review and is payable throughout the unexpired lease term;

(i) in the case of blocks of flats or maisonettes of over six dwellings, the freeholder manages the property directly or it is managed by a professional, properly bonded managing agent;

(j) where the subject property forms part of a mixed residential or commercially used block or development, there will be no significant changes in the existing use pattern therein;

(k) where the property forms part of a development containing separate blocks of dwellings, the lease terms of the subject property apply only to the subject block, and there will be no requirement to contribute towards costs relating to other parts of the development, other than in respect of common roads, paths, communal grounds and services;

(l) where the property forms part of a larger development the ownership of which has since been divided, all necessary rights and reservations have been reserved;

(m) there are no unusual restrictions on assignment or subletting of the subject property for residential purposes;

(n) there are no outstanding claims or litigation concerning the lease of the subject property or any others within the same development;

(o) where the subject property benefits from additional facilities within the development, the lease makes adequate provision for the lessee to continue to enjoy them without exceptional restriction, and for the facilities to be maintained adequately, and that there are no charges over and above the service charge for such use and maintenance; and

(p) in respect of insurance:

    (i)   the property will be insured under all risks cover, which includes subsidence, landslip and heave, for the current reinstatement cost;

    (ii) the cover assumed is available on normal terms;

    (iii) there are no outstanding claims or disputes;

    (iv) where individuals in a block make separate insurance arrangements, the leases make provision for mutual enforceability of insurance and repairing obligations; and

    (v) the landlord obliged to insure is required to rebuild the property with such alterations as may be necessary to comply with then current building regulations and planning requirements.

4.2   Among the relevant factors to be taken into account in the valuation are:

    4.2.1   the tenure of the interest to be offered as security and, if known, the terms of any tenancies to which that interest is subject;

    4.2.2   the age, type, accommodation, siting, amenities, fixtures and features of the property and other significant environmental factors within the locality; and

    4.2.3   the apparent general state of and liability for repair, the construction and apparent major defects, liability to subsidence, flooding, and/or other risks. Particular care is needed with non-traditional construction.

4.3   Unless otherwise instructed, any value for development which has or requires planning permission is to be excluded from the 'open market valuation' and the Valuer is not to include any element of value attributable to furnishings, removable fittings and sales incentives of any description when arriving at an opinion of the value. Portable and temporary structures are to be excluded also.

4.4   The definition of 'Open Market Value' is the Valuer's opinion of the best price at which the sale of an interest in property would have been completed unconditionally for cash consideration at the date of the valuation assuming:

4.4.1   a willing seller;

4.4.2   that, prior to the date of valuation, there had been a reasonable period (having regard to the nature of the property and the state of the market) for the proper marketing of the interest, for the agreement of price and terms and for the completion of the sale;

4.4.3   that the state of the market, level of values and other circumstances were, on any earlier assumed date of exchange of contracts, the same as on the date of valuation;

4.4.4   that no account is taken of any additional bid by a prospective purchaser with a special interest; and

4.4.5   that both parties to the transaction had acted knowledgeably, prudently and without compulsion.

5   Estimate for insurance purposes

In assessing the current reinstatement cost (see paragraph 1.1.3 above) the Valuer should have regard where relevant to the ABI/BCIS/House Rebuilding Cost Index.

6   The Valuer's record of inspection and valuation

6.1   The Valuer is to make and retain legible notes as to his/her findings and, particularly, the limits of the inspection and the circumstances in which it was carried out.

6.2   The Valuer is to keep a record of the comparable transactions and/ or valuations to which he/she has had regard in arriving at his/her valuation.

7   The variation of instructions

The Service is to be in accordance with this Specification unless variations are notified to or agreed with the Valuer in writing.

☆ ☆ ☆ ☆ ☆

Guidance Note 1: Additional general guidance on valuation and appraisal practice

[Revised 6/96 and effective from 1/8/96]

GN 1.1   Application of Guidance Notes

The application of the Guidance Notes, which comprise Section Two of this Manual, is not restricted by PS 1.3. Moreover, much of the material in Section One is good practice in respect of valuations carried out for purposes and in circumstances exempted by PS 1.3 and the definition of valuation (i.e. excluding oral valuations) from the mandatory status of Section One.

GN 1.2   Knowing your client

Valuers produce valuations and appraisals and associated reports for an enormous range of Clients, from those who have a deep understanding of property to those wholly unfamiliar with it or with the property market and the terms used and concepts embraced by valuers. It helps the provision of a good and suitable service if the Valuer knows the Client's ability to understand and benefit from the advice given, and grasps the importance of the advice. A process of 'getting to know your Client' is therefore advocated. Valuers may wish to establish check-lists of questions to ask or matters to discuss with Clients, the answers to which may influence their subsequent investigations and reporting. Some organisations may wish to establish standard forms for record purposes, but in any event it is desirable that the Valuer be able to show from his papers how he has responded to what he has learnt.

GN 1.3   Conditions of engagement

Where appropriate, Valuers may wish to use the Institution's publications *The Valuation of Residential Property* and *The Valuation of Business Property* reproduced at PSA 2 and PSA 4 herein or their own similar documentation, to ensure that acceptable conditions of engagement are defined and that proper limitations of liability and responsibility are achieved.

GN 1.4   Memoranda of instruction

The Annex to this Guidance Note provides a Memorandum of Valuation Instruction which Valuers and their Clients may find of assistance in establishing the key elements of the service to be provided.

GN 1.5   Financial Services Act 1986

If the Valuer's activities are to go beyond the provision of the valuation of the underlying property, the Valuer may need, in order to comply with the Financial Services Act 1986, to be a registered member of an authorised Self Regulatory Organisation. On occasion the following may be examples:

(a) attendances at meetings with Clients and other advisers such as lawyers, stockbrokers, accountants and merchant bankers, if he moves into any role where he might be regarded as a 'financial adviser'. (It is not possible to be precise but involvement in discussions on profit forecasts or tactics are likely to fall within the Act.)

If the Valuer has any doubt about his position he should take legal advice, preferably before attending any meeting. Financial advisers need to be familiar with the City Code on Take-overs and Mergers as this Manual refers only to the involvement of the Valuer as a provider of valuations; and

(b) advice regarding loans linked into a present or future equity participation, or ranking as a security, i.e. a debenture (quoted or unquoted).

GN 1.6   Legal issues

GN 1.6.1   Clients will expect Valuers to express opinions (and, in turn, Valuers will wish to express their opinion) upon legal issues affecting their valuations, but the Valuers should take care to state that any interpretation of legal documents and legal assumptions made must be checked by the Client with a suitably qualified lawyer, if they are to be relied upon. The Valuer should state that no responsibility or liability is accepted for the true interpretation of the legal position of the Client or other parties. If this is not done, the Valuer will assume no less a burden than the law imposes upon a competent lawyer, if and in so far as legal advice is expressly or impliedly given.

GN 1.6.2   The general assumption will be that the title is free from onerous and unusual restrictions, but restrictive covenants, easements, servitudes, other rights (such as those pertaining to way, light and drainage) and other obligations associated with tenure can have a material effect on and influence value and marketability. Specific enquiries should be made as to whether they are perpetual or determinable. Similarly, specific user and other restrictions in leases may influence the interest of a prospective purchaser; for instance, a very tightly-drawn user clause inevitably reduces the number and range of potential assignees/sub-lessees interested in the property.

GN 1.6.3   When valuing leases and reversions, particular care needs to be exercised in ascertaining what is to be valued; for example, the effect, if any, of past improvements which may have been carried out by the lessees. What is seen and measured on the ground by way of buildings may not be what has to be reflected in the valuation. If, due to the absence of documented licences, the extent of improvements cannot be confirmed, the Valuer should proceed on the basis of stated assumptions.

GN 1.6.4   The Valuer should ascertain what minerals, rights of support and compensation attach to the land and whether rights of use and re-entry have been reserved.

GN 1.7   Records

It is good practice for the Valuer to record for his own future reference (and to assist any investigation or litigation) the steps taken in carrying out the valuation/appraisal process, any steps which have been consciously omitted and why, and the judgements made, with reasons for them.

GN 1.8   Referencing

GN 1.8.1   The initial task in fulfilling any valuation instruction is to determine precisely the subject matter of the valuation. This requires an inspection of the property and the Valuer should have regard to the RICS/ISVA *Code of Measuring Practice* or such other relevant codes where applicable.

GN 1.8.2   Where it is appropriate to zone the floor area for valuation purposes, the depth of the zone chosen to reflect closely the market should be complete metres, i.e. not including any decimal points.

GN 1.8.3   From the inspection, a number of queries are likely to arise relative to such matters as future changes in the locality or the adjoining land or the economic and physical future of the property being valued.

GN 1.8.4   When inspecting the property and its surroundings the Valuer should record appropriate information about other property which may be used as 'comparables' in making the valuation.

GN 1.9   Physical factors

GN 1.9.1   A principal matter of concern is the state of repair and condition of the property, and its relevance to value.

GN 1.9.2 If a building survey has not been undertaken the Valuer should, subject to the proviso in the first sentence of PS 7.5, refer in the Report to the general state of repair of the property apparent from his inspection and take such defects and wants of repair apparent from it into account.

Four situations are likely to be met in practice:

(a) a failure to redecorate resulting in an unsatisfactory appearance;

(b) a neglect of periodic maintenance, the effect of which is mainly superficial and capable of being remedied;

(c) a failure to repair over a prolonged period to the extent that renovation ceases to be possible or economic; and

(d) a basic structural defect(s).

GN 1.10   Town planning and regulatory issues

GN 1.10.1 Town planning policies, proposals and subsisting permissions are nearly always of prime concern in valuations. There may be times when the Valuer is entitled to rely on local knowledge in deciding that there are no special planning problems which need to be reflected in the valuation.

GN 1.10.2 With fully developed properties, the concern must be to establish that present uses are free from enforcement action. Consideration should also be given to the effect on value of any conditions attaching to relevant planning permissions.

GN 1.10.3 The use/development and enjoyment of buildings and land are subject to general and/or specific legislation and regulations, noncompliance with which may result in cessation of occupation pending conformity, which usually involves capital expenditure. It is not practicable to identify here all the statutes and regulations which may affect all property. Many of them are specific to the class of property being valued, eg garages and service stations where the Valuer must consider the regulations concerning petroleum or cellulose spraying (if that is carried out); in the case of hotels, the presence of the appropriate fire certificate is vital if valuing on the basis of the existing use—but possibly of no concern if valuing for an alternative use. Where appropriate the Valuer should seek to be supplied with current certificates of compliance with all pertinent regulations.

GN 1.11   Valuation and Rating Lists

GN 1.11.1 Where appropriate, the Valuer needs to obtain details from the local Billing Authority of the current Council Tax banding in the Valuation List, or current description and assessment in the Rating List (Roll in Scotland). If a new Valuation or Rating List has been deposited with the Billing Authority, the Valuer should obtain details of the new banding or description and assessment.

GN 1.11.2   The description and assessment, or banding, may not provide an accurate indication of the rates or council tax bill because of the transitional arrangements made by the Government from time to time. A valuer should enquire as to the current rates or council tax payable in respect of the property. This liability should be compared with the council tax or rates payable in respect of any comparable properties, since the liability in respect of the property being valued and the comparable properties may be significantly different with consequential effects on rental and/or capital value.

GN 1.11.3   The description and assessment in the Rating List or the banding in the Valuation List ascribed to the property, are based upon what the Valuation Officer or Listing Officer has reason to believe properly describes the use to which the property is put, and its Rateable Value or Council Tax band. Valuers should treat these with caution. The Valuation Officer should value what he finds for rating purposes. Thus, if a property is occupied and used for a particular use, the Valuation Officer will value it for that purpose even if it has no planning permission for that use. A property which is empty should be valued for its most valuable permitted use. The Valuation Officer may not, however, be aware that the use of a property has changed or that it has become empty, and the current description and assessment may therefore not reflect the current actual use.

GN 1.11.4   The value and description, or band in the Rating or Valuation Lists may be inaccurate for a number of other reasons including the fact that a new assessment, description or band may have been negotiated but the List not altered, or the Valuation Officer or Listing Officer may be unaware of changes in circumstance. Valuers should treat entries in the Rating or Valuation Lists with care, and where necessary, satisfy themselves that the property and its value in the List is accurate. They should not assume that the List is correct.

GN 1.12   Insurances

The Valuer need make no enquiry, unless specifically instructed, as to insurances and the amount of cover.

GN 1.13   Other factors

There are various other factors which may need to be considered and reported by the Valuer. For example:

> (a) the practicability or otherwise of establishing the presence or absence of potentially deleterious or hazardous materials or techniques;

(b) whether reports have been obtained concerning past, present and future mining and quarrying activities; copies should be attached to the Report;

(c) the distinction, for certain valuation purposes between land, buildings, plant and machinery. This arises largely in respect of industrial and some commercial property;

(d) what reliance the market would place on 'buy-out' clauses arising on developments, rental guarantees and their covenants; and

(e) public perception that higher than normal electro-magnetic fields caused by the presence of high voltage cables and/or an electricity transformer in close proximity to the subject property may affect marketability and future value. Where the Valuer's remit includes giving advice on the suitability of the property as security for a loan, identifying factors likely materially to affect value, and/or his Report is likely to be relied upon by a prospective purchaser, the Valuer should include a statement in his Report on the lines of PSA 3.7 where he considers it applicable.

GN 1.14 Material valuation considerations

GN 1.14.1 Evidence of actual transactions is at the heart of the formulation of valuation figures, as it provides the Valuer with hard facts quite independent of his own opinion. However, the appropriate valuation figure is not arrived at purely by the interpretation of comparable evidence; it involves the consideration of other market criteria which, in particular circumstances and markets, may include the following:

(a) local economic factors, planning policies, catchment areas and supply and demand;

(b) changes in the economy and in investment markets (property and competing areas such as gilts and equities) since the dates of the comparable evidence;

(c) the state of mind of prospective vendors and purchasers in 'thin' markets, where there are few comparables, although, because their concerns have not been translated into fact, they should be given cautious weight; and

(d) the fact that certain types of property are acquired and operated other than for purely commercial reasons, eg for personal enjoyment, status, pride of ownership or charitable purposes. The Valuer should be sufficiently experienced to identify such properties and, where appropriate, to value them by reference to analysis of comparable transactions having regard to the potential motivation of a purchaser, in addition to such considerations as physical factors and/or trading profitability.

GN 1.14.2 If the Valuer has reason to believe that there has been a recent sale of the subject property, he should do his best to establish the sale price and that it does not disguise inducements or other significant considerations. He should also, unless under express instructions to the contrary, explore as carefully as he is able the marketing history, to establish whether it was freely and competently offered on the open market, that the sale was at arm's length and that the purchaser was not one with a special interest. Such an exploration, in respect of the subject property, does not relieve the Valuer of the need to consider comparables and, if they suggest a value which differs materially from the recent sale price, he has to consider all the evidence to decide why the discrepancy exists and whether it justifies abandoning such sale price as *prima facie* best evidence of value. The Valuer will be well advised to record his reasoning in his papers.

GN 1.15   Turnover rents

A rent determined having regard to trading potential should not be confused with turnover-related rent. A valuer involved in valuing either the freehold/feuhold or leasehold interest of a property let wholly or partly on a turnover-related rent will need to have knowledge of the particular trade and consider the prospects for turnover *vis-à-vis* expected movements in the property market generally. It should be noted that a turnover-related rent could be or become either substantially above or below market rental value without a turnover-related element and valuations may need to be adjusted to reflect this.

GN 1.16   Portfolio valuations

Depending on market circumstances at the time, the valuation of a portfolio as a whole or in parts may produce a greater or a lesser figure than the aggregate value of the separate properties it contains. It would be entirely appropriate for a Valuer to comment on such a situation. It is suggested that Valuers consider the implications closely with their Clients before expressing such comments on portfolios in their Reports.

GN 1.17   Professional Indemnity Insurance

GN 1.17.1   The Valuer should consider and investigate as necessary the adequacy of his insurance policy in respect of the undertaking of work, with relevant caveats, and also as to his advising upon or actually appointing and supervising specialist consultants. If the services the Valuer offers change, the insurer must be notified.

GN 1.17.2   The Valuer should keep in mind that any insurances which he has effected to protect himself against claims for negligence under professional indemnity policies may contain requirements as to the Valuer's qualifications and the inclusion of certain saving clauses in every Report and valuation. If this is the case such words should be repeated unless the insurers agree either to modification or to a complete waiver.

GN 1.18   Possible involvement of syndicates

Where the Client is a Lender, the Lender may be part of a syndicate or, having lent on property, decide to sell on tranches of the loan to other Lenders. Although the third party limitation clause should provide protection, the Valuer may therefore become exposed to the risk of a duty of care to unknown third parties. Therefore, particularly in the case of valuations for lending on commercial property, Valuers may wish to add to the usual limitations clause a statement that, in the event of a proposal to place the loan on the subject property in a syndicate, the Client must notify the Valuer, with a view to responsibility to the further, named parties being agreed.

2   Manual of Valuation Guidance Notes (1992)

Valuation Guidance Note 1: Valuation—general principles

[Revised October 1993]

1   Introduction

1.1   This Guidance Note, dealing with general principles of valuation, is intended to cover valuations of interests in land and buildings for *most* purposes. But there are additional guidance notes dealing with:
   (a) valuations for residential mortgage purposes of the kind carried out for building societies and other lending institutions (see VGN 2), *except* insofar as the matters referred to in this Guidance Note are relevant to the consideration of value;
   (b) the valuation of mineral-bearing land, (see VGN 5);
   (c) insurance—reinstatement cost (see VGN 7);
   (d) valuation of local authority assets (see VGN 8).

1.2   In those cases where valuations are covered by the *Statements of Asset Valuation Practice and Guidance Notes—Third Edition* (the 'Red Book') published by the Institution and in particular those which relate to asset valuations which are undertaken in the preparation of financial accounts, this Guidance Note should be regarded as only supplementary.

2   Conditions of engagement

2.1   Use should be made of the Institution's publications *The Valuation of Residential Property* and *The Valuation of Commercial and Industrial Property*, reproduced at Appendices 2 and 1 herein, where appropriate. The use of these should ensure that acceptable conditions of engagement are defined and proper limitations of liability and of responsibility are achieved.

2.2   Where these publications are inapplicable, the terms of the agreement and of proper limitation of liability and responsibility should be achieved by obtaining instructions in writing or by confirming verbal instructions in writing prior to undertaking the work. This will prevent uncertainty about the instructions between the Valuer and the Client and provide evidence of a fair agreement.

3   Unusual assumptions

3.1   Sometimes a Valuer will be instructed to make unusual assumptions or will be instructed not to carry out normal investigatory procedures. In such cases it is essential to confirm those instructions in writing and to repeat in the report not only what has been done, but also what the Valuer was instructed *not* to do. **Where the Valuer is concerned as to the assumptions or limitations, consideration should be given as to whether to seek to obtain amended instructions or, if necessary, the Valuer must refuse to act for the Client.**

3.2   Valuers are advised to avoid giving unusually qualified reports wherever possible.

4.   Third party (matters)

4.1   Even though the Valuer may have endeavoured to contract out of any responsibility to a third party, it may well be that the third party will not fully appreciate the implications of any qualifications in the report, as referred to in paragraph 3.1 above. If such a valuation becomes available to a third party, there is a danger of it being misunderstood or misquoted. This may bring into question the standing of the Valuer and the profession. Valuers are advised, therefore, not to provide unusually qualified reports or valuations, except where justified by the circumstances. When a Valuer does provide an unusually qualified valuation, it is particularly important that it is not to be used other than for the originally agreed purpose by the original Client.

4.2   As a valuation is normally reported in confidence to a particular Client and for the purposes of that Client, a valuation report will usually contain a paragraph relating to confidentiality on the lines recommended in the Conditions of Engagement.

5 Legal issues

5.1 Clients will expect Valuers to express opinions (and Valuers will in turn wish to express their opinion) upon legal issues affecting their valuations, but the Valuers should take care to state that any interpretation of legal documents and legal assumptions made must be checked by the Client with a suitably qualified lawyer, if they are to be relied upon. The Valuer should state that no responsibility or liability is accepted for the true interpretation of the legal position of the Client or other parties. **If this is not done, the Valuer will assume no less a burden than the law imposes upon a competent lawyer, if and in so far as they expressly or impliedly give legal advice.**

6 Valuation considerations

6.1 It is important that this paragraph is read together with the Background Notes to VGN 1.
6.2 The matters referred to below are those which a Valuer should consider in preparing a valuation. It is recognised that some valuations may call for additional considerations.
  (a) *Referencing*
      (i) Characteristics of locality and availability of communications and facilities affecting value.
      (ii) Age, description, use, accommodation, construction of any buildings, installations, amenities and services.
      (iii) Dimensions and areas of the land and buildings, confirming basis of calculation used.
      (iv) Apparent state of repair and condition.
      (v) Site stability (including the effects of mining and quarrying).
  (b) *Nature of interest*
      (i) Tenure, with reference to relevant restrictions, terms of leases (if leasehold), easements, rights of way, etc.
      (ii) Details of lettings and other occupations.
  (c) *Planning and statutory requirements*
      (i) Results of town planning, environmental, highway and other enquiries.
      (ii) Apparent contraventions of any statutory requirements.
      (iii) Outstanding statutory notices.
  (d) *Other factors*
      (i) Rating assessments and any outgoings.
      (ii) Any plant and machinery which would normally form an integral part of the building and is therefore included in the valuation.
      (iii) Fixtures, fittings and improvements.

(iv) Presence of potentially deleterious or hazardous materials or techniques; any non-standard methods of construction.

(v) Allowances for disrepair.

(vi) Any development potential.

(vii)   Any possible 'marriage' or 'break-up' value.

(e) *Marketing analysis*

(i) Details of comparable market transactions for either existing use or alternative use(s).

(ii) Market conditions and trends.

(iii) Consideration as to the period of validity.

7   The valuation report

7.1   The general form of the valuation report should have been agreed with the Client when taking instructions. No standard form of report is suitable for all occasions, but generally it should cover the matters set out below and any other specific requirements of the Client.

7.2   The presentation of the valuation report will have regard to the need for any special format but most reports should contain those items marked with an asterisk(*):

		Paragraph VGN 1	Ref BN
*1	The source of the instructions and the identity of the Client.	2	2
*2	The purpose of the valuation.	1	
*3	The date of valuation.		
*4	The basis of valuation.		
*5	Any special instructions, unusual assumptions or omissions.	3	2
*6	The date and extent of inspection.	6	3
7	Situation and amenities.	6	3
8	Description, construction, accommodation, services, areas and a site plan.	6	3
9	Plant and machinery—included/excluded.	6	9
10	Apparent state of repair.	6	4
11	Use.		6
*12	Comment on planning and environmental issues.	6	6
13	Rating description and assessment.	6	8
14	Any licences, permits, consents or certificates.	6	7
15	Other statutory controls.	6	7

		Paragraph VGN 1	Ref BN
*16	Tenure. If with vacant possession, whether whole or in part with a list of all known tenancies.	6	5
17	Any taxation implications	11	
18	Summary with any other relevant matters.	6	9
*19	*Assumptions and caveats relating to limitations of responsibility:*	4&5	5&9

*19 *Assumptions and caveats relating to limitations of responsibility:*

• Assumptions as to good title and freedom from any borrowings and encumbrances.

• Matters that would be revealed by a local search, replies to usual enquiries or by any statutory notice.

• For examination of the structure and of inaccessible parts and of latent defects including rot and inherently dangerous or unsuitable materials and techniques (i.e. ensuring that the report cannot be construed as a structural survey).

• As to whether the presence of contamination has been investigated or whether it is assumed not to be present.

• To the Client and, where appropriate, the Client's immediate professional advisers, but excluding responsibility to third parties and preserving confidentiality.

• Non-publication of the valuation and/or report in whole or in part without prior consent.

• Special clauses required for professional indemnity policy.

• For assumptions of fact and law, eg present lawful user.

• Non-disclosure of material facts to the Valuer.

20 Consideration as to the period of validity.

*21 The opinion of value in words and figures.

*22 The Valuer's/firm's name and address, qualifications and signature.

*23 The date of the report.

☆ ☆ ☆ ☆ ☆

Background Notes to VGN 1

[April 1992]

1 Introduction

1.1 These Background Notes are intended to amplify the matters contained in VGN 1 and to assist the Valuer in carrying out instructions. VGN 1 is a guide to valuation practice which by its nature omits matters of detail and specific examples of practical situations.

1.2 It should be emphasised that neither VGN 1, nor this paper, is directly concerned with valuation theory or method, but with the mechanics of practice, including the assembly, interpretation and reporting of information relevant to the task of valuation. These Notes are not fully comprehensive of all the valuation practice embraced in VGN 1 and offer comment upon selected aspects only. Where appropriate, reference is made to the paragraphs in VGN 1.

2 The Valuer and the Client

2.1 Certainty and clarity in the terms of the agreement between the Valuer and the Client should be primary objectives of the Valuer. Clients should know in advance what they can reasonably expect to receive and what responsibilities the Valuer will and will not accept. Since disputes may arise many years after a valuation has been provided, it is important to ensure that the agreement between the parties is contained in, or evidenced by, comprehensive documents, and the use of the Institution's publications is recommended. Where these are inapplicable, the principles underlying them, especially those concerned with the definition of assumptions of responsibility and exclusions of responsibility, can be adopted or adapted to meet the needs of the situation. However, if the publications or some terms in the publications are to be of contractual effect, **it is essential that they are expressly incorporated in the agreement when it is being formed**, rather than being introduced at a later stage.

2.2 The Valuer should accept responsibility for exercising all reasonable professional skill and care and should not attempt to contract on a basis which would provide the Client with something substantially different from what could reasonably be expected from a competent Valuer. However, the Valuer may, in accepting instructions, properly define and limit responsibilities, identifying any reasonable assumptions which will be made.

3 Referencing (paragraph 6.2(a) of VGN 1)

3.1 The initial task in any valuation is to determine precisely what is the subject matter of the valuation. This requires an inspection of the property and the Valuer should have regard to the RICS/ISVA *Code of Measuring Practice* or such other relevant codes where applicable.

3.2 From this inspection a number of queries may arise relative to such matters as future changes in the locality or the adjoining land or concerning the economic and physical future of the property being valued.

3.3 When inspecting the property and its surroundings the Valuer should record appropriate information about other premises which may be used as 'comparables' in making the valuation.

4 Physical factors (paragraph 6.2(a) of VGN 1)

4.1 A principal matter of concern is the state of repair and condition of buildings and structures comprising the property, and its relevance to value.

4.2 Four situations are likely to be met in practice:
- (a) A failure to redecorate resulting in an unsatisfactory appearance.
- (b) A neglect of periodic maintenance, the effect of which is mainly superficial and capable of being remedied.
- (c) A failure to repair over a prolonged period to the extent that renovation ceases to be possible or economic.
- (d) A basic structural defect in the building.

4.3 The Valuer, particularly if commenting on the apparent state of repair of a property in a report, should make it clear that the inspection and report do not purport to be a structural survey.

5 Nature of interest (paragraph 6.2(b) of VGN 1)

5.1 It is essential for the Valuer to understand clearly the nature of the relevant interest in the property which is being valued.

5.2 Valuers will, of course, wish to make assumptions as to the true legal position in order to assist their Clients in the circumstances which give rise to the need for the valuation. **It must be appreciated that the proper interpretation of legal documents and the proper legal inferences to be drawn from the relevant circumstances are especially the province of lawyers.** Valuers who presume to advise upon what they reasonably believe to be the legal position will probably be assuming the very heavy burden of acting as competent qualified lawyers, unless they make it plain that their assumptions of law and assumptions of legal inferences should only be relied upon if and when they have been confirmed by a solicitor (or counsel).

5.3 The general assumption will be that the title is free from onerous and unusual restrictions, but restrictive covenants and other obligations associated with tenure can influence value and marketability. Similarly, specific user and other restrictions in leases may influence the interest of a prospective purchaser. A very tightly-drawn user clause inevitably reduces the number and range of potential assignees/sub-lessees interested in the property.

5.4   When valuing leases and reversions, particular care needs to be exercised in ascertaining what is to be valued owing, for example, to past improvements which may have been carried out by the lessees. What is seen and measured on the ground by way of buildings may not be what has to be reflected in the valuation.

5.5   The details of lettings and sub-lettings of properties which are not being valued on the basis of vacant possession, will influence value and the Valuer should obtain full particulars. Preferably this should be done by extracting the necessary information from original documents with assistance on interpretation from legal advisers, but in many cases a summary of such information provided by the Client or the Client's advisers will suffice.

5.6   Easements and other rights such as those pertaining to way, light and drainage can have a material influence upon the value of freehold and leasehold interests and specific enquiries should be made as to whether they are perpetual or determinable.

5.7   The Valuer should ascertain what minerals, rights of support and compensation attach to the land, and whether rights of use and re-entry have been reserved.

5.8   **Where the Valuer relies on information provided, he or she should indicate in the report the source of and responsibility for such information.**

5.9   The duty of the Valuer in valuing leases and reversions is referred to above. Doubt has been cast on this statement in two ways: one view points out the peril if the Valuer purports to act as a lawyer and advises his or her Client on legal technicalities. If the Valuer acts in a manner which gives the appearance of giving legal advice the Valuer must be judged by the same standards as the lawyer. The other view is that a Valuer cannot value term or reversion without a total knowledge of the terms of the lease and this can only be gathered from the document.

5.10   It is suggested that the proper view is that the Valuer must read the lease when valuing either term or reversion but that interpretations of the law are matters for discussion between the Valuer and the Client's lawyer. It is appreciated that the lawyer is unlikely to foresee all the economic consequences of interpretation, and discussion is the best solution. If the Client does not give enough time to permit reading of the lease, or the Client is unwilling or unable to produce it, or if the Client does not wish to engage a qualified lawyer, a valuation must be given as referred to in paragraphs 3 and 4 of VGN 1.

6 Town planning and environmental issues (paragraph 6.2(c)(i) of VGN 1)

6.1 Town planning policies, proposals and subsisting permissions are nearly always of prime concern in valuations. There may be times when the Valuer is entitled to rely on local knowledge in deciding that there are no special planning problems which need to be reflected in the valuation.

6.2 With fully developed properties, the concern must be to establish that present uses are free from enforcement action. Consideration should also be given to the effect on value of any conditions attached to relevant planning permissions.

6.3 Should the Valuer be in any doubt as to the legality of any use or building operation, investigation should be made. If this is not practicable, attention must be drawn to the possibility that planning legislation may have an impact on the property and its value.

6.4 It is not the Valuer's task to undertake searches (which are normally made by a solicitor) but there are situations when absence of knowledge of the planning proposals will be so fundamental that failure to make enquiries would expose the Valuer to criticism, if not to an action in negligence.

6.5 In the valuation of land for development, planning considerations are paramount, but it is not possible to lay down a general rule for all cases. The Valuer must make up his or her own mind as to the extent of planning enquiries in each case. What can be said is that, whatever line he or she takes, **it is vital that the Valuer explains what has, and what has not been done.**

7 Other regulatory measures (paragraph 6.2(c) of VGN 1)

7.1 All buildings and many activities on open land are subject to specific legislation and regulations, non-compliance with which may result in cessation of occupation pending conformity, which in the event usually involves capital expenditure. It is not practicable to identify in the Notes all the statutes and regulations which may affect all classes of property. Many of these are specific to the class of property being valued, eg for garages the Valuer must consider the regulations concerning petroleum or cellulose spraying (if that is carried out); in the case of hotels the presence of the appropriate fire certificate is vital if valuing on the basis of the existing use—but possibly of no concern if valuing for an alternative use.

7.2 The Valuer must have regard to the nature of the property, the purposes of the valuation, the extent of the property and the size of the undertaking in determining the extent to which he or she ought to investigate the regulatory measures which can or might affect it. The Valuer should consider whether the inspection revealed any apparent breaches and where appropriate seek to be supplied with current certificates of compliance.

7.3   If the Valuer is in any doubt as to the need for investigation, he or she is advised to check. **If the Valuer cannot check, he or she must state in the report the matters which he or she thinks might affect the valuation and, if appropriate, suggest that the Client's legal advisers refer back to him or her if searches reveal matters which might affect value.**

8   Assessments for local taxation, etc (paragraph 6.2(d)(i) of VGN 1)

8.1   When the Valuer has not inspected the Valuation List in person and is including details of rating assessments in a report, it is recommended that the matter is dealt with by a statement on the following lines:

> 'As a result of a verbal enquiry only, we are informed that the entries appearing in the Valuation List of the relevant local authority at the date of inspection of the List were ...'.

The Valuer should be aware that, at any time, the List may be subject to a proposal to alter a particular entry.

8.2   In certain areas it may also be appropriate for the Valuer to refer to the assessments for drainage rates.

8.3   The description of the hereditament in the Valuation List may have implications for value where it does not coincide with the permitted town planning use.

8.4   The Valuer should consider whether the scope of the Client's instructions extends to comment on the correctness of the assessment listed.

9   Other factors (paragraphs 6.2(d) of VGN 1)

9.1   There are various other factors which may need to be considered. For example:

(a) Comment may be required on the impracticability of establishing the presence or absence of potentially deleterious or hazardous materials or techniques.[1]

(b) Where appropriate the Valuer should state whether reports have been obtained concerning past, present and future mining and quarrying activities and should attach copies to the valuation report.

(c) For certain purposes the valuation may need to distinguish between land, buildings, plant and machinery. This arises largely in respect of industrial property.[2]

[1] For further information see the Institution's leaflets, *The Valuation of Residential Property*, *The Valuation of Commercial and Industrial Property* and any other similar publications by the Institution.
[2] For further information see VGN 3 and Statement of Asset Valuation and Practice No 16 on the Valuation of Plant and Machinery for the purpose of incorporating or referring to such value in company accounts, directors' reports and other published financial statements.

10 Marketing analysis (paragraph 6.2(e)(iii) of VGN 1)

10.1 Advice provided to Clients in respect of the marketing of property interests as part of a Valuation report may bring the Valuer within the provisions of the Estate Agents Act 1979 and the statutory instruments which have been made under this legislation. It is essential that Valuers and their staff are fully aware of the requirements of the law in this respect. Breaches can lead to a Prohibition Order banning the offenders from acting in an estate agency capacity. Use should be made of the Institution's publication *Putting the Estate Agents Act 1979 and the Property Misdescriptions Act 1991 into Practice*.

11 Taxation implications

11.1 A valuation does not normally have regard to the Client's personal tax position. There are occasions when the nature of the property and the transaction contemplated will prompt the Valuer to suggest that tax implications should be considered. It is not normally the Valuer's function to act as a tax adviser and, except in special cases, the Valuer should not be drawn into tax advice. However, if it appears that taxation might seriously affect the nature of the transaction in pursuit of which valuation advice is sought, the Valuer should refer in the report to the desirability of obtaining appropriate advice from a specialist tax adviser.

☆ ☆ ☆ ☆ ☆

3 The Guide to the Professional Conduct of Solicitors (1996)

Annex 25F: Guidance—mortgage fraud—variation in purchase price

[12 December 1990, Revised January 1996]

This guidance deals with the solicitor's duty in conduct when acting for lender and borrower when there is some variation in the purchase price.

Professional Ethics is frequently asked to advise on a solicitor's duty to the lender in conduct when there is some variation in the purchase price of a property of which the lender may be unaware. The Standards and Guidance Committee has therefore prepared the following guidance (which is supported by the Council of Mortgage Lenders) on the professional conduct issues involved.

Solicitors acting contemporaneously for a buyer and a lender should consider their position very carefully if there is any change in the purchase price, or if the solicitors become aware of any other information which they would reasonably expect the lender to consider important in deciding whether, or on what terms, it would make the mortgage advance available. In such circumstances the solicitor's duty to act in the best interests of the lender would require him or her to pass on such information to the lender.

Solicitors have a duty of confidentiality to clients, but this does not affect their duty to act in the best interests of each client. Therefore any such information concerning variations to the purchase price should be forwarded to the lender with the consent of the buyer. If the buyer will not agree to the information being given to the lender, then there will be a conflict between the solicitor's duty of confidentiality to the buyer and the duty to act in the best interests of the lender. Solicitors must therefore cease acting for the lender and must consider carefully whether they are able to continue acting for the buyer, bearing in mind **15.02** note 1, p 275 in the Guide and also **12.01** note 1 referred to below.

Solicitors must not withhold information relevant to a transaction from any client. Where the client is a lender, this includes not only straightforward price reductions but may also include other allowances (eg for repairs, payment of costs, the inclusion of chattels in the price and incentives of the kind offered by builders such as free holidays and part-subsidisation of mortgage payments) which amount to a price reduction and which would affect the lender's decision to make the advance. Solicitors should not attempt to arbitrate on whether the price change is material but should notify the lender. It is recommended that solicitors advise their clients as soon as practicable that it would be regarded as fraud to misrepresent the purchase price and that a solicitor is under a duty to inform the lender of the true price being paid for a property.

Solicitors who are party to an attempt to deceive a lender may be exposing both the buyer and themselves to criminal prosecution and/or civil action and will be liable to be disciplined for having breached the principles of professional conduct (see **12.01** note 1, p 211 in the Guide). If a solicitor is aware that his or her client is attempting to perpetrate fraud in any form he or she must immediately cease acting for that client.

☆ ☆ ☆ ☆ ☆

Annex 25G: 'Green card' warning on property fraud—practice information

[March 1991, Revised January 1996]

Could you be involved or implicated?

Could you be unwittingly assisting in a fraud? The general assumption is that if there has been a property fraud a solicitor *must* have been involved. Solicitors should therefore be vigilant to protect both their clients and themselves. Steps can be taken to minimise the risk of being involved or implicated in a fraud (see below).

Could you spot a property fraud?

The signs to watch for include the following (but this list is not exhaustive):

Fraudulent buyer or fictitious solicitors—especially if the buyer is introduced to your practice by a third party (for example a broker or estate agent) who is not well known to you. Beware of clients whom you never meet and solicitors not known to you.

Unusual instructions—for example a solicitor being instructed by the seller to remit the net proceeds of sale to anyone other than the seller.

Misrepresentation of the purchase price—ensure that the true cash price actually to be paid is stated as the consideration in the contract and transfer and is identical to the price shown in the mortgage instructions and in the report on title to the lender.

A deposit or any part of purchase price paid direct—a deposit or the difference between the mortgage advance and the price, paid direct, or said to be paid direct, to the seller.

Incomplete contract documentation—contract documents not fully completed by the seller's representative, i.e. dates missing or the identity of the parties not fully described or financial details not fully stated.

Changes in the purchase price—adjustments to the purchase price, particularly in high percentage mortgage cases, or allowances off the purchase price, for example, for works to be carried out.

Unusual transactions—transactions which do not follow their normal course or the usual pattern of events:

(a) client with current mortgage on two or more properties
(b) client using alias
(c) client buying several properties from same person or two or more persons using same solicitor
(d) client reselling property at a substantial profit, for which no explanation has been provided.

What steps can I take to minimise the risk of fraud?

Be vigilant: if you have any doubts about a transaction, consider whether any of the following steps could be taken to minimise the risk of fraud:

Verify the identity and *bona fides* of your client and solicitors' firms you do not know—meet the clients where possible and get to know them a little. Check that the solicitor's firm and office address appear in the *Directory of Solicitors and Barristers* or contact the Law Society's Records Centre (PSD) (tel: 0171–242 1222).

Question unusual instructions—if you receive unusual instructions from your client discuss them with your client fully.

Discuss with your client any aspects of the transaction which worry you—if, for example, you have any suspicion that your client may have submitted a false mortgage application or references, of if the lender's valuation exceeds the actual price paid, discuss this with your client. If you believe that the client intends to proceed with a fraudulent application, you must refuse to continue to act for the buyer and the lender.

Check that the true price is shown in all documentation—check that the actual price paid is stated in the contract, transfer and mortgage instructions. Where you are also acting for a lender, tell your client that you will have to cease acting unless the client permits you to report to the lender all allowances and incentives. See also the guidance printed in [1990] *Gazette*, 12 December, 16 [see Annex 25F, p 426 in the Guide].

Do not witness pre-signed documentation—no document should be witnessed by a solicitor or his or her staff unless the person signing does so in the presence of the witness. If the document is pre-signed, ensure that it is re-signed in the presence of a witness.

Verify signature—consider whether signatures on all documents connected with a transaction should be examined and compared with signatures on any other available documentation.

Make a company search—where a private company is the seller, or the seller has purchased from a private company in the recent past, and you suspect that the sale may not be on proper arm's length terms, you should make a search in the Companies Register to ascertain the names and addresses of the officers and shareholders, which can then be compared with the names of those connected with the transaction and the seller and buyer.

Remember that, even where investigations result in a solicitor ceasing to act for a client, the solicitor will still owe a duty of confidentiality which would prevent the solicitor passing on information to the lender. It is only where the solicitor is satisfied that there is a strong *prima facie* case that the client was using the solicitor to further a fraud or other criminal purpose that the duty of confidentiality would not apply.

Any failure to observe these signs and to take the appropriate steps may be used in court as evidence against you if you and your client are prosecuted, or if you are sued for negligence.

Further guidance can be obtained from the Law Society's Practice Advice Service (tel: 0171-242 1222).

☆ ☆ ☆ ☆ ☆

Reproduced by permission of The Royal Institution of Chartered Surveyors which owns the copyright.

Annex 25 F and G are reproduced by permission of The Law Society which owns the copyright.

Authors' note

In many property finance negligence cases, plaintiffs seek to support their case on liability by showing that the defendants did not comply with their own professional guidelines. In this Appendix, various documents are extracted from the *RICS Appraisal and Valuation Manual* (1995, 1st edn), the *RICS Manual of Valuation Guidance Notes* (1992, 3rd edn) and the Law Society's *Guide to the Professional Conduct of Solicitors* (1996, 7th edn). All the documents extracted are subject to regular amendment, and practitioners should be careful to identify the version relevant to the particular action (whether earlier or later than the version extracted below). The inclusion of VGN1 (dating from 1993) from the *Manual of Valuation Guidance Notes* is intended to alert readers to the historical progression of the RIC's professional literature. The date of the document is given at the head of each one.

Index